Microsoft® Office

Word 2007

Introductory Concepts and Techniques

Gary B. Shelly
Thomas J. Cashman
Misty E. Vermaat

THOMSON COURSE TECHNOLOGY

SHELLY CASHMAN SERIES®

THOMSON COURSE TECHNOLOGY   25 THOMSON PLACE   BOSTON MA 02210

Australia • Canada • Denmark • Japan • Mexico • New Zealand • Philippines • Puerto Rico • Singapore • South Africa • Spain • United Kingdom • United States

Microsoft Office Word 2007
Introductory Concepts and Techniques

Gary B. Shelly

Thomas J. Cashman

Misty E. Vermaat

Executive Editor
Alexandra Arnold

Senior Product Manager
Reed Curry

Associate Product Manager
Klenda Martinez

Editorial Assistant
Jon Farnham

Senior Marketing Manager
Joy Stark-Vancs

Marketing Coordinator
Julie Schuster

Print Buyer
Julio Esperas

Director of Production
Patty Stephan

Production Editor
Jill Klaffky

Developmental Editor
Jill Batistick

Proofreader
Kim Kosmatka

Indexer
Rich Carlson

QA Manuscript Reviewers
**John Freitas, Serge Palladino,
Chris Scriver, Danielle Shaw,
Marianne Snow, Teresa Storch**

Art Director
Bruce Bond

Cover and Text Design
Joel Sadagursky

Cover Photo
Jon Chomitz

Compositor
GEX Publishing Services

Printer
Banta Menasha

ISBN-13: 978-1-4188-4336-6
ISBN-10: 1-4188-4336-9

Microsoft® Office

Word 2007
Introductory Concepts and Techniques

Contents

Appendices

Preface

The Shelly Cashman Series® offers the finest textbooks in computer education. We are proud of the fact that our series of Microsoft Office 4.3, Microsoft Office 95, Microsoft Office 97, Microsoft Office 2000, Microsoft Office XP, and Microsoft Office 2003 textbooks have been the most widely used books in education. With each new edition of our Office books, we have made significant improvements based on the software and comments made by instructors and students.

Microsoft Office 2007 contains more changes in the user interface and feature set than all other previous versions combined. Recognizing that the new features and functionality of Microsoft Office 2007 would impact the way that students are taught skills, the Shelly Cashman Series development team carefully reviewed our pedagogy and analyzed its effectiveness in teaching today's Office student. An extensive customer survey produced results confirming what the series is best known for: its step-by-step, screen-by-screen instructions, its project-oriented approach, and the quality of its content.

We learned, though, that students entering computer courses today are different than students taking these classes just a few years ago. Students today read less, but need to retain more. They need not only to be able to perform skills, but to retain those skills and know how to apply them to different settings. Today's students need to be continually engaged and challenged to retain what they're learning.

As a result, we've renewed our commitment to focusing on the user and how they learn best. This commitment is reflected in every change we've made to our Office 2007 books.

Objectives of This Textbook

Microsoft Office Word 2007: Introductory Concepts and Techniques is intended for a course that includes an introduction to Word 2007. No experience with a computer is assumed, and no mathematics beyond the high school freshman level is required. The objectives of this book are:

- To teach the fundamentals of Microsoft Office Word 2007

- To expose students to practical examples of the computer as a useful tool

- To acquaint students with the proper procedures to create documents suitable for coursework, professional purposes, and personal use

- To help students discover the underlying functionality of Word 2007 so they can become more productive

- To develop an exercise-oriented approach that allows learning by doing

The Shelly Cashman Approach

Features of the Shelly Cashman Series Microsoft Office Word 2007 books include:

- **Project Orientation** Each chapter in the book presents a project with a practical problem and complete solution in an easy-to-understand approach.

- **Plan Ahead Boxes** The project orientation is enhanced by the inclusion of Plan Ahead boxes. These new features prepare students to create successful projects by encouraging them to think strategically about what they are trying to accomplish before they begin working.

- **Step-by-Step, Screen-by-Screen Instructions** Each of the tasks required to complete a project is clearly identified throughout the chapter. Now, the step-by-step instructions provide a context beyond point-and-click. Each step explains why students are performing a task, or the result of performing a certain action. Found on the screens accompanying each step, call-outs give students the information they need to know when they need to know it. Now, we've used color to distinguish the content in the call-outs. The Explanatory call-outs (in black) summarize what is happening on the screen and the Navigational call-outs (in red) show students where to click.

- **Q&A** Found within many of the step-by-step sequences, Q&As raise the kinds of questions students may ask when working through a step sequence and provide answers about what they are doing, why they are doing it, and how that task might be approached differently.

- **Experimental Steps** These new steps, within our step-by-step instructions, encourage students to explore, experiment, and take advantage of the features of the Office 2007 new user interface. These steps are not necessary to complete the projects, but are designed to increase the confidence with the software and build problem-solving skills.

- **Thoroughly Tested Projects** Unparalleled quality is ensured because every screen in the book is produced by the author only after performing a step, and then each project must pass Thomson Course Technology's Quality Assurance program.

- **Other Ways Boxes and Quick Reference Summary** The Other Ways boxes displayed at the end of most of the step-by-step sequences specify the other ways to do the task completed in the steps. Thus, the steps and the Other Ways box make a comprehensive reference unit. A Quick Reference Summary at the end of the book contains all of the tasks presented in the chapters, and all ways identified of accomplishing the tasks.

- **BTW** These marginal annotations provide background information, tips, and answers to common questions that complement the topics covered, adding depth and perspective to the learning process.

- **Integration of the World Wide Web** The World Wide Web is integrated into the Word 2007 learning experience by (1) BTW annotations that send students to Web sites for up-to-date information and alternative approaches to tasks; (2) a Microsoft Business Certification Program Web page so students can prepare for the certification examinations; (3) a Quick Reference Summary Web page that summarizes the ways to complete tasks (mouse, Ribbon, shortcut menu, and keyboard); and (4) the Learn It Online section at the end of each chapter, which has chapter reinforcement exercises, learning games, and other types of student activities.

- **End-of-Chapter Student Activities** Extensive student activities at the end of each chapter provide the student with plenty of opportunities to reinforce the materials learned in the chapter through hands-on assignments. Several new types of activities have been added that challenge the student in new ways to expand their knowledge, and to apply their new skills to a project with personal relevance.

 Q&A What is a maximized window?

A maximized window fills the entire screen. When you maximize a window, the Maximize button changes to a Restore Down button.

Other Ways

1. Click Italic button on Mini toolbar
2. Right-click selected text, click Font on shortcut menu, click Font tab, click Italic in Font style list, click OK button
3. Click Font Dialog Box Launcher, click Font tab, click Italic in Font style list, click OK button
4. Press CTRL+I

 BTW **Minimizing the Ribbon** If you want to minimize the Ribbon, right-click the Ribbon and then click Minimize the Ribbon on the shortcut menu, double-click the active tab, or press CTRL+F1. To restore a minimized Ribbon, right-click the Ribbon and then click Minimize the Ribbon on the shortcut menu, double-click any top-level tab, or press CTRL+F1. To use commands on a minimized Ribbon, click the top-level tab.

Organization of This Textbook

Microsoft Office Word 2007: Introductory Concepts and Techniques consists of three chapters on Microsoft Office Word 2007, one special feature emphasizing Web-related topics, seven appendices, and a Quick Reference Summary.

End-of-Chapter Student Activities

A notable strength of the Shelly Cashman Series Microsoft Office 2007 books is the extensive student activities at the end of each chapter. Well-structured student activities can

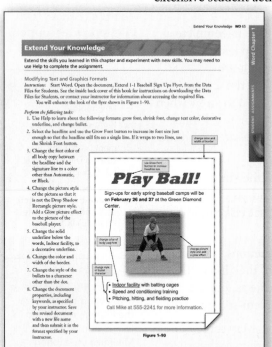

make the difference between students merely participating in a class and students retaining the information they learn. The activities in the Shelly Cashman Series Office books include the following.

CHAPTER SUMMARY A concluding paragraph, followed by a listing of the tasks completed within a chapter together with the pages on which the step-by-step, screen-by-screen explanations appear.

LEARN IT ONLINE Every chapter features a Learn It Online section that is comprised of six exercises. These exercises include True/False, Multiple Choice, Short Answer, Flash Cards, Practice Test, and Learning Games.

APPLY YOUR KNOWLEDGE This exercise usually requires students to open and manipulate a file from the Data Files that parallels the activities learned in the chapter. To obtain a copy of the Data Files for Students, follow the instructions on the inside back cover of this text.

EXTEND YOUR KNOWLEDGE This exercise allows students to extend and expand on the skills learned within the chapter.

MAKE IT RIGHT This exercise requires students to analyze a document, identify errors and issues, and correct those errors and issues using skills learned in the chapter.

IN THE LAB Three all new in-depth assignments per chapter require students to utilize the chapter concepts and techniques to solve problems on a computer.

CASES AND PLACES Five unique real-world case-study situations, including Make It Personal, an open-ended project that relates to student's personal lives, and one small-group activity.

Instructor Resources CD-ROM

The Shelly Cashman Series is dedicated to providing you with all of the tools you need to make your class a success. Information about all supplementary materials is available through your Thomson Course Technology representative or by calling one of the following telephone numbers: Colleges, Universities, and Continuing Ed departments, 1-800-648-7450; High Schools, 1-800-824-5179; and Career Colleges, Business, Government, Library and Resellers, 1-800-477-3692.

The Instructor Resources CD-ROM for this textbook include both teaching and testing aids. The contents of each item on the Instructor Resources CD-ROM (ISBN 1-4239-1226-8) are described on the following pages.

INSTRUCTOR'S MANUAL The Instructor's Manual consists of Microsoft Word files, which include chapter objectives, lecture notes, teaching tips, classroom activities, lab activities, quick quizzes, figures and boxed elements summarized in the chapters, and a glossary page. The new format of the Instructor's Manual will allow you to map through every chapter easily.

LECTURE SUCCESS SYSTEM The Lecture Success System consists of intermediate files that correspond to certain figures in the book, allowing you to step through the creation of a project in a chapter during a lecture without entering large amounts of data.

SYLLABUS Sample syllabi, which can be customized easily to a course, are included. The syllabi cover policies, class and lab assignments and exams, and procedural information.

FIGURE FILES Illustrations for every figure in the textbook are available in electronic form. Use this ancillary to present a slide show in lecture or to print transparencies for use in lecture with an overhead projector. If you have a personal computer and LCD device, this ancillary can be an effective tool for presenting lectures.

POWERPOINT PRESENTATIONS PowerPoint Presentations is a multimedia lecture presentation system that provides slides for each chapter. Presentations are based on chapter objectives. Use this presentation system to present well-organized lectures that are both interesting and knowledge based. PowerPoint Presentations provides consistent coverage at schools that use multiple lecturers.

SOLUTIONS TO EXERCISES Solutions are included for the end-of-chapter exercises, as well as the Chapter Reinforcement exercises. Rubrics and annotated solution files, as described below, are also included.

RUBRICS AND ANNOTATED SOLUTION FILES The grading rubrics provide a customizable framework for assigning point values to the laboratory exercises. Annotated solution files that correspond to the grading rubrics make it easy for you to compare students' results with the correct solutions whether you receive their homework as hard copy or via e-mail.

TEST BANK & TEST ENGINE In the ExamView test bank, you will find our standard question types (40 multiple-choice, 25 true/false, 20 completion) and new objective-based question types (5 modified multiple-choice, 5 modified true/false and 10 matching). Critical Thinking questions are also included (3 essays and 2 cases with 2 questions each) totaling the test bank to 112 questions for every chapter with page number references, and when appropriate, figure references. A version of the test bank you can print also is included. The test bank comes with a copy of the test engine, ExamView, the ultimate tool for your objective-based testing needs. ExamView is a state-of-the-art test builder that is easy to use. ExamView enables you to create paper-, LAN-, or Web-based tests from test banks designed specifically for your Thomson Course Technology textbook. Utilize the ultra-efficient QuickTest Wizard to create tests in less than five minutes by taking advantage of Thomson Course Technology's question banks, or customize your own exams from scratch.

LAB TESTS/TEST OUT The Lab Tests/Test Out exercises parallel the In the Lab assignments and are supplied for the purpose of testing students in the laboratory on the material covered in the chapter or testing students out of the course.

DATA FILES FOR STUDENTS All the files that are required by students to complete the exercises are included. You can distribute the files on the Instructor Resources CD-ROM to your students over a network, or you can have them follow the instructions on the inside back cover of this book to obtain a copy of the Data Files for Students.

ADDITIONAL ACTIVITIES FOR STUDENTS These additional activities consist of Chapter Reinforcement Exercises, which are true/false, multiple-choice, and short answer questions that help students gain confidence in the material learned.

Assessment & Training Solutions

SAM 2007

SAM 2007 helps bridge the gap between the classroom and the real world by allowing students to train and test on important computer skills in an active, hands-on environment.

SAM 2007's easy-to-use system includes powerful interactive exams, training or projects on critical applications such as Word, Excel, Access, PowerPoint, Outlook, Windows, the Internet, and much more. SAM simulates the application environment, allowing students to demonstrate their knowledge and think through the skills by performing real-world tasks.

Designed to be used with the Shelly Cashman series, SAM 2007 includes built-in page references so students can print helpful study guides that match the Shelly Cashman series textbooks used in class. Powerful administrative options allow instructors to schedule exams and assignments, secure tests, and run reports with almost limitless flexibility.

Student Edition Labs

Our Web-based interactive labs help students master hundreds of computer concepts, including input and output devices, file management and desktop applications, computer ethics, virus protection, and much more. Featuring up-to-the-minute content, eye-popping graphics, and rich animation, the highly interactive Student Edition Labs offer students an alternative way to learn through dynamic observation, step-by-step practice, and challenging review questions.

Online Content

Blackboard is the leading distance learning solution provider and class-management platform today. Thomson Course Technology has partnered with Blackboard to bring you premium online content. Instructors: Content for use with *Microsoft Office 2007: Introductory Concepts and Techniques, Windows Vista Edition* is available in a Blackboard Course Cartridge and may include topic reviews, case projects, review questions, test banks, practice tests, custom syllabi, and more.

Thomson Course Technology also has solutions for several other learning management systems. Please visit http://www.course.com today to see what's available for this title.

Workbook for Microsoft Office 2007: Introductory Concepts and Techniques

This highly popular supplement (ISBN 1-4188-4335-0) includes a variety of activities that help students recall, review, and master the concepts presented. The Workbook complements the end-of-chapter material with an outline; a self-test consisting of true/false, multiple-choice, short answer, and matching questions; and activities calculated to help students develop a deeper understanding of the information presented.

Preface

CourseCasts Learning on the Go. Always Available...Always Relevant.

Want to keep up with the latest technology trends relevant to you? Visit our site to find a library of podcasts, CourseCasts, featuring a "CourseCast of the Week," and download them to your portable media player at http://coursecasts.course.com.

Our fast-paced world is driven by technology. You know because you are an active participant — always on the go, always keeping up with technological trends, and always learning new ways to embrace technology to power your life.

Ken Baldauf, a faculty member of the Florida State University (FSU) Computer Science Department, is responsible for teaching technology classes to thousands of FSU students each year. He knows what you know; he knows what you want to learn. He is also an expert in the latest technology and will sort through and aggregate the most pertinent news and information so you can spend your time enjoying technology, rather than trying to figure it out.

Visit us at http://coursecasts.course.com to learn on the go!

CourseNotes

Course Technology's CourseNotes are six-panel quick reference cards that reinforce the most important and widely used features of a software application in a visual and user-friendly format. CourseNotes will serve as a great reference tool during and after the student completes the course. CourseNotes for Microsoft Office 2007, Word 2007, Excel 2007, Access 2007, PowerPoint 2007, Windows Vista, and more are available now!

To the Student . . . Getting the Most Out of Your Book

Welcome to *Microsoft Office Word 2007: Introductory Concepts and Techniques*. You can save yourself a lot of time and gain a better understanding of the Office 2007 programs if you spend a few minutes reviewing the figures and callouts in this section.

1 PROJECT ORIENTATION

Each chapter's project presents a practical problem and shows the solution in the first figure of the chapter. The project orientation lets you see firsthand how problems are solved from start to finish using application software and computers.

2 PROJECT PLANNING GUIDELINES AND PLAN AHEAD BOXES

Overall planning guidelines at the beginning of a chapter and Plan Ahead boxes throughout encourage you to think critically about how to accomplish the next goal before you actually begin working.

3 CONSISTENT STEP-BY-STEP, SCREEN-BY-SCREEN PRESENTATION

Chapter solutions are built using a step-by-step, screen-by-screen approach. This pedagogy allows you to build the solution on a computer as you read through the chapter. Generally, each step includes an explanation that indicates the result of the step.

4 MORE THAN JUST STEP-BY-STEP

BTW annotations in the margins of the book, Q&As in the steps, and substantive text in the paragraphs provide background information, tips, and answers to common questions that complement the topics covered, adding depth and perspective. When you finish with this book, you will be ready to use the Office programs to solve problems on your own. Experimental steps provide you with opportunities to step out on your own to try features of the programs, and pick up right where you left off in the chapter.

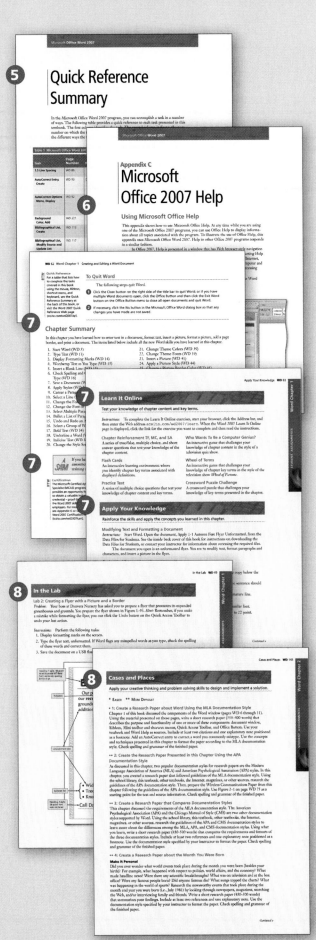

5 OTHER WAYS BOXES AND QUICK REFERENCE SUMMARY

Other Ways boxes that follow many of the step sequences and a Quick Reference Summary at the back of the book explain the other ways to complete the task presented, such as using the mouse, Ribbon, shortcut menu, and keyboard.

6 EMPHASIS ON GETTING HELP WHEN YOU NEED IT

The first project of each application and Appendix C show you how to use all the elements of Office Help. Being able to answer your own questions will increase your productivity and reduce your frustrations by minimizing the time it takes to learn how to complete a task.

7 REVIEW, REINFORCEMENT, AND EXTENSION

After you successfully step through a project in a chapter, a section titled Chapter Summary identifies the tasks with which you should be familiar. Terms you should know for test purposes are bold in the text. The SAM Training feature provides the opportunity for addional reinforcement on important skills covered in each chapter. The Learn It Online section at the end of each chapter offers reinforcement in the form of review questions, learning games, and practice tests. Also included are exercises that require you to extend your learning beyond the book.

8 LABORATORY EXERCISES

If you really want to learn how to use the programs, then you must design and implement solutions to problems on your own. Every chapter concludes with several carefully developed laboratory assignments that increase in complexity.

Learning styles of students have changed, but the Shelly Cashman Series' dedication to their success has remained steadfast for over 30 years. We are committed to continually updating our approach and content to reflect the way today's students learn and experience new technology.

This focus on the user is reflected in our bold new cover design, which features photographs of real students using the Shelly Cashman Series in their courses. Each book features a different user, reflecting the many ages, experiences, and backgrounds of all of the students learning with our books. When you use the Shelly Cashman Series, you can be assured that you are learning computer skills using the most effective courseware available.

We would like to thank the administration and faculty at the participating schools for their help in making our vision a reality. Most of all, we'd like to thank the wonderful students from all over the world who learn from our texts and now appear on our covers.

Microsoft Office Word 2007

1 Creating and Editing a Word Document

Objectives

You will have mastered the material in this chapter when you can:

- Start and quit Word
- Describe the Word window
- Enter text in a document
- Check spelling as you type
- Save a document
- Format text, paragraphs, and document elements
- Undo and redo commands or actions

- Insert a picture and format it
- Print a document
- Change document properties
- Open a document
- Correct errors in a document
- Use Word's Help

1 | Creating and Editing a Word Document

What Is Microsoft Office Word 2007?

Microsoft Office Word 2007 is a full-featured word processing program that allows you to create professional-looking documents and revise them easily. A document is a printed or electronic medium people use to communicate with others. With Word, you can develop many types of documents, including flyers, letters, memos, resumes, reports, fax cover sheets, mailing labels, and newsletters. Word also provides tools that enable you to create Web pages. From within Word, you can place these Web pages directly on a Web server.

Word has many features designed to simplify the production of documents and make documents look visually appealing. Using Word, you easily can change the shape, size, and color of text. You can include borders, shading, tables, images, pictures, charts, and Web addresses in documents.

While you are typing, Word performs many tasks automatically. For example, Word detects and corrects spelling and grammar errors in several languages. Word's thesaurus allows you to add variety and precision to your writing. Word also can format text, such as headings, lists, fractions, borders, and Web addresses, as you type.

This latest version of Word has many new features to make you more productive. For example, Word has many predefined text and graphical elements designed to assist you with preparing documents. Word also includes new charting and diagramming tools; uses themes so that you can coordinate colors, fonts, and graphics; and has a tool that enables you to convert a document to a PDF format.

To illustrate the features of Word, this book presents a series of projects that use Word to create documents similar to those you will encounter in academic and business environments.

Project Planning Guidelines

The process of developing a document that communicates specific information requires careful analysis and planning. As a starting point, establish why the document is needed. Once the purpose is determined, analyze the intended readers of the document and their unique needs. Then, gather information about the topic and decide what to include in the document. Finally, determine the document design and style that will be most successful at delivering the message. Details of these guidelines are provided in Appendix A. In addition, each project in this book provides practical applications of these planning considerations.

Project — Document with a Picture

To advertise a sale, promote a business, publicize an event, or convey a message to the community, you may want to create a flyer and post it in a public location. Libraries, schools, churches, grocery stores, and other places often provide bulletin boards or windows for flyers. These flyers announce personal items for sale or rent (car, boat, apartment); garage or block sales; services being offered (animal care, housecleaning, lessons); membership, sponsorship, or donation requests (club, church, charity); and other messages. Flyers are an inexpensive means of reaching the community, yet many go unnoticed because they are designed poorly.

The project in this chapter follows general guidelines and uses Word to create the flyer shown in Figure 1–1. This colorful, eye-catching flyer advertises horseback riding lessons at Tri-Valley Stables. The picture of the horse and rider entices passersby to stop and look at the flyer. The headline on the flyer is large and colorful to draw attention into the text. The body copy below the headline briefly describes key points of the riding lessons, and the bulleted list below the picture concisely highlights important additional information. The signature line of the flyer calls attention to the stable name and telephone number. Finally, the graphical page border nicely frames and complements the contents of the flyer.

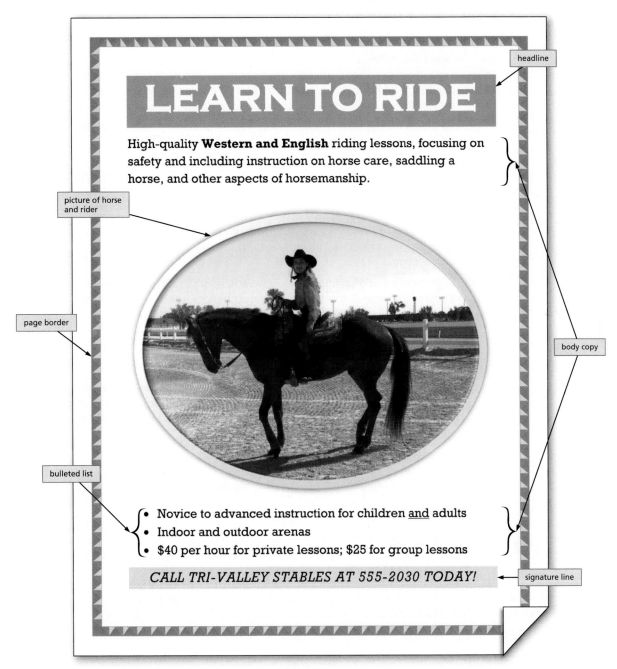

Figure 1–1

Overview

As you read this chapter, you will learn how to create the flyer shown in Figure 1–1 on the previous page by performing these general tasks:

- Enter text in the document.
- Save the document.
- Format the text in the document.
- Insert a picture in the document.
- Format the picture.
- Add a border to the page.
- Print the document.

Plan Ahead

General Project Guidelines

When creating a Word document, the actions you perform and decisions you make will affect the appearance and characteristics of the finished document. As you create a flyer, such as the project shown in Figure 1–1, you should follow these general guidelines:

1. **Choose the words for the text.** Follow the *less is more* principle. The less text, the more likely the flyer will be read. Use as few words as possible to make a point.

2. **Determine where to save the flyer.** You can store a document permanently, or **save** it, on a variety of storage media including a hard disk, USB flash drive, or CD. You also can indicate a specific location on the storage media for saving the document.

3. **Identify how to format various elements of the text.** The overall appearance of a document significantly affects its ability to communicate clearly. Examples of how you can modify the appearance, or **format**, of text include changing its shape, size, color, and position on the page.

4. **Find the appropriate graphical image.** An eye-catching graphical image should convey the flyer's overall message. It could show a product, service, result, or benefit, or visually convey a message that is not expressed easily with words.

5. **Establish where to position and how to format the graphical image.** The position and format of the graphical image should grab the attention of passersby and draw them into reading the flyer.

6. **Determine whether the flyer needs a page border, and if so, its style and format.** A graphical, color-coordinated page border can further draw attention to a flyer and nicely frame its contents. Be careful, however, that a page border does not make the flyer look too cluttered.

When necessary, more specific details concerning the above guidelines are presented at appropriate points in the chapter. The chapter also will identify the actions performed and decisions made regarding these guidelines during the creation of the flyer shown in Figure 1–1.

Starting Word

BTW

The Word Window
The screen in Figure 1-3 shows how the Word window looks the first time you start Word after installation on most computers. Your screen may look different depending on your screen resolution and Word settings.

If you are using a computer to step through the project in this chapter and you want your screen to match the figures in this book, you should change your screen's resolution to 1024 × 768. For information about how to change a computer's resolution, read Appendix E.

Note: If you are using Windows XP, see Appendix F for alternate steps.

To Start Word

The following steps, which assume Windows Vista is running, start Word based on a typical installation. You may need to ask your instructor how to start Word for your computer.

- Click the Start button on the Windows Vista taskbar to display the Start menu.

- Click All Programs at the bottom of the left pane on the Start menu to display the All Programs list.

- Click Microsoft Office in the All Programs list to display the Microsoft Office list (Figure 1–2).

Figure 1–2

- Click Microsoft Office Word 2007 to start Word and display a new blank document in the Word window (Figure 1–3).

- If the Word window is not maximized, click the Maximize button next to the Close button on its title bar to maximize the window.

Q&A What is a maximized window?

A maximized window fills the entire screen. When you maximize a window, the Maximize button changes to a Restore Down button.

- If the Print Layout button is not selected, click it so that your screen layout matches Figure 1–3.

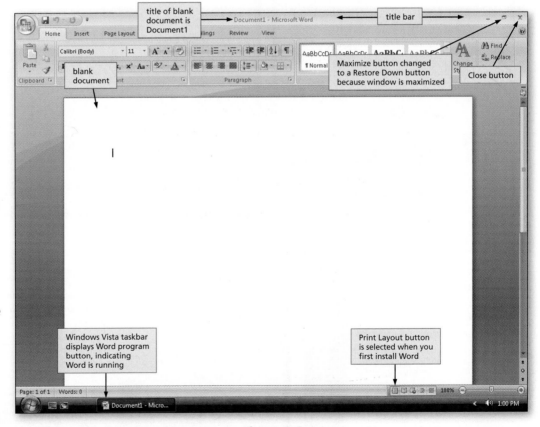

Figure 1–3

Other Ways
1. Double-click Word icon on desktop, if one is present   2. Click Microsoft Office Word 2007 on Start menu

The Word Window

The Word window consists of a variety of components to make your work more efficient and documents more professional. These include the document window, Ribbon, Mini toolbar and shortcut menus, Quick Access Toolbar, and Office Button. Some of these components are common to other Microsoft Office 2007 programs; others are unique to Word.

Document Window

You view a portion of a document on the screen through a **document window** (Figure 1–4). The default (preset) view is **Print Layout view**, which shows the document on a mock sheet of paper in the document window.

The Word document window in Figure 1–4 contains an insertion point, mouse pointer, scroll bar, and status bar. Other elements that may appear in the document window are discussed later in this and subsequent chapters.

Insertion Point The **insertion point** is a blinking vertical bar that indicates where text, graphics, and other items will be inserted. As you type, the insertion point moves to the right, and when you reach the end of a line, it moves downward to the beginning of the next line.

Figure 1–4

Mouse Pointer The **mouse pointer** becomes different shapes depending on the task you are performing in Word and the pointer's location on the screen. The mouse pointer in Figure 1–4 is the shape of an I-beam.

Scroll Bar You use a **scroll bar** to display different portions of a document in the document window. At the right edge of the document window is a vertical scroll bar. If a document is too wide to fit in the document window, a horizontal scroll bar also appears at the bottom of the document window. On a scroll bar, the position of the **scroll box** reflects the location of the portion of the document that is displayed in the document window. A **scroll arrow** is located at each end of a scroll bar. To scroll through, or display different portions of the document in the document window, you can click a scroll arrow or drag the scroll box.

Status Bar The **status bar**, located at the bottom of the document window above the Windows Vista taskbar, presents information about the document, the progress of current tasks, and the status of certain commands and keys; it also provides controls for viewing the document. As you type text or perform certain commands, various indicators and buttons may appear on the status bar.

The left edge of the status bar in Figure 1–4 shows the current page followed by the total number of pages in the document, the number of words in the document, and a button to check spelling and grammar. Toward the right edge are buttons and controls you can use to change the view of a document and adjust the size of the displayed document.

Ribbon

The **Ribbon**, located near the top of the Word window, is the control center in Word (Figure 1–5a). The Ribbon provides easy, central access to the tasks you perform while creating a document. The Ribbon consists of tabs, groups, and commands. Each **tab** surrounds a collection of groups, and each group contains related commands.

When you start Word, the Ribbon displays seven top-level tabs: Home, Insert, Page Layout, References, Mailings, Review, and View. The **Home tab**, called the primary tab, contains the more frequently used commands. To display a different tab on the Ribbon, click the top-level tab. That is, to display the Insert tab, click Insert on the Ribbon. To return to the Home tab, click Home on the Ribbon. The tab currently displayed is called the **active tab**.

To display more of the document in the document window, some users prefer to minimize the Ribbon, which hides the groups on the Ribbon and displays only the top-level tabs (Figure 1–5b). To use commands on a minimized Ribbon, click the top-level tab.

BTW

Minimizing the Ribbon
If you want to minimize the Ribbon, right-click the Ribbon and then click Minimize the Ribbon on the shortcut menu, double-click the active tab, or press CTRL+F1. To restore a minimized Ribbon, right-click the Ribbon and then click Minimize the Ribbon on the shortcut menu, double-click any top-level tab, or press CTRL+F1. To use commands on a minimized Ribbon, click the top-level tab.

Figure 1–5

Each time you start Word, the Ribbon appears the same way it did the last time you used Word. The chapters in this book, however, begin with the Ribbon appearing as it did at the initial installation of the software. If you are stepping through this chapter on a computer and you want your Ribbon to match the figures in this book, read Appendix E.

In addition to the top-level tabs, Word displays other tabs, called **contextual tabs**, when you perform certain tasks or work with objects such as pictures or tables. If you insert a picture in the document, for example, the Picture Tools tab and its related subordinate Format tab appear (Figure 1–6). When you are finished working with the picture, the Picture Tools and Format tabs disappear from the Ribbon. Word determines when contextual tabs should appear and disappear based on tasks you perform. Some contextual tabs, such as the Table Tools tab, have more than one related subordinate tab.

Figure 1–6

Commands on the Ribbon include buttons, boxes (text boxes, check boxes, etc.), and galleries (Figure 1–6). A **gallery** is a set of choices, often graphical, arranged in a grid or in a list. You can scroll through choices on an in-Ribbon gallery by clicking the gallery's scroll arrows. Or, you can click a gallery's More button to view more gallery options on the screen at a time. Some buttons and boxes have arrows that, when clicked, also display a gallery; others always cause a gallery to be displayed when clicked. Most galleries support **live preview**, which is a feature that allows you to point to a gallery choice and see its effect in the document — without actually selecting the choice (Figure 1–7).

Figure 1–7

Some commands on the Ribbon display an image to help you remember their function. When you point to a command on the Ribbon, all or part of the command glows in shades of yellow and orange, and an Enhanced ScreenTip appears on the screen. An **Enhanced ScreenTip** is an on-screen note that provides the name of the command, available keyboard shortcut(s), a description of the command, and sometimes instructions for how to obtain help about the command (Figure 1–8). Enhanced ScreenTips are more detailed than a typical ScreenTip, which usually only displays the name of the command.

Figure 1–8

The lower-right corner of some groups on the Ribbon has a small arrow, called a **Dialog Box Launcher**, that when clicked, displays a dialog box or a task pane with additional options for the group (Figure 1–9). When presented with a dialog box, you make selections and must close the dialog box before returning to the document. A **task pane**, by contrast, is a window that can remain open and visible while you work in the document.

Figure 1–9

Mini Toolbar and Shortcut Menus

The **Mini toolbar**, which appears automatically based on tasks you perform, contains commands related to changing the appearance of text in a document. All commands on the Mini toolbar also exist on the Ribbon. The purpose of the Mini toolbar is to minimize mouse movement. For example, if you want to use a command that currently is not displayed on the active tab, you can use the command on the Mini toolbar — instead of switching to a different tab to use the command.

When the Mini toolbar appears, it initially is transparent (Figure 1–10a). If you do not use the transparent Mini toolbar, it disappears from the screen. To use the Mini toolbar, move the mouse pointer into the toolbar, which causes the Mini toolbar to change from a transparent to bright appearance (Figure 1–10b).

Figure 1–10

A **shortcut menu**, which appears when you right-click an object, is a list of frequently used commands that relate to the right-clicked object. When you right-click a scroll bar, for example, a shortcut menu appears with commands related to the scroll bar. If you right-click an item in the document window, Word displays both the Mini toolbar and a shortcut menu (Figure 1–11).

Figure 1–11

Quick Access Toolbar

The **Quick Access Toolbar**, located by default above the Ribbon, provides easy access to frequently used commands (Figure 1–12a). The commands on the Quick Access Toolbar always are available, regardless of the task you are performing. Initially, the Quick Access Toolbar contains the Save, Undo, and Redo commands. If you click the Customize Quick Access Toolbar button, Word provides a list of commands you quickly can add to and remove from the Quick Access Toolbar (Figure 1–12b).

Figure 1–12

You also can add other commands to or delete commands from the Quick Access Toolbar so that it contains the commands you use most often. As you add commands to the Quick Access Toolbar, its commands may interfere with the document title on the title bar. For this reason, Word provides an option of displaying the Quick Access Toolbar below the Ribbon (Figure 1–13).

Figure 1–13

BTW

Quick Access Toolbar Commands
To add a Ribbon command to the Quick Access Toolbar, right-click the command on the Ribbon and then click Add to Quick Access Toolbar on the shortcut menu. To delete a command from the Quick Access Toolbar, right-click the command on the Quick Access Toolbar and then click Remove from Quick Access Toolbar on the shortcut menu. To display the Quick Access Toolbar below the Ribbon, right-click the Quick Access Toolbar and then click Show Quick Access Toolbar Below the Ribbon on the shortcut menu.

Each time you start Word, the Quick Access Toolbar appears the same way it did the last time you used Word. The chapters in this book, however, begin with the Quick Access Toolbar appearing as it did at the initial installation of the software. If you are stepping through this chapter on a computer and you want your Quick Access Toolbar to match the figures in this book, you should reset your Quick Access Toolbar. For more information about how to reset the Quick Access Toolbar, read Appendix E.

Office Button

While the Ribbon is a control center for creating documents, the **Office Button** is a central location for managing and sharing documents. When you click the Office Button, located in the upper-left corner of the window, Word displays the Office Button menu (Figure 1–14a). A **menu** contains a list of commands.

When you click the New, Open, Save As, and Print commands on the Office Button menu, Word displays a dialog box with additional options. The Save As, Print, Prepare, Send, and Publish commands have an arrow to their right. If you point to this arrow, Word displays a **submenu**, which is a list of additional commands associated with the selected command (Figure 1–14b). For the Prepare, Send, and Publish commands that do not display a dialog box when clicked, you can point either to the command or the arrow to display the submenu.

(a)

(b)

Figure 1–14

Key Tips

If you prefer using the keyboard instead of the mouse, you can press the ALT key on the keyboard to display a **Key Tip badge**, or keyboard code icon, for certain commands (Figure 1–15). To select a command using the keyboard, press its displayed code letter, or **Key Tip**. When you press a Key Tip, additional Key Tips related to the selected command may appear. For example, to select the New command on the Office Button menu, press the ALT key, then press the F key, and then press the N key.

To remove the Key Tip badges from the screen, press the ALT key or the ESC key until all Key Tip badges disappear, or click the mouse anywhere in the Word window.

Figure 1–15

Entering Text

The first step in creating a document is to enter its text by typing on the keyboard. By default, Word positions text you type at the left margin. In a later section of this chapter, you will learn how to format, or change the appearance of, the entered text.

BTW

Zooming
If text is too small for you to read on the screen, you can zoom the document by dragging the Zoom slider on the status bar or clicking the Zoom Out or Zoom In buttons on the status bar. Changing the zoom has no effect on the printed document.

Plan Ahead

> **Choose the words for the text.**
> The text in a flyer is organized into three areas: headline, body copy, and signature line.
>
> - The headline is the first line of text on the flyer. It conveys the product or service being offered, such as a car for sale or personal lessons, or the benefit that will be gained, such as a convenience, better performance, greater security, higher earnings, or more comfort.
>
> - The body text consists of all text between the headline and the signature line. This text highlights the key points of the message in as few words as possible. It should be easy to read and follow. While emphasizing the positive, the body text must be realistic, truthful, and believable.
>
> - The signature line, which is the last line of text on the flyer, contains contact information or identifies a call to action.

To Type Text

To begin creating the flyer in this chapter, you type the headline in the document window. The following steps type this first line of text in the document.

1

- Type Learn to Ride as the headline (Figure 1–16).

What if I make an error while typing?

You can press the **BACKSPACE** key until you have deleted the text in error and then retype the text correctly.

Why did the Spelling and Grammar Check icon appear on the status bar?

When you begin typing text, the **Spelling and Grammar Check icon** appears on the status bar with an animated pencil writing on paper that indicates Word is checking for spelling and grammar errors. When you stop typing, the pencil changes to a blue check mark (no errors) or a red X (potential errors found). Word flags potential errors in the document with a red or green wavy underline. Later, this chapter shows how to fix flagged errors.

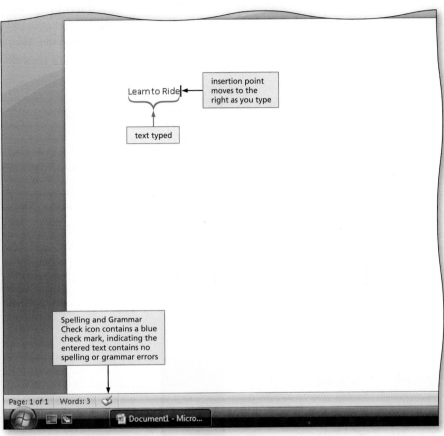

Figure 1–16

2

- Press the ENTER key to move the insertion point to the beginning of the next line (Figure 1–17).

Why did blank space appear between the headline and the insertion point?

Each time you press the ENTER key, Word creates a new paragraph and inserts blank space between the two paragraphs. Later in this chapter, you will learn how to adjust the spacing between paragraphs.

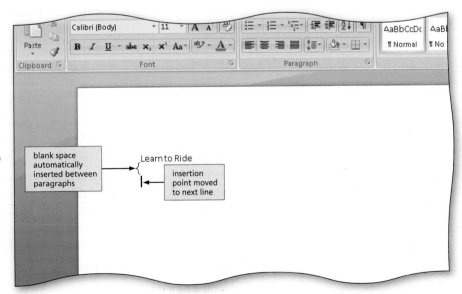

Figure 1–17

To Display Formatting Marks

To indicate where in a document you press the ENTER key or SPACEBAR, you may find it helpful to display formatting marks. A **formatting mark**, sometimes called a **nonprinting character**, is a character that Word displays on the screen but is not visible on a printed document. For example, the paragraph mark (¶) is a formatting mark that indicates where you pressed the ENTER key. A raised dot (·) shows where you pressed the SPACEBAR. Other formatting marks are discussed as they appear on the screen.

Depending on settings made during previous Word sessions, your Word screen already may display formatting marks (Figure 1–18). The following step displays formatting marks, if they do not show already on the screen.

1

- If necessary, click Home on the Ribbon to display the Home tab.

- If it is not selected already, click the Show/Hide ¶ button on the Home tab to display formatting marks on the screen (Figure 1–18).

Q&A

What if I do not want formatting marks to show on the screen?

If you feel the formatting marks clutter the screen, you can hide them by clicking the Show/Hide ¶ button again. It is recommended that you display formatting marks so that you visually can identify when you press the ENTER key, SPACEBAR, and other keys associated with nonprinting characters; therefore, the document windows presented in this book show the formatting marks.

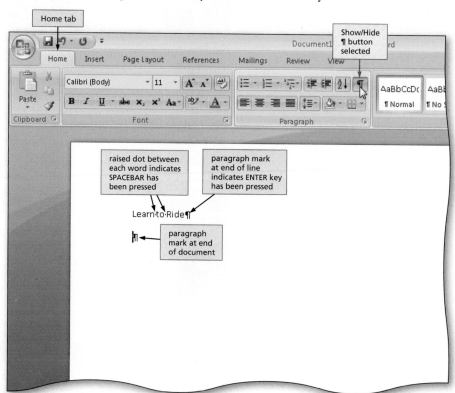

Figure 1–18

BTW

Strange Formatting Marks

With some fonts, the formatting marks are not displayed on the screen properly. For example, the raised dot in each space may be displayed behind a character instead of in the space between two characters, causing the characters to look incorrect.

Wordwrap

Wordwrap allows you to type words in a paragraph continually without pressing the ENTER key at the end of each line. When the insertion point reaches the right margin, Word automatically positions the insertion point at the beginning of the next line. As you type, if a word extends beyond the right margin, Word also automatically positions that word on the next line along with the insertion point.

Word creates a new paragraph each time you press the ENTER key. Thus, as you type text in the document window, do not press the ENTER key when the insertion point reaches the right margin. Instead, press the ENTER key only in these circumstances:

1. To insert blank lines in a document

2. To begin a new paragraph

3. To terminate a short line of text and advance to the next line

4. To respond to questions or prompts in Word dialog boxes, task panes, and other on-screen objects

To Wordwrap Text as You Type

The next step in creating the flyer is to type the body copy. The following step wordwraps the text in the body copy.

- **Type** High-quality Western and English riding lessons, focusing on safety and including instruction on horse care, saddling a horse, and other aspects of horsemanship.

Q&A

Why does my document wrap on different words?

Differences in wordwrap relate to the printer used by your computer. That is, the printer controls where wordwrap occurs for each line in your document. Thus, it is possible that the same document could wordwrap differently if printed on different printers.

- Press the ENTER key to position the insertion point on the next line in the document (Figure 1–19).

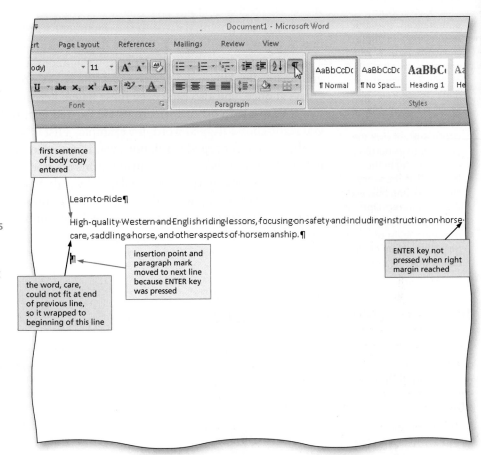

Figure 1–19

To Insert a Blank Line

In the flyer, the picture of the horse and rider should be positioned below the paragraph just entered. The picture will be inserted after all text is entered and formatted. Thus, you will leave a blank line in the document for the picture. To enter a blank line in a document, press the ENTER key without typing any text on the line. The following step inserts one blank line below the first paragraph of body copy.

- Press the ENTER key to insert a blank line in the document (Figure 1–20).

Figure 1–20

BTW

Automatic Spelling Correction

As you type, Word automatically corrects some misspelled words. For example, if you type recieve, Word automatically fixes the misspelling and displays the word, receive, when you press the SPACEBAR or type a punctuation mark. To see a complete list of automatically corrected words, click Office Button, click the Word Options button, click Proofing in the left pane of the Word Options dialog box, click the AutoCorrect Options button, and then scroll through the list of words near the bottom of the dialog box.

Spelling and Grammar Check

As you type text in a document, Word checks your typing for possible spelling and grammar errors. If all of the words you have typed are in Word's dictionary and your grammar is correct, as mentioned earlier, the Spelling and Grammar Check icon on the status bar displays a blue check mark. Otherwise, the icon shows a red X. In this case, Word flags the potential error in the document window with a red or green wavy underline. A red wavy underline means the flagged text is not in Word's dictionary (because it is a proper name or misspelled). A green wavy underline indicates the text may be incorrect grammatically. Although you can check the entire document for spelling and grammar errors at once, you also can check these flagged errors as they appear on the screen.

To display a list of corrections for flagged text, right-click the flagged text. When you right-click a flagged word, for example, a list of suggested spelling corrections appears on the screen. A flagged word, however, is not necessarily misspelled. For example, many names, abbreviations, and specialized terms are not in Word's main dictionary. In these cases, you tell Word to ignore the flagged word. As you type, Word also detects duplicate words while checking for spelling errors. For example, if your document contains the phrase, to the the store, Word places a red wavy underline below the second occurrence of the word, the.

To Check Spelling and Grammar as You Type

In the following steps, the word, instruction, has been misspelled intentionally as intrution to illustrate Word's check spelling as you type feature. If you are doing this project on a computer, your flyer may contain other misspelled words, depending on the accuracy of your typing.

- **Type** Novice to advanced intrution **and then press the** SPACEBAR (Figure 1–21).

Q&A

What if Word does not flag my spelling and grammar errors with wavy underlines?

To verify that the check spelling and grammar as you type features are enabled, click the Office Button and then click the Word Options button. When the Word Options dialog box is displayed, click Proofing, and then ensure the 'Check spelling as you type' and 'Mark grammar errors as you type' check boxes have check marks. Also ensure the 'Hide spelling errors in this document only' and 'Hide grammar errors in this document only' check boxes do not have check marks. Click the OK button.

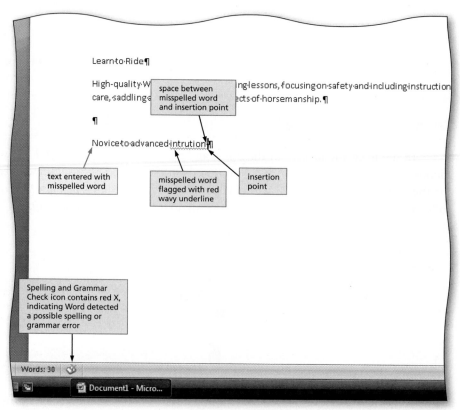

Figure 1–21

2

- Right-click the flagged word (intrution, in this case) to display a shortcut menu that includes a list of suggested spelling corrections for the flagged word (Figure 1–22).

What if, when I right-click the misspelled word, my desired correction is not in the list on the shortcut menu?

You can click outside the shortcut menu to close the menu and then retype the correct word, or you can click Spelling on the shortcut menu to display the Spelling dialog box. Chapter 2 discusses the Spelling dialog box.

What if a flagged word actually is, for example, a proper name and spelled correctly?

Right-click it and then click Ignore All on the shortcut menu to instruct Word not to flag future occurrences of the same word.

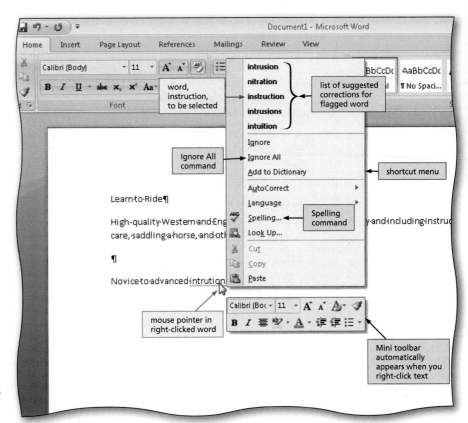

Figure 1–22

3

- Click instruction on the shortcut menu to replace the misspelled word in the document (intrution) with the word, instruction (Figure 1–23).

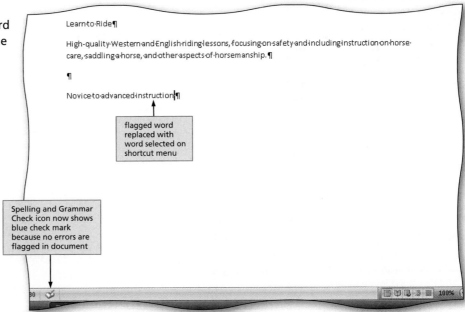

Figure 1–23

Other Ways

1. Click Spelling and Grammar Check icon on status bar, click correct word on shortcut menu

To Enter More Text

In the flyer, the text yet to be entered includes the remainder of the body copy, which will be formatted as a bulleted list, and the signature line. The following steps enter the remainder of text in the flyer.

1 Press the END key to move the insertion point to the end of the current line.

2 Type `for children and adults` and then press the ENTER key.

3 Type `Indoor and outdoor arenas` and then press the ENTER key.

4 Type `$40 per hour for private lessons; $25 for group lessons` and then press the ENTER key.

5 To complete the text in the flyer, type `Call Tri-Valley Stables at 555-2030 today!` (Figure 1–24).

Character Widths
Many word processing documents use variable character fonts, where some characters are wider than others; for example, the letter w takes up more space than the letter i.

Figure 1–24

Saving the Project

File Type
Depending on your Windows Vista settings, the file type .docx may be displayed immediately to the right of the file name after you save the file. The file type .docx is a Word 2007 document. Previous versions of Word had a file type of .doc.

While you are creating a document, the computer stores it in memory. When you save a document, the computer places it on a storage medium such as a USB flash drive, CD, or hard disk. A saved document is referred to as a **file**. A **file name** is the name assigned to a file when it is saved.

It is important to save a document frequently for the following reasons:

• The document in memory will be lost if the computer is turned off or you lose electrical power while Word is open.

• If you run out of time before completing your project, you may finish your document at a future time without starting over.

Determine where to save the document.
When saving a document, you must decide which storage medium to use.

- If you always work on the same computer and have no need to transport your projects to a different location, then your computer's hard disk will suffice as a storage location. It is a good idea, however, to save a backup copy of your projects on a separate medium in case the file becomes corrupted or the computer's hard disk fails.

- If you plan to work on your projects in various locations or on multiple computers, then you should save your projects on a portable medium, such as a USB flash drive or CD. The projects in this book use a USB flash drive, which saves files quickly and reliably and can be reused. CDs are easily portable and serve as good backups for the final versions of projects because they generally can save files only one time.

To Save a Document

You have performed many tasks while creating this project and do not want to risk losing the work completed thus far. Accordingly, you should save the document. The following steps save a document on a USB flash drive using the file name, Horseback Riding Lessons Flyer.

Note: If you are using Windows XP, see Appendix F for alternate steps.

1

- With a USB flash drive connected to one of the computer's USB ports, click the Save button on the Quick Access Toolbar to display the Save As dialog box (Figure 1–25).

- If the Navigation pane is not displayed in the Save As dialog box, click the Browse Folders button to expand the dialog box.

- If a Folders list is displayed below the Folders button, click the Folders button to remove the Folders list.

Q&A

Do I have to save to a USB flash drive?

No. You can save to any device or folder. A **folder** is a specific location on a storage medium. You can save to the default folder or a different folder. You also can create your own folders, which is explained later in this book.

Figure 1–25

• **Type** Horseback Riding Lessons Flyer **in the File name text box to change the file name. Do not press the ENTER key after typing the file name (Figure 1–26).**

Q&A

What characters can I use in a file name?

A file name can have a maximum of 260 characters, including spaces. The only invalid characters are the backslash (\), slash (/), colon (:), asterisk (*), question mark (?), quotation mark ("), less than symbol (<), greater than symbol (>), and vertical bar (|).

Q&A

What are file properties and tags?

File properties contain information about a file such as the file name, author name, date the file was modified, and tags. A tag is a file property that contains a word or phrase about a file. You can organize and locate files based on their file properties.

Figure 1–26

• **If Computer is not displayed in the Favorite Links section, drag the top or bottom edge of the Save As dialog box until Computer is displayed.**

• **Click Computer in the Favorite Links section to display a list of available drives (Figure 1–27).**

• **If necessary, scroll until UDISK 2.0 (E:) appears in the list of available drives.**

Q&A

Why is my list of drives arranged and named differently?

The size of the Save As dialog box and your computer's configuration determine how the list is displayed and how the drives are named.

Q&A

How do I save the file if I am not using a USB flash drive?

Use the same process, but select your desired save location in the Favorite Links section.

Figure 1–27

4

- Double-click UDISK 2.0 (E:) in the Computer list to select the USB flash drive, Drive E in this case, as the new save location (Figure 1–28).

What if my USB flash drive has a different name or letter?

It is very likely that your USB flash drive will have a different name and drive letter and be connected to a different port. Verify the device in your Computer list is correct.

Figure 1–28

5

- Click the Save button in the Save As dialog box to save the document on the USB flash drive with the file name, Horseback Riding Lessons Flyer (Figure 1–29).

How do I know that the project is saved?

While Word is saving your file, it briefly displays a message on the status bar indicating the amount of the file saved. In addition, your USB drive may have a light that flashes during the save process.

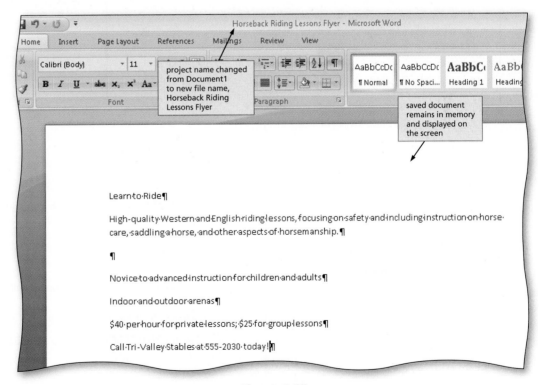

Figure 1–29

Other Ways
1. Click Office Button, click Save, type file name, click Computer, select drive or folder, click Save button   2. Press CTRL+S or press SHIFT+F12, type file name, click Computer, select drive or folder, click Save button

Formatting Paragraphs and Characters in a Document

With the text for the flyer entered, the next step is to format its paragraphs and characters. Paragraphs encompass the text from the first character in a paragraph up to and including a paragraph mark (¶). **Paragraph formatting** is the process of changing the appearance of a paragraph. For example, you can center or indent a paragraph. Characters include letters, numbers, punctuation marks, and symbols. **Character formatting** is the process of changing the way characters appear on the screen and in print. You use character formatting to emphasize certain words and improve readability of a document. For example, you can italicize or underline characters. Often, you apply both paragraph and character formatting to the same text. For example, you may center a paragraph (paragraph formatting) and bold some of the characters in a paragraph (character formatting).

Although you can format paragraphs and characters before you type, many Word users enter text first and then format the existing text. Figure 1–30a shows the flyer in this chapter before formatting its paragraphs and characters. Figure 1–30b shows the flyer after formatting. As you can see from the two figures, a document that is formatted is easier to read and looks more professional. The following pages discuss how to format the flyer so that it looks like Figure 1–30b.

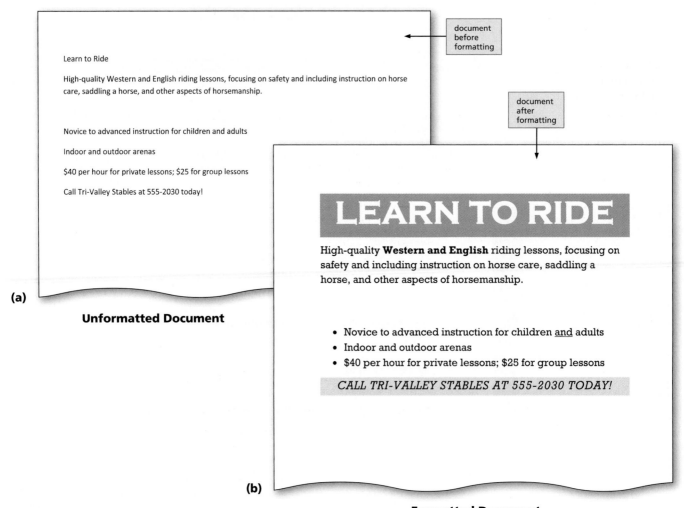

(a) **Unformatted Document**

(b) **Formatted Document**

Figure 1–30

Fonts, Font Sizes, Styles, and Themes

Characters that appear on the screen are a specific shape and size. The **font**, or typeface, defines the appearance and shape of the letters, numbers, and special characters. In Word, the default font usually is Calibri (Figure 1–31 on the next page). You can leave characters in the default font or change them to a different font. **Font size** specifies the size of the characters and is determined by a measurement system called points. A single **point** is about 1/72 of one inch in height. The default font size in Word typically is 11 (Figure 1–31). A character with a font size of 11 is about 11/72 or a little less than 1/6 of one inch in height. You can increase or decrease the font size of characters in a document.

When you create a document, Word formats the text using a particular style. A **style** is a named group of formatting characteristics, including font and font size. The default style in Word is called the **Normal style**, which most likely uses 11-point Calibri font. If you do not specify a style for text you type, Word applies the Normal style to the text. In addition to the Normal style, Word has many other built-in, or predefined, styles that you can use to format text. You also can create your own styles. Styles make it easy to apply many formats at once to text. After you apply a style to text, you easily can modify the text to include additional formats. You also can modify the style.

To assist you with coordinating colors and fonts and other formats, Word uses document themes. A document **theme** is a set of unified formats for fonts, colors, and graphics. The default theme fonts are Cambria for headings and Calibri for body text (Figure 1–31). Word includes a variety of document themes. By changing the document theme, you quickly give your document a new look. You also can define your own document themes.

Identify how to format various elements of the text.

By formatting the characters and paragraphs in a document, you can improve its overall appearance. In a flyer, consider the following formatting suggestions.

- **Increase the font size of characters.** Flyers usually are posted on a bulletin board or in a window. Thus, the font size should be as large as possible so that passersby easily can read the flyer. To give the headline more impact, its font size should be larger than the font size of the text in the body copy. If possible, make the font size of the signature line larger than the body copy but smaller than the headline.

- **Change the font of characters.** Use fonts that are easy to read. Try to use only two different fonts in a flyer, for example, one for the headline and the other for all other text. Too many fonts can make the flyer visually confusing.

- **Change paragraph alignment.** The default alignment for paragraphs in a document is **left-aligned**, that is, flush at the left margin of the document with uneven right edges. Consider changing the alignment of some of the paragraphs to add interest and variety to the flyer.

- **Highlight key paragraphs with bullets.** A **bullet** is a dot or other symbol positioned at the beginning of a paragraph. Use bullets to highlight important paragraphs in a flyer.

- **Emphasize important words.** To call attention to certain words or lines, you can underline them, italicize them, or bold them. Use these formats sparingly, however, because overuse will minimize their effect and make the flyer look too busy.

- **Use color.** Use colors that complement each other and convey the meaning of the flyer. Vary colors in terms of hue and brightness. Headline colors, for example, can be bold and bright. Signature lines should stand out more than body copy but less than headlines. Keep in mind that too many colors can detract from the flyer and make it difficult to read.

Plan Ahead

To Apply Styles

In the flyer, you want the headline and the signature line to be emphasized more than the other text. Word provides heading styles designed to emphasize this type of text. The first step in formatting the flyer is to apply the Heading 1 style to the headline and the Heading 2 style to the signature line. The default Heading 1 style is a 14-point Cambria bold font. The default Heading 2 style is a 13-point Cambria bold font. The default theme color scheme uses shades of blue for headings.

To apply a style to a paragraph, you first position the insertion point in the paragraph and then apply the style. The following steps apply heading styles to paragraphs.

- Press CTRL+HOME (that is, press and hold down the CTRL key, press the HOME key, and then release both keys) to position the insertion point at the top of the document (Figure 1–31).

Figure 1–31

- Point to Heading 1 in the Styles gallery to display a live preview in the document of the Heading 1 style (Figure 1–32).

What happens if I move the mouse pointer?

If you move the mouse pointer away from the gallery, the text containing the insertion point returns to the Normal style.

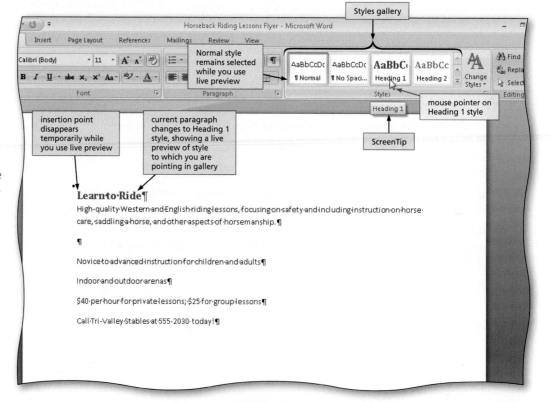

Figure 1–32

3
- Click Heading 1 in the Styles gallery to apply the Heading 1 style to the headline (Figure 1–33).

Why did a square appear on the screen near the left edge of the headline?

The square is a nonprinting character, like the paragraph mark, that indicates text to its right has a special paragraph format applied to it.

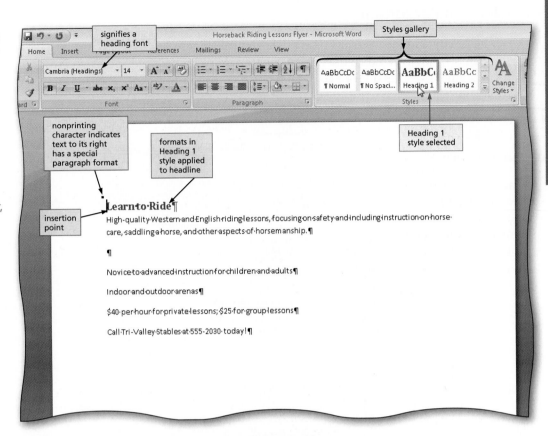

Figure 1–33

4
- Press CTRL+END (that is, press and hold down the CTRL key, press the END key, and then release both keys) to position the insertion point at the end of the document.

- Click Heading 2 in the Styles gallery to apply the Heading 2 style to the signature line (Figure 1–34).

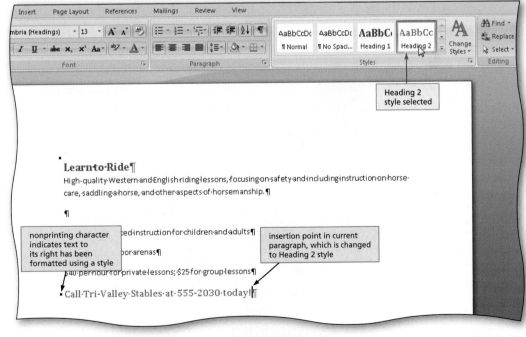

Figure 1–34

Other Ways
1. Click Styles Dialog Box Launcher, click desired style in Styles task pane	2. Press CTRL+SHIFT+S, click Style Name box arrow in Apply Styles task pane, click desired style in list

To Center a Paragraph

The headline in the flyer currently is left-aligned (Figure 1–35). You want the headline to be **centered**, that is, positioned horizontally between the left and right margins on the page. Thus, you will center the paragraph containing the headline. Recall that Word considers a single short line of text, such as the three-word headline, a paragraph. The following steps center a paragraph.

- Click somewhere in the paragraph to be centered (in this case, the headline) to position the insertion point in the paragraph to be formatted (Figure 1–35).

Figure 1–35

2

- Click the Center button on the Home tab to center the headline (Figure 1–36).

Q&A

What if I want to return the paragraph to left-aligned?

Click the Align Text Left button on the Home tab.

Figure 1–36

Other Ways

1. Right-click paragraph, click Center button on Mini toolbar

2. Right-click paragraph, click Paragraph on shortcut menu, click Indents and Spacing tab, click Alignment box arrow, click Centered, click OK button

3. Click Paragraph Dialog Box Launcher, click Indents and Spacing tab, click Alignment box arrow, click Centered, click OK button

4. Press CTRL+E

Formatting Single Versus Multiple Paragraphs and Characters

As shown in the previous pages, to format a single paragraph, simply move the insertion point in the paragraph and then format the paragraph. Likewise, to format a single word, position the insertion point in the word and then format the word.

        To format *multiple* paragraphs or words, however, you first must select the paragraphs or words you want to format and then format the selection. If your screen normally displays dark letters on a light background, which is the default setting in Word, then selected text displays light letters on a dark background.

To Select a Line

        The font size of characters in the Heading 1 style, 14 point, is too small for passersby to read in the headline of the flyer. To increase the font size of the characters in the headline, you must first select the line of text containing the headline. The following steps select a line.

1
- Move the mouse pointer to the left of the line to be selected (in this case, the headline) until the mouse pointer changes to a right-pointing block arrow (Figure 1–37).

Figure 1–37

2
- While the mouse pointer is a right-pointing block arrow, click the mouse to select the entire line to the right of the mouse pointer (Figure 1–38).

Figure 1–38

Other Ways	
1. Drag mouse through line	2. With insertion point at beginning of desired line, press SHIFT+DOWN ARROW

To Change the Font Size of Selected Text

The next step is to increase the font size of the characters in the selected headline. You would like the headline to be as large as possible and still fit on a single line, which in this case is 48 point. The following steps increase the font size of the headline from 14 to 48 point.

● With the text selected, click the Font Size box arrow on the Home tab to display the Font Size gallery (Figure 1–39).

Q&A Why are the font sizes in my Font Size gallery different from those in Figure 1–39?

Font sizes may vary depending on the current font and your printer driver.

Q&A What happened to the Mini toolbar?

The Mini toolbar disappears if you do not use it. These steps use the Font Size box arrow on the Home tab instead of the Font Size box arrow on the Mini toolbar. If a command exists both on the currently displayed tab and the Mini toolbar, this book uses the command on the tab. When the command is not on the currently displayed tab, the Mini toolbar is used.

Figure 1–39

❷
● Point to 48 in the Font Size gallery to display a live preview of the headline at 48 point (Figure 1–40).

🔎 **Experiment**

● Point to various font sizes in the Font Size gallery and watch the font size of the headline change in the document window.

❸
● Click 48 in the Font Size gallery to increase the font size of the selected text to 48.

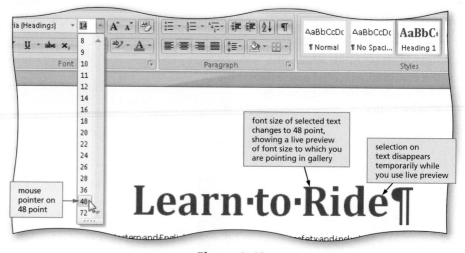

Figure 1–40

Other Ways

1. Click Font Size box arrow on Mini toolbar, click desired font size in Font Size gallery

2. Right-click selected text, click Font on shortcut menu, click Font tab, select desired font size in Size list, click OK button

3. Click Font Dialog Box Launcher, click Font tab, select desired font size in Size list, click OK button

4. Press CTRL+SHIFT+P, click Font tab, select desired font size in Size list, click OK button

To Change the Font of Selected Text

As mentioned earlier, the default Heading 1 style uses the font called Cambria. Word, however, provides many other fonts to add variety to your documents. To draw more attention to the headline, you change its font so it differs from the font of other text in the flyer. The following steps change the font from Cambria to Copperplate Gothic Bold.

1

• With the text selected, click the Font box arrow on the Home tab to display the Font gallery (Figure 1–41).

Will the fonts in my Font gallery be the same as those in Figure 1–41?

Your list of available fonts may differ, depending on the type of printer you are using.

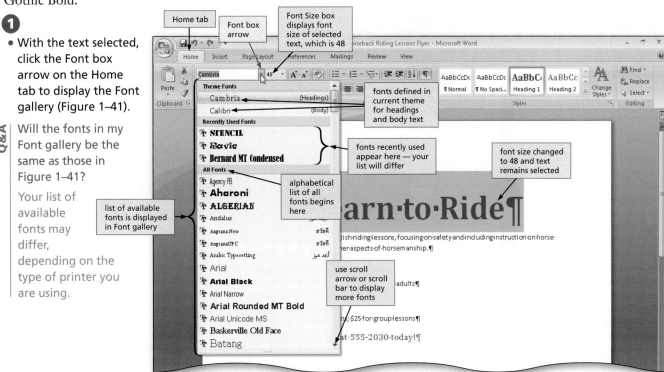

Figure 1–41

2

• Scroll through the Font gallery, if necessary, and then point to Copperplate Gothic Bold (or a similar font) to display a live preview of the headline in Copperplate Gothic Bold font (Figure 1–42).

Experiment

• Point to various fonts in the Font gallery and watch the font of the headline change in the document window.

3

• Click Copperplate Gothic Bold (or a similar font) to change the font of the selected text to Copperplate Gothic Bold.

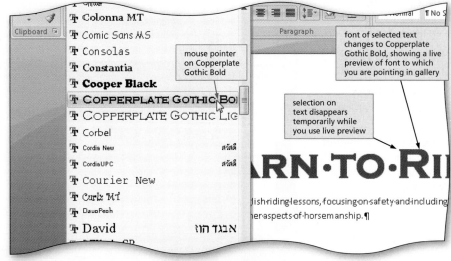

Figure 1–42

Other Ways

1. Click Font box arrow on Mini toolbar, click desired font in Font gallery
2. Right-click selected text, click Font on shortcut menu, click
Font tab, select desired font in Font list, click OK button
3. Click Font Dialog Box Launcher, click Font tab, select desired font in Font list, click OK button
4. Press CTRL+SHIFT+F, click Font tab, select desired font in the Font list, click OK button

To Select Multiple Paragraphs

The next formatting step in creating the flyer is to increase the font size of the characters between the headline and the signature line so that they are easier to read from a distance. To change the font size of the characters in multiple lines, you first must select all the lines to be formatted. The following steps select multiple lines.

- Move the mouse pointer to the left of the first paragraph to be selected until the mouse pointer changes to a right-pointing block arrow (Figure 1–43).

Figure 1–43

- Drag downward to select all lines that will be formatted (Figure 1–44).

Q&A

How do I *drag* the mouse?

Dragging is the process of holding down the mouse button while moving the mouse and then releasing the mouse button.

Figure 1–44

Other Ways

1. With insertion point at beginning of desired line, press SHIFT+DOWN ARROW repeatedly until all lines are selected

To Change the Font Size of Selected Text

The characters between the headline and the signature line in the flyer currently are 11 point. To make them easier to read from a distance, this flyer uses 16 point for these characters. The following steps change the font size of the selected text.

1 With the text selected, click the Font Size box arrow on the Home tab to display the Font Size gallery.

2 Click 16 in the Font Size gallery to increase the font size of the selected text to 16.

To Format a Line

In the flyer, the signature line is to be centered to match the paragraph alignment of the headline. Also, its text should have a font size larger than the rest of the body copy. The following steps center the line and increase its font size to 18.

1 Click somewhere in the paragraph to be centered (in this case, the signature line) to position the insertion point in the paragraph to be formatted.

2 Click the Center button on the Home tab to center the signature line.

3 Move the mouse pointer to the left of the line to be selected (in this case, the signature line) until the mouse pointer changes to a right-pointing block arrow and then click to select the line.

4 With the signature line selected, click the Font Size box arrow on the Home tab and then click 18 in the Font Size gallery to increase the font size of the selected text to 18 (Figure 1–45).

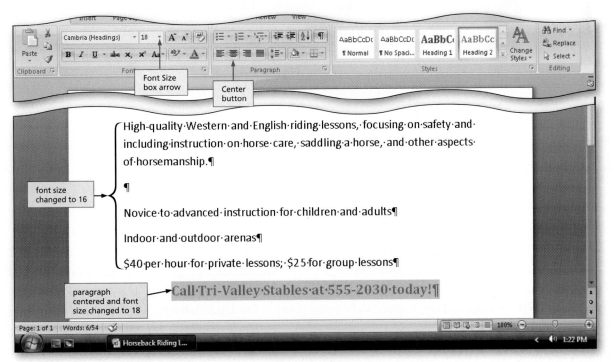

Figure 1–45

To Bullet a List of Paragraphs

The next step is to format the three important points above the signature line in the flyer as a bulleted list. A **bulleted list** is a series of paragraphs, each beginning with a bullet character. The three lines each end with a paragraph mark because you pressed the ENTER key at the end of each line. Thus, these three lines actually are three separate paragraphs.

To format a list of paragraphs with bullets, you first must select all the lines in the paragraphs. The following steps bullet a list of paragraphs.

1
- Move the mouse pointer to the left of the first paragraph to be selected until the mouse pointer changes to a right-pointing block arrow.

- Drag downward until all paragraphs (lines) that will be formatted with a bullet character are selected.

2
- Click the Bullets button on the Home tab to place a bullet character at the beginning of each selected paragraph (Figure 1–46).

Q&A

How do I remove bullets from a list or paragraph?

Select the list or paragraph and click the Bullets button again.

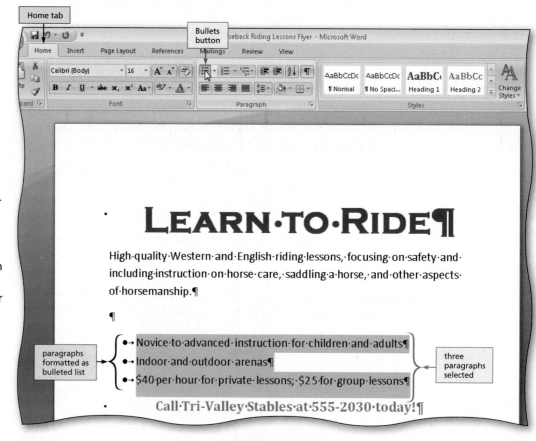

Figure 1–46

Other Ways

1. Right-click selected paragraphs, click Bullets button on Mini toolbar

2. Right-click selected paragraphs, point to Bullets on shortcut menu, click desired bullet style

To Undo and Redo an Action

Word provides a means of canceling your recent command(s) or action(s). For example, if you format text incorrectly, you can undo the format and try it again. When you point to the Undo button, Word displays the action you can undo as part of the ScreenTip.

If, after you undo an action, you decide you did not want to perform the undo, you can redo the undone action. Word does not allow you to undo or redo some actions, such as saving or printing a document. The next steps undo the bullet format just applied and then redo the bullet format.

1

• Click the Undo button on the Quick Access Toolbar to remove the bullets from the selected paragraphs (Figure 1–47).

2

• Click the Redo button on the Quick Access Toolbar to place a bullet character at the beginning of each selected paragraph again (shown in Figure 1–46).

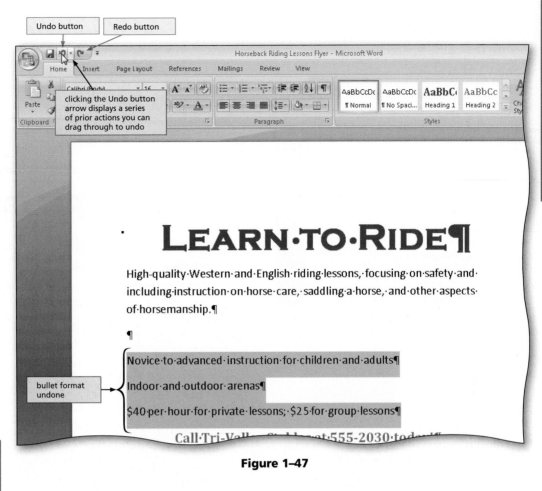

Figure 1–47

Other Ways

1. Press CTRL+Z; press CTRL+Y

To Select a Group of Words

To emphasize the types of riding lessons, Western and English, these words are bold in the flyer. To format a group of words, you first must select them. The following steps select a group of words.

1

• Position the mouse pointer immediately to the left of the first character of the text to be selected, in this case, the W in Western (Figure 1–48).

 Why did the shape of the mouse pointer change?

The mouse pointer's shape is an I-beam when positioned in unselected text in the document window.

Figure 1–48

2

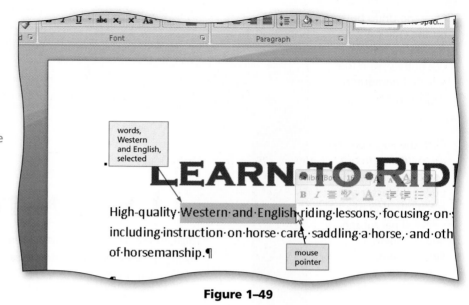

- Drag the mouse pointer through the last character of the text to be selected, in this case, the h in English (Figure 1–49).

 Q&A Why did the mouse pointer shape change again?

When the mouse pointer is positioned in selected text, its shape is a left-pointing block arrow.

Other Ways

1. With insertion point at beginning of first word in group, press CTRL+SHIFT+RIGHT ARROW repeatedly until all words are selected

Figure 1–49

To Bold Text

Bold characters display somewhat thicker and darker than those that are not bold. The following step formats the selected words, Western and English, as bold.

1

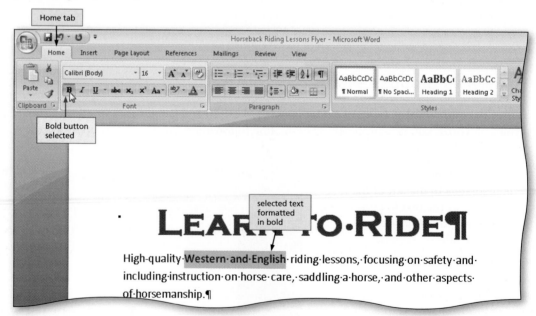

- With the text selected, click the Bold button on the Home tab to format the selected text in bold (Figure 1–50).

Q&A How would I remove a bold format?

You would click the Bold button a second time, or you immediately could click the Undo button on the Quick Access Toolbar.

Figure 1–50

Other Ways

1. Click Bold button on Mini toolbar

2. Right-click selected text, click Font on shortcut menu, click Font tab, click Bold in Font style list, click OK button

3. Click Font Dialog Box Launcher, click Font tab, click Bold in Font style list, click OK button

4. Press CTRL+B

To Underline a Word

As with bold text, underlines are used to emphasize or draw attention to specific text. **Underlined** text prints with an underscore (_) below each character. In the flyer, the word, and, in the first bulleted paragraph is emphasized with an underline.

As with a single paragraph, if you want to format a single word, you do not need to select the word. Simply position the insertion point somewhere in the word and apply the desired format. The following step formats a word with an underline.

1

- Click somewhere in the word to be underlined (and, in this case).

- Click the Underline button on the Home tab to underline the word containing the insertion point (Figure 1–51).

Q&A How would I remove an underline?

You would click the Underline button a second time, or you immediately could click the Undo button on the Quick Access Toolbar.

Q&A Are other types of underlines available?

In addition to the basic solid underline shown in Figure 1–51, Word has many decorative underlines, such as double underlines, dotted underlines, and wavy underlines. You can access the decorative underlines and also change the color of an underline through the Underline gallery.

Figure 1–51

Other Ways
1. Right-click text, click Font on shortcut menu, click Font tab, click Underline style box arrow, click desired underline style, click OK button
2. Click Font Dialog Box Launcher, click Font tab, click Underline style box arrow, click desired underline style, click OK button
3. Press CTRL+U

To Italicize Text

To further emphasize the signature line, this line is italicized in the flyer. **Italicized** text has a slanted appearance. The following steps select the text and then italicize it.

- Point to the left of the line to be selected (in this case, the signature line) and click when the mouse pointer is a right-pointing block arrow.

- Click the Italic button on the Home tab to italicize the selected text.

- Click inside the selected text to remove the selection (Figure 1–52).

Q&A How would I remove an italic format?

You would click the Italic button a second time, or you immediately could click the Undo button on the Quick Access Toolbar.

Q&A How can I tell what formatting has been applied to text?

The selected buttons and boxes on the Home tab show formatting characteristics of the location of the insertion point. With the insertion point in the signature line, the Home tab shows these formats: 18-point Cambria bold italic font, centered paragraph, and Heading 2 style.

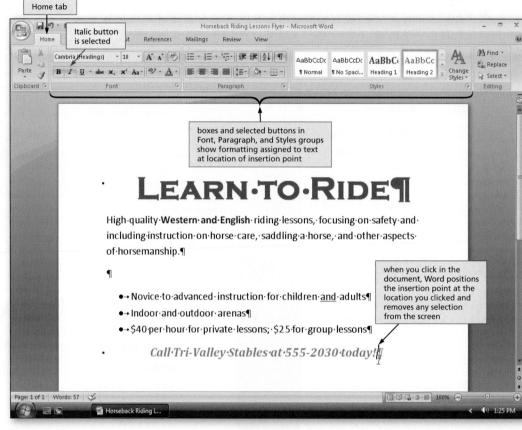

Figure 1–52

Other Ways

1. Click Italic button on Mini toolbar
2. Right-click selected text, click Font on shortcut menu, click Font tab, click Italic in Font style list, click OK button
3. Click Font Dialog Box Launcher, click Font tab, click Italic in Font style list, click OK button
4. Press CTRL+I

Document Formats

One advantage of using styles to format text is that you easily can change the formats of styles and themes in your document to give it a different or new look. Recall that a style is a named group of formatting characteristics and a theme is a set of unified formats for fonts, colors, and graphics. In Word, you can change the style set, theme colors, and theme fonts.

- The predefined styles in the Styles gallery, such as Heading 1 and Heading 2, each known as a **Quick Style**, are part of a style set. A **style set** consists of a group of frequently used styles formatted so they look pleasing when used together. When you change the style set, formats assigned to each Quick Style also change.

- Each **color scheme** in a theme identifies 12 complementary colors for text, background, accents, and links in a document. With more than 20 predefined color schemes, Word provides a simple way to select colors that work well together.

- Each theme has a **font set** that defines formats for two fonts: one for headings and another for body text. In Word, you can select from more than 20 predefined coordinated font sets to give the document's text a new look.

Use color.

When choosing color, associate the meaning of color to your message:

- Red expresses danger, power, or energy, and often is associated with sports or physical exertion.

- Brown represents simplicity, honesty, and dependability.

- Orange denotes success, victory, creativity, and enthusiasm.

- Yellow suggests sunshine, happiness, hope, liveliness, and intelligence.

- Green symbolizes growth, healthiness, harmony, blooming, and healing, and often is associated with safety or money.

- Blue indicates integrity, trust, importance, confidence, and stability.

- Purple represents wealth, power, comfort, extravagance, magic, mystery, and spirituality.

- White stands for purity, goodness, cleanliness, precision, and perfection.

- Black suggests authority, strength, elegance, power, and prestige.

- Gray conveys neutrality and thus often is found in backgrounds and other effects.

Plan Ahead

To Change the Style Set

To symbolize perfection and precision in the flyer, the characters in the headline are white. The style set, called Modern, formats Heading 1 characters in white. It also formats the Heading 1 and Heading 2 styles in all capital letters and places a background color around the paragraphs, which further emphasize the headline and signature line in the flyer. Thus, you will change the style set from Default to Modern. The following steps change a style set.

- Click the Change Styles button on the Home tab to display the Change Styles menu (Figure 1–53).

Figure 1–53

2

- Point to Style Set on the Change Styles menu to display the Style Set gallery.

- Point to Modern in the Style Set gallery to display a live preview of the formats associated with the Modern style set (Figure 1–54).

 Experiment

- Point to various style sets in the Style Set gallery and watch the formats of the styled text change in the document window.

3

- Click Modern in the Style Set gallery to change the document style set to Modern.

Q&A What if I want to return to the original style set?

You would click the Change Styles button, click Style Set on the Change Styles menu, and then click Default in the Style Set gallery, or you could click the Undo button on the Quick Access Toolbar.

Figure 1–54

BTW

Style Formats

To see the formats assigned to a particular style in a document, click the Styles Dialog Box Launcher on the Home tab and then click the Style Inspector button in the Styles task pane. Position the insertion point in the style and then point to the Paragraph formatting or Text level formatting areas in the Style Inspector task pane to display an Enhanced ScreenTip describing formats assigned to the location of the insertion point. You also can click the Reveal Formatting button in the Style Inspector to display the Reveal Formatting task pane.

To Change Theme Colors

To suggest enthusiasm, success, and honesty, the background colors around the headline and signature line paragraphs in the flyer use shades of orange and brown. In Word, the color scheme called Aspect uses these colors. Thus, you will change the color scheme to Aspect. The following steps change theme colors.

1

- Click the Change Styles button on the Home tab to display the Change Styles menu.

- Point to Colors on the Change Styles menu to display the Colors gallery.

- Point to Aspect in the Colors gallery to display a live preview of the Aspect color scheme (Figure 1–55).

  Experiment

- Point to various color schemes in the Colors gallery and watch the paragraph background colors change in the document window.

2

- Click Aspect in the Colors gallery to change the document theme colors to Aspect.

Figure 1–55

Q&A What if I want to return to the original color scheme?

You would click the Change Styles button, click Colors on the Change Styles menu, and then click Office in the Colors gallery.

Other Ways

1. Click Theme Colors button arrow on Page Layout tab, select desired color scheme

To Change Theme Fonts

Earlier in this chapter, you changed the font of the headline to Copperplate Gothic Bold. In this flyer, all text below the headline should be the Rockwell font, instead of the Calibri font, because it better matches the western tone of the flyer. Thus, the next step is to change the current font set, which is called Office, to a font set called Foundry, which uses the Rockwell font for headings and body text.

If you previously changed a font using buttons on the Ribbon or Mini toolbar, Word will not alter those when you change the font set because changes to the font set are not applied to fonts changed individually. This means the font headline in the flyer will stay as Copperplate Gothic Bold when you change the font set. The following steps change the font set to Foundry.

- Click the Change Styles button on the Home tab.

- Point to Fonts on the Change Styles menu to display the Fonts gallery.

- Scroll through the Fonts gallery until Foundry is displayed and then point to Foundry to display a live preview of the Foundry font set (Figure 1–56).

Experiment

- Point to various font sets in the Fonts gallery and watch the fonts below the headline change in the document window.

Figure 1–56

- Click Foundry in the Fonts gallery to change the document theme fonts to Foundry.

Q&A

What if I want to return to the original font set?

You would click the Change Styles button, click Fonts on the Change Styles menu, and then click Office in the Fonts gallery.

Other Ways
1. Click Theme Fonts button arrow on Page Layout tab, select desired font set

Inserting and Formatting a Picture in a Word Document

With the text formatted in the flyer, the next step is to insert a picture in the flyer and format the picture. Flyers usually contain graphical images, such as a picture, to attract the attention of passersby.

Note: If you are using Windows XP, see Appendix F for alternate steps.

<table>
<tr><td>

Find the appropriate graphical image.
To use graphical images, also called graphics, in a Word document, the image must be stored digitally in a file. Files containing graphical images are available from a variety of sources:

- Word includes a collection of predefined graphical images that you can insert in a document.

- Microsoft has free digital images on the Web for use in a document. Other Web sites also have images available, some of which are free, while others require a fee.

- You can take a picture with a digital camera and **download** it, which is the process of copying the digital picture from the camera to your computer.

- With a scanner, you can convert a printed picture, drawing, or diagram to a digital file.

   If you receive a picture from a source other than yourself, do not use the file until you are certain it does not contain a virus. A **virus** is a computer program that can damage files and programs on your computer. Use an antivirus program to verify that any files you use are virus free.

</td><td>

Plan
Ahead

</td></tr>
</table>

<table>
<tr><td>

Establish where to position and how to format the graphical image.
The content, size, shape, position, and format of a graphic should capture the interest of passersby, enticing them to stop and read the flyer. Often, the graphic is the center of attraction and visually the largest element on a flyer. If you use colors in the graphical image, be sure they are part of the document's color scheme.

</td><td>

Plan
Ahead

</td></tr>
</table>

To Insert a Picture

The next step in creating the flyer is to insert the picture of the horse and rider so that it is centered on the blank line above the bulleted list. The picture, which was taken with a digital camera, is available on the Data Files for Students. See the inside back cover of this book for instructions on downloading the Data Files for Students, or contact your instructor for information about accessing the required files. The following steps insert a centered picture, which, in this example, is located on the same USB flash drive that contains the saved flyer.

1

- To position the insertion point where you want the picture to be located, press CTRL+HOME and then press the DOWN ARROW key four times.

- Click the Center button on the Home tab to center the paragraph that will contain the picture.

- Click Insert on the Ribbon to display the Insert tab (Figure 1–57).

Figure 1–57

2

- With your USB flash drive connected to one of the computer's USB ports, click the Insert Picture from File button on the Insert tab to display the Insert Picture dialog box.

- If the Folders list is displayed below the Folders button, click the Folders button to remove the Folders list.

- If necessary, click Computer in the Favorite Links section and then scroll until UDISK 2.0 (E:) appears in the list of available drives.

- Double-click UDISK 2.0 (E:) to select the USB flash drive, Drive E in this case, as the device that contains the picture.

- Click Horse and Rider to select the file name (Figure 1–58).

Q&A | What if the picture is not on a USB flash drive?

Use the same process, but select the device containing the picture in the Favorite Links section.

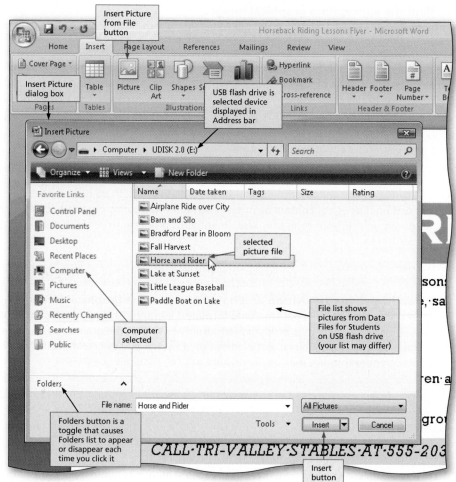

Figure 1–58

3

- Click the Insert button in the dialog box to insert the picture at the location of the insertion point in the document (Figure 1–59).

Q&A | What are the symbols around the picture?

A selected graphic appears surrounded by a **selection rectangle**, which has small squares and circles, called **sizing handles**, at each corner and middle location.

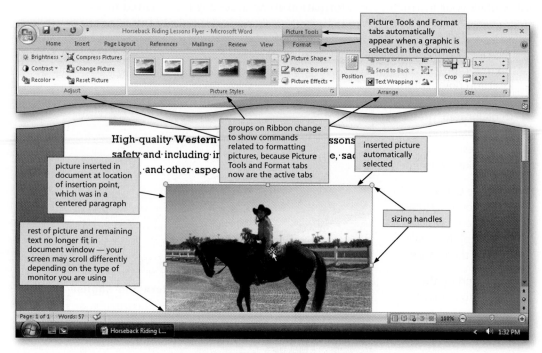

Figure 1–59

Scrolling

As mentioned at the beginning of this chapter, you view only a portion of a document on the screen through the document window. At some point when you type text or insert graphics, Word will **scroll** the top or bottom portion of the document off the screen. Although you cannot see the text and graphics once they scroll off the screen, they remain in the document.

As shown in Figure 1–59, when you insert the picture in the flyer, the text and graphics are too long to fit in the document window. Thus, to see the bottom of the flyer, you will need to scroll downward.

You may use either the mouse or the keyboard to scroll to a different location in a document. With the mouse, you can use the scroll arrows or the scroll box on the scroll bar to display a different portion of the document in the document window, and then click the mouse to move the insertion point to that location. Table 1–1 explains various techniques for using the scroll bar to scroll vertically with the mouse.

BTW

Minimize Wrist Injury
Computer users frequently switch between the keyboard and the mouse during a word processing session; such switching strains the wrist. To help prevent wrist injury, minimize switching. For instance, if your fingers already are on the keyboard, use keyboard keys to scroll. If your hand already is on the mouse, use the mouse to scroll.

Table 1–1 Using the Scroll Bar to Scroll with the Mouse	
SCROLL DIRECTION	**MOUSE ACTION**
Up	Drag the scroll box upward.
Down	Drag the scroll box downward.
Up one screen	Click anywhere above the scroll box on the vertical scroll bar.
Down one screen	Click anywhere below the scroll box on the vertical scroll bar.
Up one line	Click the scroll arrow at the top of the vertical scroll bar.
Down one line	Click the scroll arrow at the bottom of the vertical scroll bar.

When you use the keyboard to scroll, the insertion point automatically moves when you press the appropriate keys. Table 1–2 outlines various techniques to scroll through a document using the keyboard, some of which you have seen used in this chapter.

Table 1–2 Scrolling with the Keyboard	
SCROLL DIRECTION	**KEY(S) TO PRESS**
Left one character	LEFT ARROW
Right one character	RIGHT ARROW
Left one word	CTRL+LEFT ARROW
Right one word	CTRL+RIGHT ARROW
Up one line	UP ARROW
Down one line	DOWN ARROW
To end of line	END
To beginning of line	HOME
Up one paragraph	CTRL+UP ARROW
Down one paragraph	CTRL+DOWN ARROW
Up one screen	PAGE UP
Down one screen	PAGE DOWN
To top of document window	ALT+CTRL+PAGE UP
To bottom of document window	ALT+CTRL+PAGE DOWN
To beginning of document	CTRL+HOME
To end of document	CTRL+END

To Apply a Picture Style

Earlier in this chapter, you applied the heading styles to the headline and signature line in the flyer. Word also provides styles for pictures, allowing you easily to change the basic rectangle format to a more visually appealing style. Word provides a gallery of more than 25 picture styles, which include a variety of shapes, angles, borders, and reflections. The flyer in this chapter uses an oval picture style that has a border around its edges. The following steps apply a picture style to the picture in the flyer.

1

- Click the down scroll arrow on the vertical scroll bar as many times as necessary until the entire picture is displayed in the document window (Figure 1–60).

Q&A

What if the Picture Tools and Format tabs no longer are displayed on my Ribbon?

Double-click the picture to display the Picture Tools and Format tabs.

Figure 1–60

2

- Click the More button in the Picture Styles gallery, which shows more gallery options.

- Point to Metal Oval in the Picture Styles gallery to display a live preview of that style applied to the picture in the document (Figure 1–61).

Experiment

- Point to various picture styles in the Picture Styles gallery and watch the format of the picture change in the document window.

3

- Click Metal Oval in the Picture Styles gallery to apply the selected style to the picture.

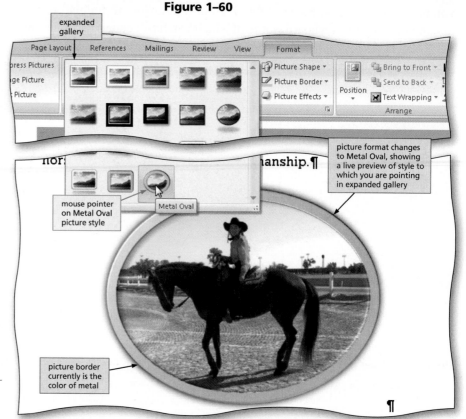

Figure 1–61

To Change a Picture Border Color

The flyer in this chapter has a tan border around the picture. Earlier in this chapter, you changed the color scheme to Aspect. To coordinate the border color with the other colors in the document, you will use a shade of tan in Aspect color scheme for the picture border. Any color galleries you display show colors defined in this current color scheme. The following steps change the picture border color.

1

- Click the Picture Border button arrow on the Format tab to display the Picture Border gallery.

Q&A

What if the Picture Tools and Format tabs no longer are displayed on my Ribbon?

Double-click the picture to display the Picture Tools and Format tabs.

- Point to Tan, Background 2 (third theme color from left in the first row) in the Picture Border gallery to display a live preview of that border color on the picture (Figure 1–62).

Experiment

- Point to various colors in the Picture Border gallery and watch the border color on the picture change in the document window.

2

- Click Tan, Background 2 in the Picture Styles gallery to change the picture border color.

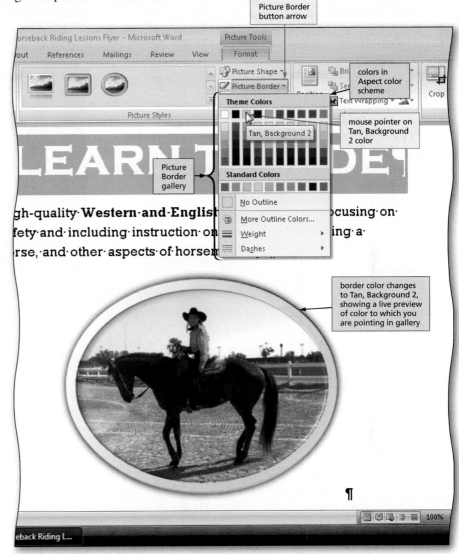

Figure 1–62

To Zoom the Document

The next step in formatting the picture is to resize it. Specifically, you will increase the size of the picture. You do not want it so large, however, that it causes the flyer text to flow to a second page. You can change the zoom so that you can see the entire document on the screen at once. Seeing the entire document at once helps you determine the appropriate size of the picture. The steps on the next page zoom the document.

1

Experiment

- Repeatedly click the Zoom Out and Zoom In buttons on the status bar and watch the size of the document change in the document window.

2

- Click the Zoom Out or Zoom In button as many times as necessary until the Zoom level button displays 50% on its face (Figure 1–63).

Q&A

If I change the zoom percentage, will the document print differently?

Changing the zoom has no effect on the printed document.

Figure 1–63

Other Ways
1. Drag Zoom slider on status bar	2. Click Zoom level button on status bar, select desired zoom percent or type, click OK button	3. Click Zoom button on View tab, select desired zoom percent or type, click OK button

To Resize a Graphic

The next step is to resize the picture. **Resizing** includes both enlarging and reducing the size of a graphic. The picture in the flyer should be as large as possible, without causing any flyer text to flow to a second page.

With the entire document displaying in the document window, you will be able to see how the resized graphic will look on the entire page. The following steps resize a selected graphic.

1

- With the graphic still selected, point to the upper-right corner sizing handle on the picture so that the mouse pointer shape changes to a two-headed arrow (Figure 1–64).

Q&A

What if my graphic (picture) is not selected?

To select a graphic, click it.

Figure 1–64

2
- Drag the sizing handle diagonally outward until the crosshair mouse pointer is positioned approximately as shown in Figure 1–65.

3
- Release the mouse button to resize the graphic.

Q&A What if the graphic is the wrong size?

Repeat Steps 1, 2, and 3.

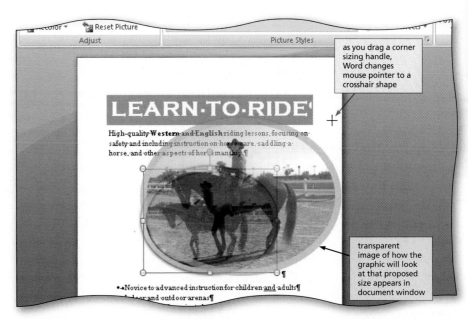

Figure 1–65

4
- Click outside the graphic to deselect it (Figure 1–66).

Q&A What happened to the Picture Tools and Format tabs?

When you click outside of a graphic or press a key to scroll through a document, Word deselects the graphic and removes the Picture Tools and Format tabs from the screen.

Q&A What if I want to return a graphic to its original size and start again?

With the graphic selected, click the Size Dialog Box Launcher on the Format tab to display the Size dialog box, click the Size tab, click the Reset button, and then click the Close button.

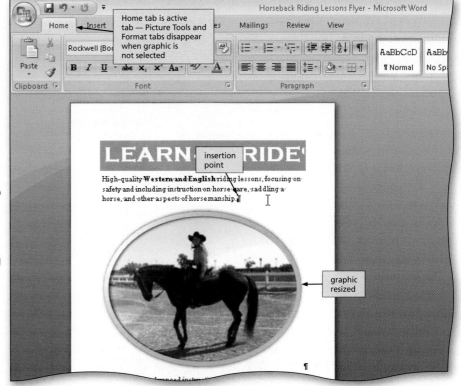

Figure 1–66

Other Ways

1. Enter graphic height and width in Shape Height and Shape Width text boxes in Size group on Format tab in Picture Tools tab

2. Click Size Dialog Box Launcher on Format tab in Picture Tools tab, click Size tab, enter desired height and width values in text boxes, click Close button

Enhancing the Page

With the text and graphics entered and formatted, the next step is to look at the page as a whole and determine if it looks finished in its current state. As you review the page, answer these questions:

- Does it need a page border to frame its contents, or would a page border make it look too busy?
- Is the spacing between paragraphs and graphics on the page adequate? Do any sections of text or graphics look as if they are positioned too closely to the items above or below them?

You determine that a graphical, color-coordinated border would enhance the flyer. You also notice that the flyer would look more proportionate if it had a little more space below the headline and above the graphic. The following pages make these enhancements to the flyer.

To Add a Page Border

In Word, you can add a border around the perimeter of an entire page. In this flyer, you add a graphical border that uses a shade of brown from the Aspect color scheme. The following steps add a graphical page border.

1
- Click Page Layout on the Ribbon to display the Page Layout tab.
- Click the Page Borders button on the Page Layout tab to display the Borders and Shading dialog box (Figure 1–67).

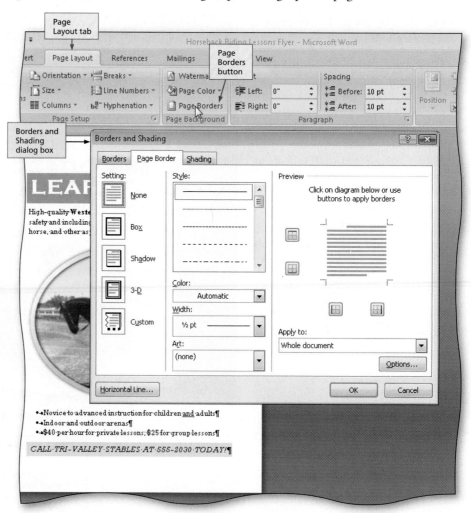

Figure 1–67

2

- Click the Art box arrow to display the Art gallery.

- Click the down scroll arrow in the Art gallery until the art border shown in Figure 1–68 appears.

Figure 1–68

3

- Click the art border shown in Figure 1–68 to display a preview of the selection in the Preview area of the dialog box.

- Click the Color box arrow to display a Color gallery (Figure 1–69).

 Do I have to use an art border?

No. You can select a solid or decorative line in the Style list.

 Can I add color to every border type?

You can color all of the line styles and many of the art borders.

Figure 1–69

4

- Click the right-most theme color (Tan, Accent 6) in the Color gallery to display a preview of the selection in the Preview area.

- Click the OK button to add the border to the page (Figure 1–70).

 What if I wanted to remove the border?

Click None in the Setting list in the Borders and Shading dialog box.

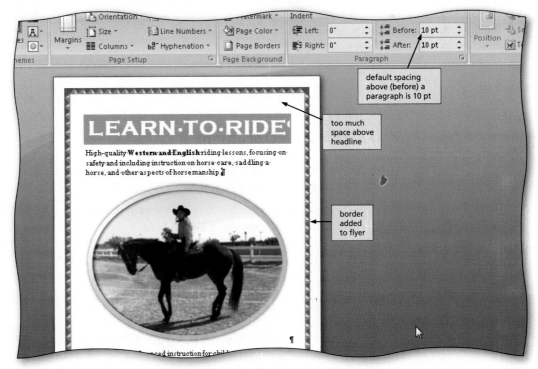

Figure 1–70

To Change Spacing Above and Below Paragraphs

The default spacing above a heading paragraph in Word is 10 points. In the flyer, you want to remove this spacing so the headline is closer to the page border. The default spacing below (after) a body text paragraph is 0 points. Below the first paragraph of body copy in the flyer, you want to increase this space. The following steps change the spacing above and below paragraphs.

1

- Position the insertion point in the paragraph to be adjusted, in this case, the headline.

- Click the Spacing Before box down arrow on the Page Layout tab as many times as necessary until 0 pt is displayed in the Spacing Before text box (Figure 1–71).

Q&A

Why is a blank space still between the border and the headline?

The space is a result of Word's preset left, right, top, and bottom margins and other settings.

2

- Position the insertion point in the paragraph below the headline.

- Click the Spacing After box up arrow on the Page Layout tab as many times as necessary until 24 pt is displayed in the Spacing After text box, shown in Figure 1–72. (If the text flows to two pages, resize the picture so that it is smaller.)

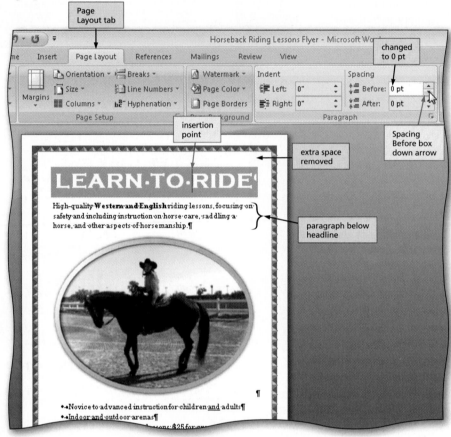

Figure 1–71

To Zoom the Document

You are finished enhancing the page and no longer need to view the entire page in the document window. Thus, the following step changes the zoom back to 100 percent.

1 Click the Zoom In button as many times as necessary until the Zoom level button displays 100% on its face, shown in Figure 1–72.

Changing Document Properties and Saving Again

Word helps you organize and identify your files by using **document properties**, which are the details about a file. Document properties, also known as **metadata**, can include such information as the project author, title, or subject. **Keywords** are words or phrases that further describe the document. For example, a class name or document topic can describe the file's purpose or content.

Document properties are valuable for a variety of reasons:

- Users can save time locating a particular file because they can view a document's properties without opening the document.
- By creating consistent properties for files having similar content, users can better organize their documents.
- Some organizations require Word users to add document properties so that other employees can view details about these files.

Five different types of document properties exist, but the more common ones used in this book are standard and automatically updated properties. **Standard properties** are associated with all Microsoft Office documents and include author, title, and subject. **Automatically updated properties** include file system properties, such as the date you create or change a file, and statistics, such as the file size.

BTW

Printing Document Properties
To print document properties, click the Office Button to display the Office Button menu, point to Print on the Office Button menu to display the Print submenu, click Print on the Print submenu to display the Print dialog box, click the Print what box arrow, click Document properties to instruct Word to print the document properties instead of the document, and then click the OK button.

To Change Document Properties

The **Document Information Panel** contains areas where you can view and enter document properties. You can view and change information in this panel at any time while you are creating a document. Before saving the flyer again, you want to add your name and course information as document properties. The following steps use the Document Information Panel to change document properties.

1

- Click the Office Button to display the Office Button menu.

- Point to Prepare on the Office Button menu to display the Prepare submenu (Figure 1–72).

Q&A

What other types of actions besides changing properties can you take to prepare a document for distribution?

The Prepare submenu provides commands related to sharing a document with others, such as allowing or restricting people to view and modify your document, checking to see if your document will open in earlier versions of Word, and searching for hidden personal information.

Figure 1–72

2

- Click Properties on the Prepare submenu to display the Document Information Panel (Figure 1–73).

Q&A

Why are some of the document properties in my Document Information Panel already filled in?

The person who installed Microsoft Office 2007 on your computer or network may have set or customized the properties.

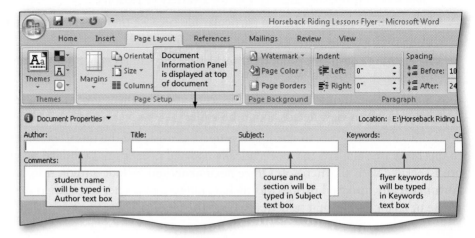

Figure 1–73

3

- Click the Author text box, if necessary, and then type your name as the Author property. If a name already is displayed in the Author text box, delete it before typing your name.

- Click the Subject text box, if necessary delete any existing text, and then type your course and section as the Subject property.

- If an AutoComplete dialog box appears, click its Yes button.

- Click the Keywords text box, if necessary delete any existing text, and then type Tri-Valley Stables as the Keywords property (Figure 1–74).

Figure 1–74

Q&A

What types of document properties does Word collect automatically?

Word records such details as how long you worked at creating your project, how many times you revised the document, and what fonts and themes are used.

4

- Click the Close the Document Information Panel button so that the Document Information Panel no longer is displayed.

To Save an Existing Document with the Same File Name

Saving frequently cannot be overemphasized. You have made several modifications to the document since you saved it earlier in the chapter. When you first saved the document, you clicked the Save button on the Quick Access Toolbar, the Save As dialog box appeared, and you entered the file name, Horseback Riding Lessons Flyer. If you want to use the same file name to save the changes made to the document, you again click the Save button on the Quick Access Toolbar. The following step saves the document again.

1

- Click the Save button on the Quick Access Toolbar to overwrite the previous Horseback Riding Lessons Flyer file on the USB flash drive (Figure 1–75).

Q&A

Why did the Save As dialog box not appear?

Word overwrites the document using the settings specified the first time you saved the document. To save the file with a different file name or on different media, display the Save As dialog box by clicking the Office Button and then clicking Save As on the Office Button menu. Then, fill in the Save As dialog box as described in Steps 2 through 5 on pages WD 20 and WD 21.

Figure 1–75

Other Ways

1. Press CTRL+S or press SHIFT+F12

Printing a Document

After you create a document, you often want to print it. A printed version of the document is called a **hard copy** or **printout**.

Printed copies of your document can be useful for the following reasons:

- Many people prefer proofreading a hard copy of the document rather than viewing it on the screen to check for errors and readability.

- Hard copies can serve as reference material if your storage medium is lost or becomes corrupted and you need to re-create the document.

It is a good practice to save a document before printing it, in the event you experience difficulties with the printer.

BTW

Conserving Ink and Toner

You can instruct Word to print draft quality documents to conserve ink or toner by clicking the Office Button, clicking the Word Options button, clicking Advanced in the left pane of the Word Options dialog box, scrolling to the Print area, placing a check mark in the 'Use draft quality' check box, and then clicking the OK button. To print the document with these settings, click the Office Button, point to Print, and then click Quick Print.

To Print a Document

With the completed document saved, you may want to print it. The following steps print the contents of the saved Horseback Riding Lessons Flyer project.

1

- Click the Office Button to display the Office Button menu.

- Point to Print on the Office Button menu to display the Print submenu (Figure 1–76).

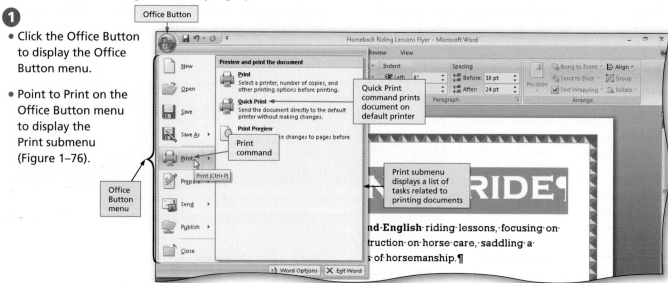

Figure 1–76

2

- Click Quick Print on the Print submenu to print the document.

- When the printer stops, retrieve the hard copy of the Horseback Riding Lessons Flyer (Figures 1–77).

Q&A | How can I print multiple copies of my document other than issuing the Quick Print command twice?

Click the Office Button, point to Print on the Office Button menu, click Print on the Print submenu, increase the number in the Number of copies box, and then click the OK button.

Q&A | Do I have to wait until my document is complete to print it?

No, you can follow these steps to print a document at any time while you are creating it.

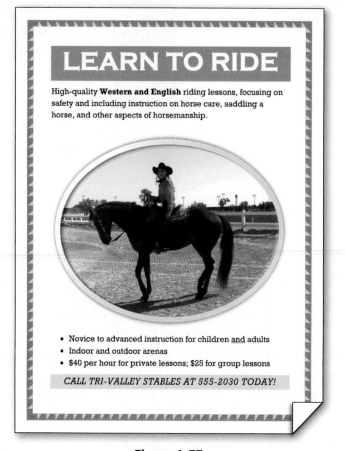

Figure 1–77

BTW | **Printed Borders**
If one or more of your borders do not print, click the Page Borders button on the Page Layout tab, click the Options button in the dialog box, click the Measure from box arrow and click Text, change the four text boxes to 15 pt, and then click the OK button in each dialog box. Try printing the document again. If the borders still do not print, adjust the text boxes in the dialog box to a number smaller than 15 point.

Other Ways

1. Press CTRL+P, press ENTER

Quitting Word

When you quit Word, if you have made changes to a document since the last time the file was saved, Word displays a dialog box asking if you want to save the changes you made to the file before it closes that window. The dialog box contains three buttons with these resulting actions: the Yes button saves the changes and then quits Word; the No button quits Word without saving changes; and the Cancel button closes the dialog box and redisplays the document without saving the changes.

If no changes have been made to an open document since the last time the file was saved, Word will close the window without displaying a dialog box.

To Quit Word with One Document Open

You saved the document prior to printing and did not make any changes to the project. The Horseback Riding Lessons Flyer project now is complete, and you are ready to quit Word. When one Word document is open, the following steps quit Word.

1
- Point to the Close button on the right side of the Word title bar (Figure 1–78).

2
- Click the Close button to quit Word.

Q&A What if I have more than one Word document open?

You would click the Close button for each open document. When you click the last open document's Close button, Word also quits. As an alternative, you could click the Office Button and then click the Exit Word button on the Office Button menu, which closes all open Word documents and then quits Word.

Figure 1–78

Other Ways

1. Double-click Office Button
2. With multiple documents open, click Office Button, click Exit Word on Office Button menu
3. Right-click Microsoft Word button on Windows Vista taskbar, click Close on shortcut menu
4. Press ALT+F4

Starting Word and Opening a Document

Once you have created and saved a document, you may need to retrieve it from your storage medium. For example, you might want to revise the document or reprint it. Opening a document requires that Word is running on your computer.

To Start Word

The following steps, which assume Windows Vista is running, start Word.

1 Click the Start button on the Windows Vista taskbar to display the Start menu.

2 Click All Programs at the bottom of the left pane on the Start menu to display the All Programs list and then click Microsoft Office in the All Programs list to display the Microsoft Office list.

3 Click Microsoft Office Word 2007 in the Microsoft Office list to start Word and display a new blank document in the Word window.

4 If the Word window is not maximized, click the Maximize button on its title bar to maximize the window.

Note: If you are using Windows XP, see Appendix F for alternate steps.

To Open a Document from Word

Earlier in this chapter you saved your project on a USB flash drive using the file name, Horseback Riding Lessons Flyer. The following steps open the Horseback Riding Lessons Flyer file from the USB flash drive.

1

- With your USB flash drive connected to one of the computer's USB ports, click the Office Button to display the Office Button menu (Figure 1–79).

Q&A

What files are shown in the Recent Documents list?

Word displays the most recently opened document file names in this list. If the name of the file you want to open appears in the Recent Documents list, you could click it to open the file.

Figure 1–79

2

- Click Open on the Office Button menu to display the Open dialog box.

- If the Folders list is displayed below the Folders button, click the Folders button to remove the Folders list.

- If necessary, click Computer in the Favorite Links section and then scroll until UDISK 2.0 (E:) appears in the list of available drives.

- Double-click UDISK 2.0 (E:) to select the USB flash drive, Drive E in this case, as the new open location.

- Click Horseback Riding Lessons Flyer to select the file name (Figure 1–80).

Q&A

How do I open the file if I am not using a USB flash drive?

Use the same process, but be certain to select your device in the Computer list.

Figure 1–80

3

- Click the Open button to open the selected file and display the Horseback Riding Lessons Flyer document in the Word window (Figure 1–81).

Q&A

Why is the Word icon and document name on the Windows Vista taskbar?

When you open a Word file, a Word program button is displayed on the taskbar. The button in Figure 1–81 contains an ellipsis because some of its contents do not fit in the allotted button space. If you point to a program button, its entire contents appear in a ScreenTip, which in this case would be the file name followed by the program name.

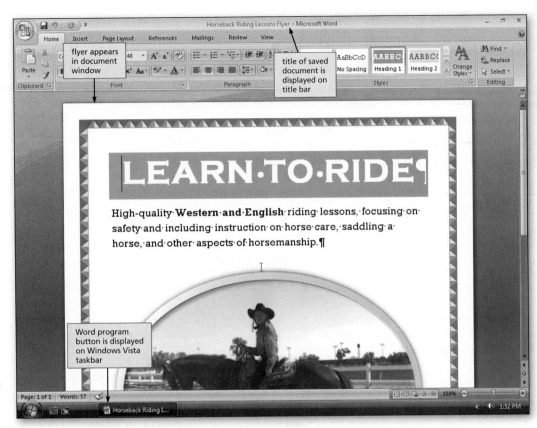

Figure 1–81

Other Ways

1. Click Office Button, click file name in Recent Documents list
2. Press CTRL+O, select file name, press ENTER

Correcting Errors

After creating a document, you often will find you must make changes to it. For example, the document may contain an error, or new circumstances may require you to add text to the document.

Types of Changes Made to Documents

The types of changes made to documents normally fall into one of the three following categories: additions, deletions, or modifications.

Additions   Additional words, sentences, or paragraphs may be required in a document. Additions occur when you omit text from a document and want to insert it later. For example, additional types of riding lessons may be offered.

BTW

Print Preview
You can preview a document before printing it by clicking the Office Button, pointing to Print, and then clicking Print Preview. When finished previewing the document, click the Close Print Preview button.

Deletions   Sometimes, text in a document is incorrect or is no longer needed. For example, group lessons might not be offered. In this case, you would delete the words, $25 for group lessons, from the flyer.

Modifications   If an error is made in a document or changes take place that affect the document, you might have to revise a word(s) in the text. For example, the fee per hour may change from $40 to $50 for private lessons.

To Insert Text in an Existing Document

Word inserts text to the left of the insertion point. The text to the right of the insertion point moves to the right and downward to fit the new text. The following steps insert the word, various, to the left of the word, aspects, in the flyer.

- Scroll through the document and then click to the left of the location of text to be inserted (in this case, the a in aspects) to position the insertion point where text should be inserted (Figure 1–82).

Figure 1–82

- Type various and then press the SPACEBAR to insert the word, various, to the left of the insertion point (Figure 1–83).

Why did the text move to the right as I typed?

In Word, the default typing mode is **insert mode**, which means as you type a character, Word moves all the characters to the right of the typed character one position to the right.

Figure 1–83

Deleting Text from an Existing Document

It is not unusual to type incorrect characters or words in a document. As discussed earlier in this chapter, you can click the Undo button on the Quick Access Toolbar to immediately undo a command or action — this includes typing. Word also provides other methods of correcting typing errors.

To delete an incorrect character in a document, simply click next to the incorrect character and then press the BACKSPACE key to erase to the left of the insertion point, or press the DELETE key to erase to the right of the insertion point.

To Select a Word and Delete It

To delete a word or phrase, you first must select the word or phrase. The following steps select the word, various, that was just added in the previous steps and then delete the selection.

- Position the mouse pointer somewhere in the word to be selected (in this case, various), as shown in Figure 1–84.

Figure 1–84

- Double-click the word to select it (Figure 1–85).

❸

- With the text selected, press the DELETE key to delete the selected text (shown in Figure 1–82).

Figure 1–85

Closing the Entire Document

Sometimes, everything goes wrong. If this happens, you may want to close the document entirely and start over with a new document. You also may want to close a document when you are finished with it so you can begin your next document. If you wanted to close a document, you would use the steps on the next page.

To Close the Entire Document and Start Over

1. Click the Office Button and then click Close.
2. If Word displays a dialog box, click the No button to ignore the changes since the last time you saved the document.
3. Click the Office Button and then click New on the Office Button menu. When Word displays the New Document dialog box, click Blank document and then click the Create button.

Word Help
The best way to become familiar with Word Help is to use it. Appendix C includes detailed information about Word Help and exercises that will help you gain confidence in using it.

Word Help

At any time while using Word, you can find answers to questions and display information about various topics through **Word Help**. Used properly, this form of assistance can increase your productivity and reduce your frustrations by minimizing the time you spend learning how to use Word.

This section introduces you to Word Help. Additional information about using Word Help is available in Appendix C.

To Search for Word Help

Using Word Help, you can search for information based on phrases such as save a document or format text, or key terms such as copy, save, or format. Word Help responds with a list of search results displayed as links to a variety of resources. The following steps, which use Word Help to search for information about selecting text, assume you are connected to the Internet.

1

- Click the Microsoft Office Word Help button near the upper-right corner of the Word window to open the Word Help window.

- Type select text in the 'Type words to search for' text box at the top of the Word Help window (Figure 1–86).

Figure 1–86

2

- Press the ENTER key to display the search results.

- Click the Maximize button on the Word Help window title bar to maximize the Help window (Figure 1–87).

Q&A

Where is the Word window with the Horseback Riding Lessons Flyer document?

Word is open in the background, but the Word Help window is overlaid on top of the Word window. When the Word Help window is closed, the document will reappear.

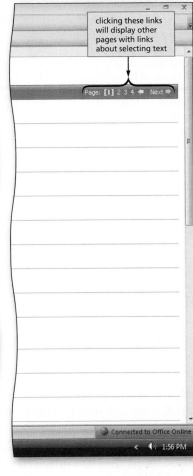

Figure 1–87

3

- Click the Select text link to display information about selecting text (Figure 1–88).

Q&A

What is the purpose of the buttons at the top of the Word Help window?

Use the buttons in the upper-left corner of the Word Help window to navigate through Help, change the display, show the Word Help table of contents, and print the contents of the window.

4

- Click the Close button on the Word Help window title bar to close the Word Help window and redisplay the Word window.

Figure 1–88

Other Ways

1. Press F1

BTW

Quick Reference
For a table that lists how to complete the tasks covered in this book using the mouse, Ribbon, shortcut menu, and keyboard, see the Quick Reference Summary at the back of this book, or visit the Word 2007 Quick Reference Web page (scsite.com/wd2007/qr).

To Quit Word

The following steps quit Word.

1 Click the Close button on the right side of the title bar to quit Word; or if you have multiple Word documents open, click the Office Button and then click the Exit Word button on the Office Button menu to close all open documents and quit Word.

2 If necessary, click the No button in the Microsoft Office Word dialog box so that any changes you have made are not saved.

Chapter Summary

In this chapter you have learned how to enter text in a document, format text, insert a picture, format a picture, add a page border, and print a document. The items listed below include all the new Word skills you have learned in this chapter.

1. Start Word (WD 5)
2. Type Text (WD 13)
3. Display Formatting Marks (WD 14)
4. Wordwrap Text as You Type (WD 15)
5. Insert a Blank Line (WD 15)
6. Check Spelling and Grammar as You Type (WD 16)
7. Save a Document (WD 19)
8. Apply Styles (WD 24)
9. Center a Paragraph (WD 26)
10. Select a Line (WD 27)
11. Change the Font Size of Selected Text (WD 28)
12. Change the Font of Selected Text (WD 29)
13. Select Multiple Paragraphs (WD 30)
14. Bullet a List of Paragraphs (WD 32)
15. Undo and Redo an Action (WD 32)
16. Select a Group of Words (WD 33)
17. Bold Text (WD 34)
18. Underline a Word (WD 35)
19. Italicize Text (WD 36)
20. Change the Style Set (WD 37)
21. Change Theme Colors (WD 39)
22. Change Theme Fonts (WD 39)
23. Insert a Picture (WD 41)
24. Apply a Picture Style (WD 44)
25. Change a Picture Border Color (WD 45)
26. Zoom the Document (WD 45)
27. Resize a Graphic (WD 46)
28. Add a Page Border (WD 48)
29. Change Spacing Above and Below Paragraphs (WD 50)
30. Change Document Properties (WD 51)
31. Save an Existing Document with the Same File Name (WD 53)
32. Print a Document (WD 54)
33. Quit Word with One Document Open (WD 55)
34. Open a Document from Word (WD 56)
35. Insert Text in an Existing Document (WD 58)
36. Select a Word and Delete It (WD 59)
37. Close the Entire Document and Start Over (WD 60)
38. Search for Word Help (WD 60)

If you have a SAM user profile, you may have access to hands-on instruction, practice, and assessment. Log in to your SAM account (http://sam2007.course.com) to launch any assigned training activities or exams that relate to the skills covered in this chapter.

BTW

Certification
The Microsoft Certified Application Specialist (MCAS) program provides an opportunity for you to obtain a valuable industry credential – proof that you have the Word 2007 skills required by employers. For more information, see Appendix G or visit the Word 2007 Certification Web page (scsite.com/wd2007/cert).

Learn It Online

Test your knowledge of chapter content and key terms.

Instructions: To complete the Learn It Online exercises, start your browser, click the Address bar, and then enter the Web address scsite.com/wd2007/learn. When the Word 2007 Learn It Online page is displayed, click the link for the exercise you want to complete and then read the instructions.

Chapter Reinforcement TF, MC, and SA

A series of true/false, multiple choice, and short answer questions that test your knowledge of the chapter content.

Flash Cards

An interactive learning environment where you identify chapter key terms associated with displayed definitions.

Practice Test

A series of multiple choice questions that test your knowledge of chapter content and key terms.

Who Wants To Be a Computer Genius?

An interactive game that challenges your knowledge of chapter content in the style of a television quiz show.

Wheel of Terms

An interactive game that challenges your knowledge of chapter key terms in the style of the television show *Wheel of Fortune*.

Crossword Puzzle Challenge

A crossword puzzle that challenges your knowledge of key terms presented in the chapter.

Apply Your Knowledge

Reinforce the skills and apply the concepts you learned in this chapter.

Modifying Text and Formatting a Document

Instructions: Start Word. Open the document, Apply 1-1 Autumn Fest Flyer Unformatted, from the Data Files for Students. See the inside back cover of this book for instructions on downloading the Data Files for Students, or contact your instructor for information about accessing the required files.

The document you open is an unformatted flyer. You are to modify text, format paragraphs and characters, and insert a picture in the flyer.

Perform the following tasks:

1. Delete the word, entire, in the sentence of body copy below the headline.

2. Insert the word, Creek, between the text, Honey Farm, in the sentence of body copy below the headline. The sentence should end: ...Honey Creek Farm.

3. At the end of the signature line, change the period to an exclamation point. The sentence should end: ...This Year's Fest!

4. Apply the Heading 1 style to the headline. Apply the Heading 2 style to the signature line.

5. Center the headline and the signature line.

6. Change the font and font size of the headline to 48-point Cooper Black, or a similar font.

7. Change the font size of body copy between the headline and the signature line to 22 point.

8. Change the font size of the signature line to 28 point.

9. Bullet the three lines (paragraphs) of text above the signature line.

10. Bold the text, October 4 and 5.

Continued >

Apply Your Knowledge *continued*

11. Underline the word, and, in the first bulleted paragraph.

12. Italicize the text in the signature line.

13. Change the theme colors to the Civic color scheme.

14. Change the theme fonts to the Opulent font set.

15. Change the zoom to 50 percent so the entire page is visible in the document window.

16. Change the spacing before the headline paragraph to 0 point. Change the spacing after the headline paragraph to 12 point.

17. Insert the picture of the combine centered on the blank line above the bulleted list. The picture is called Fall Harvest and is available on the Data Files for Students. Apply the Snip Diagonal Corner, White picture style to the inserted picture. Change the color of the picture border to Orange, Accent 6.

18. The entire flyer now should fit on a single page. If it flows to two pages, resize the picture or decrease spacing before and after paragraphs until the entire flyer text fits on a single page.

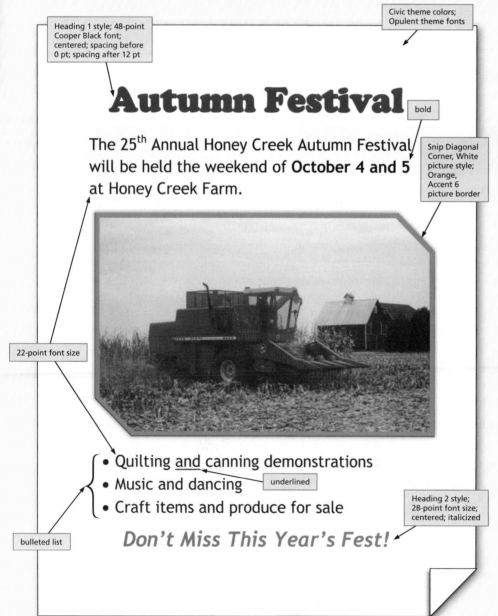

Heading 1 style; 48-point Cooper Black font; centered; spacing before 0 pt; spacing after 12 pt

Civic theme colors; Opulent theme fonts

bold

Snip Diagonal Corner, White picture style; Orange, Accent 6 picture border

22-point font size

underlined

bulleted list

Heading 2 style; 28-point font size; centered; italicized

19. Enter the text, Honey Creek, as the keywords. Change the other document properties, as specified by your instructor.

20. Click the Office Button and then click Save As. Save the document using the file name, Apply 1-1 Autumn Fest Flyer Formatted.

21. Position the Quick Access Toolbar below the Ribbon. Save the document again by clicking the Save button. Reposition the Quick Access Toolbar above the Ribbon.

22. Submit the revised document, shown in Figure 1–89, in the format specified by your instructor.

Figure 1–89

Extend Your Knowledge

Extend the skills you learned in this chapter and experiment with new skills. You may need to use Help to complete the assignment.

Modifying Text and Graphics Formats

Instructions: Start Word. Open the document, Extend 1-1 Baseball Sign Ups Flyer, from the Data Files for Students. See the inside back cover of this book for instructions on downloading the Data Files for Students, or contact your instructor for information about accessing the required files.

You will enhance the look of the flyer shown in Figure 1–90.

Perform the following tasks:

1. Use Help to learn about the following formats: grow font, shrink font, change text color, decorative underline, and change bullet.

2. Select the headline and use the Grow Font button to increase its font size just enough so that the headline still fits on a single line. If it wraps to two lines, use the Shrink Font button.

3. Change the font color of all body copy between the headline and the signature line to a color other than Automatic, or Black.

4. Change the picture style of the picture so that it is not the Drop Shadow Rectangle picture style. Add a Glow picture effect to the picture of the baseball player.

5. Change the solid underline below the words, Indoor facility, to a decorative underline.

6. Change the color and width of the border.

7. Change the style of the bullets to a character other than the dot.

8. Change the document properties, including keywords, as specified by your instructor. Save the revised document with a new file name and then submit it in the format specified by your instructor.

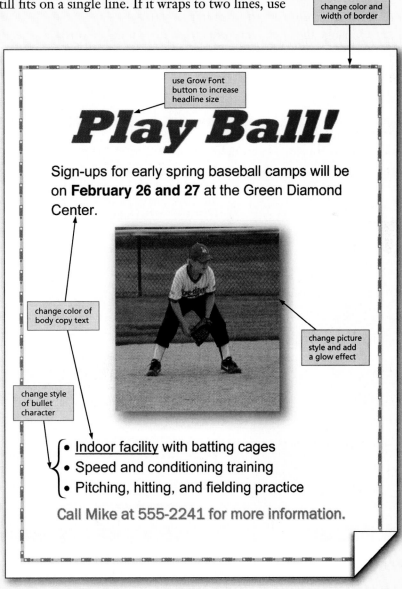

change color and width of border

use Grow Font button to increase headline size

change color of body copy text

change picture style and add a glow effect

change style of bullet character

Figure 1–90

Make It Right

Analyze a document and correct all errors and/or improve the design.

Correcting Spelling and Grammar Errors

Instructions: Start Word. Open the document, Make It Right 1-1 New York Tour Flyer, from the Data Files for Students. See the inside back cover of this book for instructions on downloading the Data Files for Students, or contact your instructor for information on accessing the required files.

The document is a flyer that contains spelling and grammar errors, as shown in Figure 1–91. You are to correct each spelling (red wavy underline) and grammar error (green wavy underline) by right-clicking the flagged text and then clicking the appropriate correction on the shortcut menu. If your screen does not display the wavy underlines, click the Office Button and then click the Word Options button. When the Word Options dialog box is displayed, click Proofing, be sure the 'Hide spelling errors in this document only' and 'Hide grammar errors in this document only' check boxes do not have check marks, and then click the OK button. If your screen still does not display the wavy underlines, redisplay the Word Options dialog box, click Proofing, and then click the Recheck Document button.

Change the document properties, including keywords, as specified by your instructor. Save the revised document with a new file name and then submit it in the format specified by your instructor.

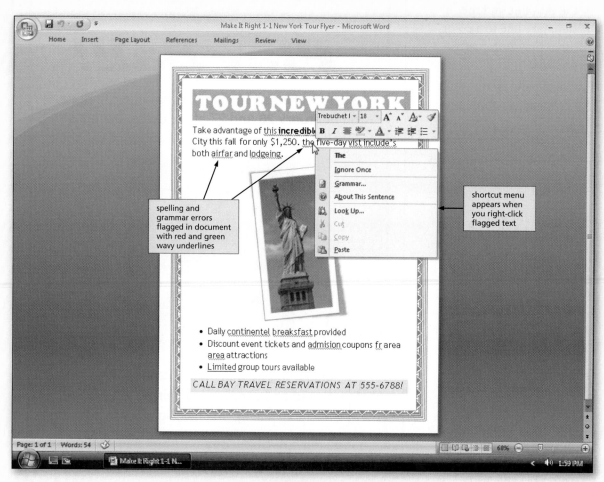

Figure 1–91

In the Lab

Design and/or create a document using the guidelines, concepts, and skills presented in this chapter. Labs are listed in order of increasing difficulty.

Lab 1: Creating a Flyer with a Picture

Problem: You work part-time at Scenic Air. Your boss has asked you to prepare a flyer that advertises aerial tours over the city of Campton. First, you prepare the unformatted flyer shown in Figure 1–92a, and then you format it so that it looks like Figure 1–92b on the next page. *Hint:* Remember, if you make a mistake while formatting the flyer, you can click the Undo button on the Quick Access Toolbar to undo your last action.

Instructions: Perform the following tasks:

1. Display formatting marks on the screen.

2. Type the flyer text, unformatted, as shown in Figure 1–92a. If Word flags any misspelled words as you type, check the spelling of these words and correct them.

3. Save the document on a USB flash drive using the file name, Lab 1-1 Airplane Rides Flyer.

4. Apply the Heading 1 style to the headline. Apply the Heading 2 style to the signature line.

5. Center the headline and the signature line.

6. Change the font and font size of the headline to 48-point Arial Rounded MT Bold, or a similar font.

7. Change the font size of body copy between the headline and the signature line to 22 point.

8. Change the font size of the signature line to 28 point.

9. Bullet the three lines (paragraphs) of text above the signature line.

10. Bold the text, change your view.

11. Italicize the word, aerial.

Airplane Rides

Gain an entirely new vision of Campton by taking an aerial tour. Visitor or local, business or pleasure, the trip will change your view of the city.

Pilots are licensed and experienced

15-, 30-, or 60-minute tours available during daylight hours

Individual and group rates

Call Scenic Air at 555-9883!

Figure 1–92a

Continued >

In the Lab *continued*

12. Underline the word, and, in the first bulleted paragraph.

13. Change the style set to Formal.

14. Change the theme fonts to the Metro font set.

15. Change the zoom to 50 percent so the entire page is visible in the document window.

16. Change the spacing before the headline to 0 point. Change the spacing after the first paragraph of body copy to 0 point. Change the spacing before the first bulleted paragraph to 12 point.

17. Insert the picture on the blank line above the bulleted list. The picture is called Airplane Ride over City and is available on the Data Files for Students. Apply the Relaxed Perspective, White picture style to the inserted picture.

18. The entire flyer should fit on a single page. If it flows to two pages, resize the picture or decrease spacing before and after paragraphs until the entire flyer text fits on a single page.

19. Change the document properties, including keywords, as specified by your instructor.

20. Save the flyer again with the same file name.

21. Submit the document, shown in Figure 1–92b, in the format specified by your instructor.

Figure 1–92b

In the Lab

Lab 2: Creating a Flyer with a Picture and a Border

Problem: Your boss at Danvers Nursery has asked you to prepare a flyer that promotes its expanded greenhouses and grounds. You prepare the flyer shown in Figure 1–93. *Hint:* Remember, if you make a mistake while formatting the flyer, you can click the Undo button on the Quick Access Toolbar to undo your last action.

Instructions: Perform the following tasks:
1. Display formatting marks on the screen.
2. Type the flyer text, unformatted. If Word flags any misspelled words as you type, check the spelling of these words and correct them.
3. Save the document on a USB flash drive using the file name, Lab 1-2 Nursery Expansion Flyer.

Figure 1–93

Continued >

In the Lab *continued*

4. Apply the Heading 1 style to the headline. Apply the Heading 2 style to the signature line.

5. Center the headline and the signature line.

6. Change the font and font size of the headline to 48-point Arial Rounded MT Bold, or a similar font.

7. Change the font size of body copy between the headline and the signature line to 22 point.

8. Change the font size of the signature line to 28 point.

9. Bullet the three lines (paragraphs) of text above the signature line.

10. Italicize the word, growing.

11. Bold the text, recently expanded.

12. Underline the word, and, in the third bulleted paragraph.

13. Change the style set to Traditional.

14. Change the theme colors to the Solstice color scheme.

15. Change the theme fonts to the Flow font set.

16. Change the zoom to 50 percent so the entire page is visible in the document window.

17. Change the spacing before the headline to 0 point. Change the spacing after the first paragraph of body copy to 24 point. Change the spacing before the first bulleted paragraph to 12 point.

18. Insert the picture on the blank line above the bulleted list. The picture is called Bradford Pear in Bloom and is available on the Data Files for Students. Apply the Soft Edge Oval picture style to the inserted picture.

19. The entire flyer should fit on a single page. If it flows to two pages, resize the picture or decrease spacing before and after paragraphs until the entire flyer text fits on a single page.

20. Add the graphic border, shown in Figure 1–93 on the previous page (about one-third down in the Art gallery). Change the color of the border to Tan, Background 2.

21. Change the document properties, including keywords, as specified by your instructor.

22. Save the flyer again with the same file name.

23. Submit the document, shown in Figure 1–93, in the format specified by your instructor.

In the Lab

Lab 3: Creating a Flyer with a Picture and Resized Border Art

Problem: Your neighbor has asked you to prepare a flyer that promotes her cabin rental business. You prepare the flyer shown in Figure 1–94.

Instructions: Enter the text in the flyer, checking spelling as you type, and then format it as shown in Figure 1–94. The picture to be inserted is called Paddle Boat on Lake and is available on the Data Files for Students. After adding the page border, reduce the point size of its width so that the border is not so predominant on the page. Change the document properties, including keywords, as specified by your instructor. Save the document on a USB flash drive using the file name, Lab 1-3 Cabin Rentals Flyer. Submit the document, shown in Figure 1–94, in the format specified by your instructor.

The flyer contains the following callouts:

- Art cabin border; color Tan, Accent 6; width 25 pt
- Heading 1 style; 48-point Ravie font; centered; spacing before 0 pt
- Aspect theme colors; Opulent theme fonts
- spacing after 18 point
- bold
- Bevel Rectangle picture style
- 20-point font size
- spacing before 18 point
- bulleted list
- underlined
- Heading 2 style; 26-point font size; centered; italicized; spacing before 18 pt

The flyer text reads:

Rent a Cabin

Enjoy the splendors of nature and relax in a beautiful setting at our **new** lakeside resort. Cabins offer kitchen facilities, water, and electricity.

- Two- and three-bedroom cabins available
- <u>All</u> cabins are lakeside and include a dock, pier, and paddleboat
- Prices start at $100 per night

Call Sunset Cabins at 555-8404 today!

Figure 1–94

Cases and Places

Apply your creative thinking and problem solving skills to design and implement a solution.

• EASIER   •• MORE DIFFICULT

• 1: Design and Create a Grand Reopening Flyer

Your friend owns the Craft Barn, a large, year-round craft fair. She recently has renovated and remodeled the facility and is planning a grand reopening. She has asked you to create a flyer advertising this fact. The flyer should contain the following headline: Craft Barn. The first paragraph of text below the headline should read: Pick up a jar of homemade jam or a handcrafted gift at the completely remodeled and renovated Craft Barn, located at 8701 County Road 300 West. Insert the photograph named, Barn and Silo, which is available on the Data Files for Students. The bullet items

Continued >

Cases and Places *continued*

under the photograph should read as follows: first bullet – Expanded and paved parking; second bullet – More than 150 booths; and third bullet – Open Monday through Saturday, 10:00 a.m. to 7:00 p.m. The last line should read: Call 555-5709 for more information! Use the concepts and techniques presented in this chapter to create and format this flyer. Be sure to check spelling and grammar.

• 2: Design and Create a Property Advertisement Flyer

As a part-time employee of Markum Realty, you have been assigned the task of preparing a flyer advertising lakefront property. The headline should read: Lakefront Lot. The first paragraph of text should read as follows: Build the house of your dreams or a weekend getaway on this beautiful lakeside property located on the north side of Lake Pleasant. Insert the photograph named, Lake at Sunset, which is available on the Data Files for Students. Below the photograph, insert the following bullet items: first bullet — City sewer and water available; second bullet – Lot size 110 × 300; third bullet – List price $65,000. The last line should read: Call Markum Realty at 555-0995 for a tour! Use the concepts and techniques presented in this chapter to create and format this flyer. Be sure to check spelling and grammar.

•• 3: Design and Create a Flyer for the Sale of a Business

After 25 years, your Uncle Mitch has decided to sell his ice cream shop and wants you to help him create a sales flyer. The shop is in a choice location at the corner of 135th and Main Street and has an established customer base. The building has an adjacent, paved parking lot, as well as an outdoor seating area. He wants to sell the store and all its contents, including the equipment, tables, booths, and chairs. The 1200-square-foot shop recently was appraised at $200,000, and your uncle is willing to sell for cash or on contract. Use the concepts and techniques presented in this chapter to create and format a sales flyer. Include a headline, descriptive body copy, a signature line, an appropriate photograph or clip art image, a bulleted list, a decorative underline, and if appropriate, a page border. Be sure to check spelling and grammar in the flyer.

•• 4: Design and Create a Flyer that Advertises You

Make It Personal

Everyone has at least one skill, talent, or special capability, which if shared with others, can lead to opportunity for growth, experience, and personal reward. Perhaps you play a musical instrument. If so, you could offer lessons. Maybe you are a skilled carpenter or other tradesman who could advertise your services. If you speak a second language, you could offer tutoring. Budding athletes might harbor a desire to pass on their knowledge by coaching a youth sports team. You may have a special knack for singing, sewing, knitting, photography, typing, housecleaning, or pet care. Carefully consider your own personal capabilities, skills, and talents and then use the concepts and techniques presented in this chapter to create a flyer advertising a service you can provide. Include a headline, descriptive body copy, a signature line, an appropriate photograph or clip art image, a bulleted list, a decorative underline, and if appropriate, a page border. Be sure to check spelling and grammar in the flyer.

•• 5: Redesign and Enhance a Poorly Designed Flyer

Working Together

Public locations, such as stores, schools, and libraries, have bulletin boards or windows for people to post flyers. Often, these bulletin boards or windows have so many flyers that some go unnoticed. Locate a posted flyer on a bulletin board or window that you think might be overlooked. Copy the text from the flyer and distribute it to each team member. Each member then independently should use this text, together with the techniques presented in this chapter, to create a flyer that would be more likely to catch the attention of passersby. Be sure to check spelling and grammar. As a group, critique each flyer and have team members redesign their flyer based on the group's recommendations. Hand in each team member's original and final flyers.

2 | Creating a Research Paper

Objectives

You will have mastered the material in this chapter when you can:

- Describe the MLA documentation style for research papers

- Change line and paragraph spacing in a document

- Use a header to number pages of a document

- Apply formatting using shortcut keys

- Modify paragraph indentation

- Create and modify styles

- Insert and edit citations and their sources

- Add a footnote to a document

- Insert a manual page break

- Create a bibliographical list of sources

- Move text

- Find and replace text

- Use the Research task pane to look up information

2 | Creating a Research Paper

Introduction

In both academic and business environments, you will be asked to write reports. Business reports range from proposals to cost justifications to five-year plans to research findings. Academic reports focus mostly on research findings. A **research paper** is a document you can use to communicate the results of research findings. To write a research paper, you learn about a particular topic from a variety of sources (research), organize your ideas from the research results, and then present relevant facts and/or opinions that support the topic. Your final research paper combines properly credited outside information along with personal insights. Thus, no two research papers — even if about the same topic — will or should be the same.

Project — Research Paper

When preparing a research paper, you should follow a standard documentation style that defines the rules for creating the paper and crediting sources. A variety of documentation styles exists, depending on the nature of the research paper. Each style requires the same basic information; the differences in styles relate to requirements for presenting the information. For example, one documentation style uses the term bibliography for the list of sources, whereas another uses references, and yet a third prefers the title works cited. Two popular documentation styles for research papers are the **Modern Language Association of America (MLA)** and **American Psychological Association (APA)** styles. This chapter uses the MLA documentation style because it is used in a wide range of disciplines.

The project in this chapter follows research paper guidelines and uses Word to create the short research paper shown in Figure 2–1. This paper, which discusses three types of wireless communications, follows the MLA documentation style. Each page contains a page number. The first two pages present the heading (name, course, and date information), paper title, an introduction with a thesis statement, details that support the thesis, and a conclusion. This section of the paper also includes references to research sources. The third page contains a detailed, alphabetical list of the sources used in the research paper.

Overview

As you read through this chapter, you will learn how to create the research paper shown in Figure 2–1 by performing these general tasks:

- Change the document settings.
- Type the research paper.
- Save the research paper.
- Create an alphabetical list of sources.
- Proof and revise the research paper.
- Print the research paper.

Pappas 3

Works Cited

Davies, Habika. "Text Messaging, Instant Messaging, and Picture Messaging Services." <u>Computing in</u>

<u>Today's World</u> January 2008: 34-42.

Podpora, Maxine C., and Adelbert D. Ruiz. <u>Advances in Wireless Internet Access Point Technology.</u>

Dallas: Wells Publishing, 2008.

Shelly, Gary B., and Thomas J. Cashman. <u>How a GPS Works.</u> Course Technology. 21 March 2008

<www.scsite.com/wd2007/pr2/wc.htm>.

alphabetical list of sources

Pappas 2

geographic location, according to Shelly and Cashman (How a GPS Works). A GPS receiver is a handheld,

mountable, or embedded device that contains an antenna, a radio receiver, and a processor. Many

mobile devices, such as mobile phones and PDAs, have GPS capability built into the device.

Mobile users communicate wirelessly through wireless messaging services, wireless Internet

access points, and global positioning systems. Anyone can take advantage of wireless communications

using mobile computers and devices.

header contains last name followed by page number

Pappas 1

Alex Pappas

Ms. Singh

English 104

28 March 2008

Wireless Communications

Wireless communications are everywhere. People around the world regularly send and receive

messages wirelessly, that is, transmitted through the air. Three types of wireless communications

include wireless messaging services, wireless Internet access points, and global positioning systems.

People use mobile phones, PDAs, and other mobile devices to access text messaging, instant

messaging, and picture messaging services (Davies 34-42). Through text messaging services, users send

and receive short text messages, which usually consist of fewer than 300 characters. Wireless instant

messaging is an Internet communications service that allows a wireless mobile device to exchange

instant messages with one or more mobile devices or online personal computers. Users send graphics,

pictures, video clips, sound files, and short text messages with picture messaging services.[1]

In many public locations, people connect to the Internet through a wireless Internet access point

using mobile computers and devices. Two types of wireless Internet access points are hot spots and 3G

networks. A hot spot is a wireless network that allows mobile users to check e-mail, browse the Web,

and access any Internet service – as long as their computers or devices have the appropriate wireless

capability. A 3G network, which uses cellular radio technology, enables users to connect to the Internet

through a mobile phone or computer equipped with an appropriate PC Card.

A global positioning system (GPS) is a navigation system that consists of one or more earth-

based receivers that accept and analyze signals sent by satellites in order to determine the receiver's

parenthetical citation

superscripted note reference mark

[1] Podpora and Ruiz indicate that some messaging services use the term, video messaging, to

refer separately to the capability of sending video clips (79-82).

explanatory note positioned as footnote

Figure 2–1

General Project Guidelines

When creating a Word document, the actions you perform and decisions you make will affect the appearance and characteristics of the finished document. As you create a research paper, such as the project shown in Figure 2–1 on the previous page, you should follow these general guidelines:

1. **Select a topic.** Spend time brainstorming ideas for a topic. Choose one you find interesting. For shorter papers, narrow down the scope of the topic; for longer papers, broaden the scope. Identify a tentative thesis statement, which is a sentence describing the paper's subject matter.

2. **Research the topic and take notes.** Gather credible, relevant information about the topic that supports the thesis statement. Sources of research include books, magazines, newspapers, and the Internet. As you record facts and ideas, list details about the source: title, author, place of publication, publisher, date of publication, etc. When taking notes, be careful not to **plagiarize**. That is, do not use someone else's work and claim it to be your own. If you copy information directly, place it in quotation marks and identify its source.

3. **Organize your ideas.** Classify your notes into related concepts. Make an outline from the categories of notes. In the outline, identify all main ideas and supporting details.

4. **Write the first draft, referencing sources.** From the outline, compose the paper. Every research paper should include an introduction containing the thesis statement, supporting details, and a conclusion. Follow the guidelines identified in the required documentation style. Reference all sources of information.

5. **Create the list of sources.** Using the formats specified in the required documentation style, completely list all sources referenced in the body of the research paper in alphabetical order.

6. **Proofread and revise the paper.** If possible, proofread the paper with a fresh set of eyes, that is, at least one to two days after completing the first draft. Proofreading involves reading the paper with the intent of identifying errors (spelling, grammar, etc.) and looking for ways to improve the paper (wording, transitions, flow, etc.). Try reading the paper out loud, which helps to identify unclear or awkward wording. Ask someone else to proofread the paper and give you suggestions for improvements.

When necessary, more specific details concerning the above guidelines are presented at appropriate points in the chapter. The chapter also will identify the actions performed and decisions made regarding these guidelines during the creation of the research paper shown in Figure 2–1.

BTW

APA Documentation Style
In the APA style, a separate title page is required instead of placing name and course information on the paper's first page. Double-space all pages of the paper with 1.5" top, bottom, left, and right margins. Indent the first word of each paragraph .5" from the left margin. In the upper-right margin of each page, including the title page, place a running head that consists of the page number double-spaced below a brief summary of the paper title.

MLA Documentation Style

The research paper in this project follows the guidelines presented by the MLA. To follow the MLA style, double-space text on all pages of the paper using one-inch top, bottom, left, and right margins. Indent the first word of each paragraph one-half inch from the left margin. At the right margin of each page, place a page number one-half inch from the top margin. On each page, precede the page number by your last name.

The MLA style does not require a title page. Instead, place your name and course information in a block at the left margin beginning one inch from the top of the page. Center the title one double-space below your name and course information.

In the text of the paper, place author references in parentheses with the page number(s) of the referenced information. The MLA style uses in-text **parenthetical citations** instead of noting each source at the bottom of the page or at the end of the paper. In the MLA style, notes are used only for optional explanatory notes.

If used, explanatory notes elaborate on points discussed in the paper. Use a super-script (raised number) to signal that an explanatory note exists, and also to sequence the notes. Position explanatory notes either at the bottom of the page as footnotes or at the end of the paper as endnotes. Indent the first line of each explanatory note one-half inch from the left margin. Place one space following the superscripted number before beginning the note text. Double-space the note text. At the end of the note text, you may list bibliographic information for further reference.

The MLA style uses the term **works cited** to refer to the bibliographic list of sources at the end of the paper. The works cited page alphabetically lists sources that are referenced directly in the paper. Place the list of sources on a separate numbered page. Center the title, Works Cited, one inch from the top margin. Double-space all lines. Begin the first line of each source at the left margin, indenting subsequent lines of the same source one-half inch from the left margin. List each source by the author's last name, or, if the author's name is not available, by the title of the source. Underline or italicize the title of each source.

Changing Document Settings

The MLA documentation style defines some global formats that apply to the entire research paper. Some of these formats are the default in Word. For example, the default left, right, top, and bottom margin settings in Word are one inch, which meets the MLA style. You will modify, however, the paragraph and line spacing and header formats as required by the MLA style.

After starting Word, the following pages adjust line and paragraph spacing and define a header for the current document.

To Start Word

If you are using a computer to step through the project in this chapter and you want your screens to match the figures in this book, you should change your computer's resolution to 1024 × 768. For information about how to change a computer's resolution, read Appendix E.

The following steps, which assume Windows Vista is running, start Word based on a typical installation. You may need to ask your instructor how to start Word for your computer.

1 Click the Start button on the Windows Vista taskbar to display the Start menu and then click All Programs at the bottom of the left pane on the Start menu to display the All Programs list.

2 Click Microsoft Office in the All Programs list to display the Microsoft Office list and then click Microsoft Office Word 2007 to start Word and display a new blank document in the Word window.

3 If the Word window is not maximized, click the Maximize button next to the Close button on its title bar to maximize the window.

4 If the Print Layout button is not selected, click it so that your screen layout matches Figure 2–2 on the next page.

5 If your zoom percent is not 100, click the Zoom Out or Zoom In button as many times as necessary until the Zoom level button displays 100% on its face.

Note: If you are using Windows XP, see Appendix F for alternate steps.

To Display Formatting Marks

As discussed in Chapter 1, it is helpful to display formatting marks that indicate where in the document you pressed the ENTER key, SPACEBAR, and other keys. The following step displays formatting marks.

1 If necessary, click Home on the Ribbon to display the Home tab. If the Show/Hide ¶ button on the Home tab is not selected already, click it to display formatting marks on the screen.

BTW

Line Spacing
If the top of a set of characters or a graphical image is chopped off, then line spacing may be set to Exactly. To remedy the problem, change line spacing to 1.0, 1.15, 1.5, 2.0, 2.5, 3.0, or At least (in the Paragraph dialog box), all of which accommodate the largest font or image.

Adjusting Line and Paragraph Spacing

Line spacing is the amount of vertical space between lines of text in a paragraph. **Paragraph spacing** is the amount of space above and below a paragraph. By default, the Normal style places 10 points of blank space after each paragraph and inserts a vertical space equal to 1.15 lines between each line of text. It also automatically adjusts line height to accommodate various font sizes and graphics.

The MLA documentation style requires that you **double-space** the entire research paper. That is, the amount of vertical space between each line of text and above and below paragraphs should be equal to one blank line. The next sets of steps adjust line spacing and paragraph spacing according to the MLA documentation style.

To Double-Space Text

To double-space the lines in the research paper, change the line spacing to 2.0. The following steps change line spacing to double.

1

- Click the Line spacing button on the Home tab to display the Line spacing gallery (Figure 2–2).

Q&A

What do the numbers in the Line spacing gallery represent?

The default line spacing is 1.15 lines. The options 1.0, 2.0, and 3.0 set line spacing to single, double, and triple, respectively. Similarly, the 1.5 and 2.5 options set line spacing to 1.5 and 2.5 lines. All these options adjust line spacing automatically to accommodate the largest font or graphic on a line.

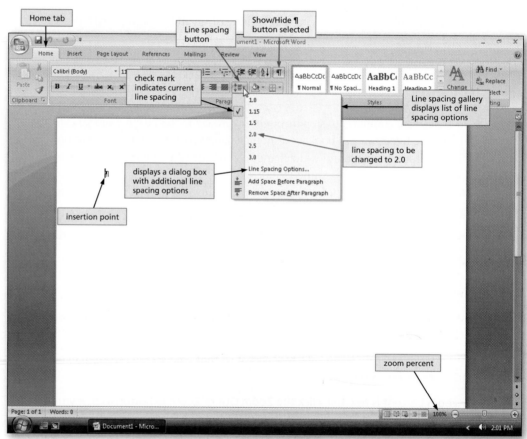

Figure 2–2

2

- Click 2.0 in the Line spacing gallery to change the line spacing to double at the location of the insertion point.

Q&A

Can I change the line spacing of existing text?

Yes. Select the text first and then change the line spacing as described in these steps.

Other Ways

1. Right-click paragraph, click Paragraph on shortcut menu, click Indents and Spacing tab, click Line

   spacing box arrow, click Double, click OK button

2. Click Paragraph Dialog Box Launcher, click Indents

   and Spacing tab, click Line spacing box arrow, click Double, click OK button

3. Press CTRL+2

To Remove Space after a Paragraph

The research paper should not have additional blank space after each paragraph. The following steps remove space after a paragraph.

- Click the Line spacing button on the Home tab to display the Line spacing gallery (Figure 2–3).

- Click Remove Space After Paragraph in the Line spacing gallery so that no blank space appears after a paragraph.

Q&A Can I remove space after existing paragraphs?

Yes. Select the paragraphs first and then remove the space as described in these steps.

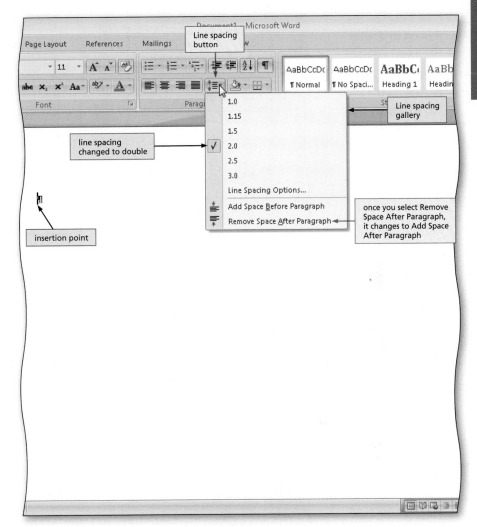

Figure 2–3

Other Ways

1. Click Spacing After box arrow on Page Layout tab until 0 pt is displayed

2. Right-click paragraph, click Paragraph on shortcut menu, click Indents and Spacing tab, click Spacing After box arrow until 0 pt is displayed, click OK button

3. Click Paragraph Dialog Box Launcher, click Indents and Spacing tab, click Spacing After box arrow until 0 pt is displayed, click OK button

---

Headers and Footers

A **header** is text and graphics that print at the top of each page in a document. Similarly, a **footer** is text and graphics that print at the bottom of every page. In Word, headers print in the top margin one-half inch from the top of every page, and footers print in the bottom margin one-half inch from the bottom of each page, which meets the MLA style. In addition to text and graphics, headers and footers can include document information such as the page number, current date, current time, and author's name.

In this research paper, you are to precede the page number with your last name placed one-half inch from the upper-right edge of each page. The procedures on the following pages enter your name and the page number in the header, as specified by the MLA style.

To Switch to the Header

To enter text in the header, you instruct Word to edit the header. The following steps switch from editing the document text to editing the header.

- Click Insert on the Ribbon to display the Insert tab.

- Click the Header button on the Insert tab to display the Header gallery (Figure 2–4).

Q&A

Can I use a built-in header for this research paper?

None of the built-in headers adhere to the MLA style. Thus, you enter your own header contents, instead of using a built-in header, for this research paper.

Figure 2–4

②

🔍 **Experiment**

- Click the down scroll arrow in the Header gallery to see the available built-in headers.

③

- Click Edit Header in the Header gallery to switch from the document text to the header, which allows you to edit the contents of the header (Figure 2–5).

Q&A

How do I remove the Header & Footer Tools and Design tabs from the Ribbon?

When you are finished editing the header, you will close it, which removes the Header & Footer Tools tabs.

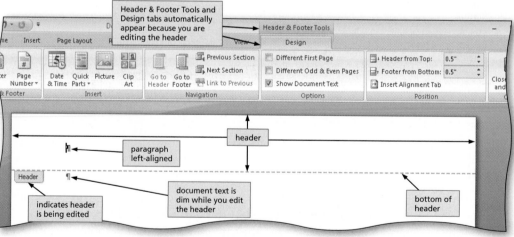

Figure 2–5

Other Ways

1. Double-click dimmed header

To Right-Align a Paragraph

The paragraph in the header currently is left-aligned (Figure 2–5). Your last name and the page number should print **right-aligned**, that is, at the right margin. The following step right-aligns a paragraph.

1

- Click Home on the Ribbon to display the Home tab.

- Click the Align Text Right button on the Home tab to right-align the paragraph in the header (Figure 2–6).

Q&A What if I wanted to return the paragraph to left-aligned?

Click the Align Text Right button again, or click the Align Text Left button.

Figure 2–6

Other Ways

1. Right-click paragraph, click Paragraph on shortcut menu, click Indents and Spacing tab, click Alignment box arrow, click Right, click OK button

2. Click Paragraph Dialog Box Launcher, click Indents and Spacing tab, click Alignment box arrow, click Right, click OK button

3. Press CTRL+R

To Enter Text

The following steps enter your last name right-aligned in the header area.

1 Click Design on the Ribbon to display the Design tab.

2 Type Pappas and then press the SPACEBAR to enter the last name in the header.

BTW **Footers**
If you wanted to create a footer, you would click the Footer button on the Insert tab and then select the desired built-in footer or click Edit Footer to create a customized footer.

To Insert a Page Number

The next task is to insert the current page number in the header. The following steps insert a page number at the location of the insertion point.

1

- Click the Insert Page Number button on the Design tab to display the Insert Page Number menu.

- Point to Current Position on the Insert Page Number menu to display the Current Position gallery (Figure 2–7).

Figure 2–7

2

 Experiment

- Click the down scroll arrow in the Current Position gallery to see the available page number formats.

3

- If necessary, scroll to the top of the Current Position gallery. Click Plain Number in the Current Position gallery to insert an unformatted page number at the location of the insertion point (Figure 2–8).

Figure 2–8

Other Ways

1. Click Insert Page Number button on Insert tab	2. Click Quick Parts button on Insert tab or on Design tab on Header & Footer Tools tab,	click Field on Quick Parts menu, select Page in Field names list, click OK button

To Close the Header

You are finished entering text in the header. Thus, the next task is to switch back to the document text. The following step closes the header.

1

- Click the Close Header and Footer button on the Design tab (shown in Figure 2–8) to close the header and switch back to the document text (Figure 2–9).

Q&A

How do I make changes to existing header text?

Switch to the header using the steps described on page WD 80, edit the header as you would edit text in the document window, and then switch back to the document text.

Figure 2–9

Other Ways

1. Double-click dimmed document text

Typing the Research Paper Text

The text of the research paper in this chapter encompasses the first two pages of the paper. You will type the text of the research paper and then modify it later in the chapter, so that it matches Figure 2–1 on page WD 75.

Plan Ahead

Write the first draft, referencing sources.
As you write the first draft of your research paper, be sure it includes the proper components, uses credible sources, and does not contain any plagiarism.

- **Include an introduction, body, and conclusion.** The first paragraph of the paper introduces the topic and captures the reader's attention. The body, which follows the introduction, consists of several paragraphs that support the topic. The conclusion summarizes the main points in the body and restates the topic.

- **Evaluate sources for authority, currency, and accuracy.** Be especially wary of information obtained from the Web. Any person, company, or organization can publish a Web page on the Internet. Ask yourself these questions about the source:

  - Authority: Does a reputable institution or group support the source? Is the information presented without bias? Are the author's credentials listed and verifiable?

  - Currency: Is the information up to date? Are dates of sources listed? What is the last date revised or updated?

  - Accuracy: Is the information free of errors? Is it verifiable? Are the sources clearly identified?

- **Acknowledge all sources of information; do not plagiarize.** Not only is plagiarism unethical, but it is considered an academic crime that can have severe punishments such as failing a course or being expelled from school.

  When you summarize, paraphrase (rewrite information in your own words), present facts, give statistics, quote exact words, or show a map, chart, or other graphical image, you

(continued)

Plan
Ahead

(continued)

must acknowledge the source. Information that commonly is known or accessible to the audience constitutes common knowledge and does not need to be acknowledged. If, however, you question whether certain information is common knowledge, you should document it — just to be safe.

To Enter Name and Course Information

As discussed earlier in this chapter, the MLA style does not require a separate title page for research papers. Instead, place your name and course information in a block at the top of the page, below the header, at the left margin. The following steps enter the name and course information in the research paper.

BTW

Date Formats
The MLA style prefers the day-month-year (28 March 2008) or month-day-year (March 28, 2008) format. Whichever format you select, use it consistently throughout the paper.

1 Type `Alex Pappas` as the student name and then press the ENTER key.

2 Type `Ms. Singh` as the instructor name and then press the ENTER key.

3 Type `English 104` as the course name and then press the ENTER key.

4 Type `28 March 2008` as the paper due date and then press the ENTER key (Figure 2–10).

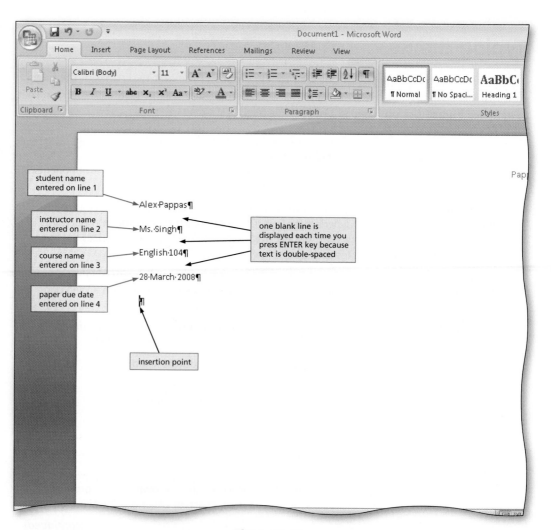

Figure 2–10

To Click and Type

The next step is to enter the title of the research paper centered between the page margins. In Chapter 1, you used the Center button on the Home tab to center text and graphics. As an alternative, you can use **Click and Type** to format and enter text, graphics, and other items. To use Click and Type, you double-click a blank area of the document window. Word automatically formats the item you enter according to the location where you just double-clicked. The following steps use Click and Type to center and then type the title of the research paper.

 1

 Experiment

- Move the mouse pointer around the document below the entered name and course information and observe the various icons that appear with the I-beam.

2

- Position the mouse pointer in the center of the document at the approximate location for the research paper title until a center icon appears below the I-beam (Figure 2–11).

Q&A

What are the other icons that appear in the Click and Type pointer?

A left-align icon appears to the right of the I-beam when the Click and Type pointer is in certain locations on the left side of the document window. A right-align icon appears to the left of the icon when the Click and Type pointer is in certain locations on the right side of the document window.

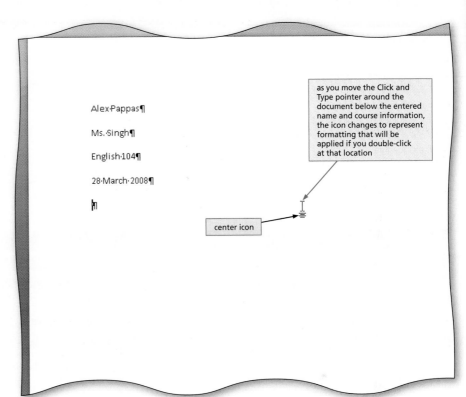

Alex·Pappas¶

Ms.·Singh¶

English·104¶

28·March·2008¶

¶

as you move the Click and Type pointer around the document below the entered name and course information, the icon changes to represent formatting that will be applied if you double-click at that location

center icon

Figure 2–11

 3

- Double-click to center the paragraph mark and insertion point between the left and right margins.

- **Type** Wireless Communications as the paper title and then press the ENTER key (Figure 2–12).

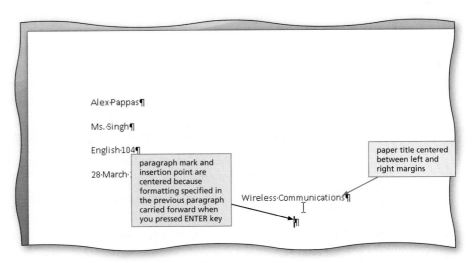

Alex·Pappas¶

Ms.·Singh¶

English·104¶

28·March·

paragraph mark and insertion point are centered because formatting specified in the previous paragraph carried forward when you pressed ENTER key

Wireless·Communications¶

paper title centered between left and right margins

¶

Figure 2–12

Shortcut Keys

Word has many shortcut keys for your convenience while typing. Table 2–1 lists the common shortcut keys for formatting characters. Table 2–2 lists common shortcut keys for formatting paragraphs.

Table 2–1 Shortcut Keys for Formatting Characters

Character Formatting Task	Shortcut Keys	Character Formatting Task	Shortcut Keys
All capital letters	CTRL+SHIFT+A	Italic	CTRL+I
Bold	CTRL+B	Remove character formatting (plain text)	CTRL+SPACEBAR
Case of letters	SHIFT+F3	Small uppercase letters	CTRL+SHIFT+K
Decrease font size	CTRL+SHIFT+<	Subscript	CTRL+EQUAL SIGN
Decrease font size 1 point	CTRL+[	Superscript	CTRL+SHIFT+PLUS SIGN
Double-underline	CTRL+SHIFT+D	Underline	CTRL+U
Increase font size	CTRL+SHIFT+>	Underline words, not spaces	CTRL+SHIFT+W
Increase font size 1 point	CTRL+]		

Table 2–2 Shortcut Keys for Formatting Paragraphs

Paragraph Formatting	Shortcut Keys	Paragraph Formatting	Shortcut Keys
1.5 line spacing	CTRL+5	Justify paragraph	CTRL+J
Add/remove one line above paragraph	CTRL+0 (ZERO)	Left-align paragraph	CTRL+L
Center paragraph	CTRL+E	Remove hanging indent	CTRL+SHIFT+T
Decrease paragraph indent	CTRL+SHIFT+M	Remove paragraph formatting	CTRL+Q
Double-space lines	CTRL+2	Right-align paragraph	CTRL+R
Hanging indent	CTRL+T	Single-space lines	CTRL+1
Increase paragraph indent	CTRL+M		

BTW

Shortcut Keys
To print a complete list of shortcut keys in Word, click the Microsoft Office Word Help button near the upper-right corner of the Word window, type shortcut keys in the 'Type words to search for' text box at the top of the Word Help window, press the ENTER key, click the Keyboard shortcuts for Microsoft Office Word link, click the Show All link in the upper-right corner of the Help window, click the Print button in the Help window, and then click the Print button in the Print dialog box.

To Format Text Using Shortcut Keys

The paragraphs below the paper title should be left-aligned, instead of centered. Thus, the next step is to left-align the paragraph below the paper title. When your fingers are already on the keyboard, you may prefer using **shortcut keys**, or keyboard key combinations, to format text as you type it. The following step left-aligns a paragraph using the shortcut keys CTRL+L. (Recall from Chapter 1 that a notation such as CTRL+L means to press the letter l on the keyboard while holding down the CTRL key.)

1 Press CTRL+L to left-align the current paragraph, that is, the paragraph containing the insertion point.

Q&A Why would I use a keyboard shortcut, instead of the Ribbon, to format text?

Switching between the mouse and the keyboard takes time. If your hands are already on the keyboard, use a keyboard shortcut. If your hand is on the mouse, use the Ribbon.

To Save a Document

You have performed many tasks while creating the research paper and do not want to risk losing the work completed thus far. Accordingly, you should save the document. For a detailed example of the procedure summarized below, refer to pages WD 19 through WD 21 in Chapter 1.

Note: If you are using Windows XP, see Appendix F for alternate steps.

1 With a USB flash drive connected to one of the computer's USB ports, click the Save button on the Quick Access Toolbar to display the Save As dialog box.

2 Type `Wireless Communications Paper` in the File name text box to change the file name.

3 If Computer is not displayed in the Favorite Links section, drag the top or bottom edge of the Save As dialog box until Computer is displayed. Click Computer in the Favorite Links section and then double-click your USB flash drive in the list of available drives.

4 Click the Save button in the Save As dialog box to save the document on the USB flash drive with the file name, Wireless Communications Paper.

To Display the Rulers

According to the MLA style, the first line of each paragraph in the research paper is to be indented one-half inch from the left margin. Although you can use a dialog box to indent paragraphs, Word provides a quicker way through the **horizontal ruler**. This ruler displays at the top edge of the document window just below the Ribbon. Word also provides a **vertical ruler** that displays along the left edge of the Word window. The following steps display the rulers.

1

Experiment

- Repeatedly click the View Ruler button on the vertical scroll bar to see the how this button is used to both show and hide the rulers.

2

- If the rulers are not displayed, click the View Ruler button on the vertical scroll bar because you want to use the ruler to indent paragraphs (Figure 2–13).

Q&A Can I use the rulers for other tasks?

In addition to indenting paragraphs, you can use the rulers to set tab stops, change page margins, and adjust column widths.

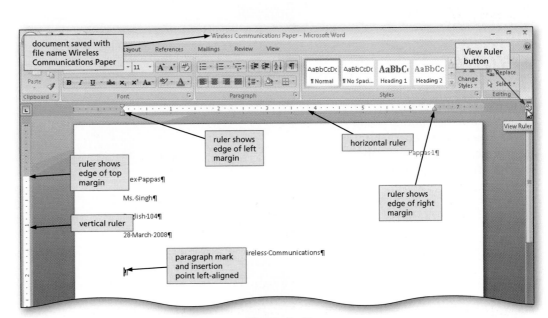

Figure 2–13

Other Ways

1. Click View Ruler check box on View tab

To First-Line Indent Paragraphs

The first line of each paragraph in the research paper is to be indented one-half inch from the left margin. You can use the horizontal ruler, usually simply called the **ruler**, to indent just the first line of a paragraph, called **first-line indent**.

The left margin on the ruler contains two triangles above a square. The **First Line Indent marker** is the top triangle at the 0" mark on the ruler (Figure 2–14). The bottom triangle is discussed later in this chapter. The small square at the 0" mark is the Left Indent marker. The **Left Indent marker** allows you to change the entire left margin, whereas the First Line Indent marker indents only the first line of the paragraph. The following steps first-line indent paragraphs in the research paper.

1

- With the insertion point on the paragraph mark below the research paper title, point to the First Line Indent marker on the ruler (Figure 2–14).

Figure 2–14

2

- Drag the First Line Indent marker to the .5" mark on the ruler to display a vertical dotted line in the document window, which indicates the proposed location of the first line of the paragraph (Figure 2–15).

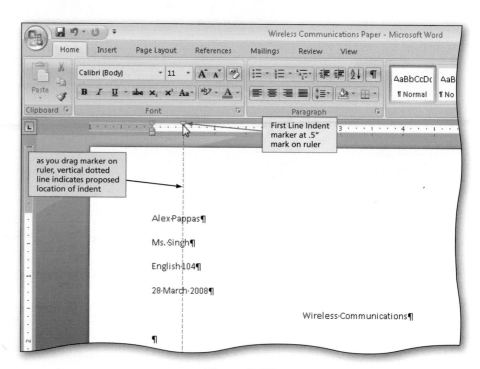

Figure 2–15

3

- Release the mouse button to place the First Line Indent marker at the .5" mark on the ruler, or one-half inch from the left margin (Figure 2–16).

First Line Indent marker .5" from left margin

Alex·Pappas¶

Ms.·Singh¶

English·104¶

28·March·2008¶

paragraph mark containing insertion point indented one-half inch

Wireless·Communications¶

Figure 2–16

4

- **Type** Wireless communications are everywhere. People around the world regularly send and receive messages wirelessly, that is, transmitted through the air. and notice that Word automatically indented the first line of the paragraph by one-half inch (Figure 2–17).

Q&A

Will I have to set first-line indent for each paragraph in the paper?

No. Each time you press the ENTER key, paragraph formatting in the previous paragraph carries forward to the next paragraph. Thus, once you set the first-line indent, its format carries forward automatically to each subsequent paragraph you type.

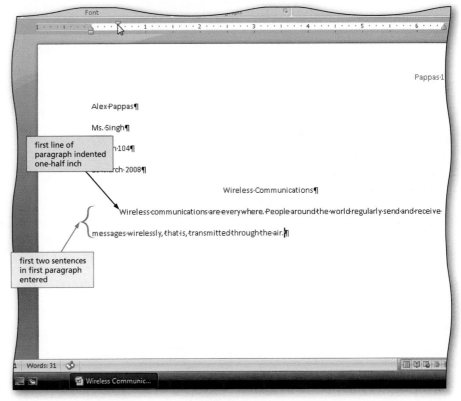

Pappas·1

Alex·Pappas¶

Ms.·Singh¶

first line of paragraph indented one-half inch

·104¶

·2008¶

Wireless·Communications¶

Wireless·communications·are·everywhere.·People·around·the·world·regularly·send·and·receive·

messages·wirelessly,·that·is,·transmitted·through·the·air.¶

first two sentences in first paragraph entered

Words: 31

Wireless Communic...

Figure 2–17

Other Ways
1. Right-click paragraph, click Paragraph on shortcut menu, click Indents and Spacing tab, click Special box arrow, click First line, click OK button	2. Click Paragraph Dialog Box Launcher, click Indents and Spacing tab, click Special box arrow, click First line, click OK button	3. Press TAB key at beginning of paragraph

To Create a Quick Style

Recall from Chapter 1 that a Quick Style is a predefined style that appears in the Styles gallery on the Ribbon. You use styles in the Styles gallery to apply defined formats to text. Later in this chapter, you will apply the formats of the research paper paragraph to the paragraphs in the footnote. To accomplish this task, you can create a Quick Style based on the formats in the current paragraph. That is, text is double-spaced with the first line of the paragraph indented and no space after the paragraph. The following steps first select the paragraph and then create a Quick Style based on the formats in the selected paragraph.

- Position the mouse pointer in the paragraph below the title and then triple-click; that is, press the mouse button three times in rapid succession, to select the paragraph.

- Right-click the selected paragraph to display a shortcut menu.

- Point to Styles on the shortcut menu to display the Styles submenu (Figure 2–18).

Figure 2–18

- Click Save Selection as a New Quick Style on the Styles submenu to display the Create New Style from Formatting dialog box.

- Type `Research Paper Paragraphs` in the Name text box (Figure 2–19).

Figure 2–19

- Click the OK button to create the new Quick Style and add it to the Styles gallery (Figure 2–20).

Q&A

How can I see the formats assigned to a Quick Style?

Click the Styles Dialog Box Launcher. When the Styles task pane appears, position the mouse pointer on any style to display its formats in a ScreenTip. When finished, click the Close button in the task pane.

Figure 2–20

Other Ways
1. Click More button in Styles gallery on Home tab, click Save Selection as a New	Quick Style, enter name of new Quick Style, click OK button

To AutoCorrect as You Type

As you type, you may make typing, spelling, capitalization, or grammar errors. For this reason, Word provides an **AutoCorrect** feature that automatically corrects these kinds of errors as you type them in the document. For example, if you type the text ahve, Word automatically changes it to the correct spelling, have, when you press the SPACEBAR or a punctuation mark key such as a period or comma.

Word has predefined many commonly misspelled words, which it automatically corrects for you. In the following steps, the word wireless is misspelled intentionally as wreless to illustrate the AutoCorrect as you type feature.

- Press CTRL+END to move the insertion point to the end of the document.

- Press the SPACEBAR.

- Type the beginning of the next sentence, misspelling the word, wireless, as follows: Three types of wireless communications include wireless messaging services, wreless (Figure 2–21).

Figure 2–21

2

- Press the SPACEBAR and watch Word automatically correct the misspelled word.

- Type the rest of the sentence (Figure 2–22): `Internet access points, and global positioning systems.`

Wireless·Communications¶

Wireless·communications·are·everywhere.·People·around·the·world·regularly·send·and·receive·messages·wirelessly,·that·is,·transmitted·through·the·air.·Three·types·of·wireless·communications· include·wireless·messaging·services,·wireless·Internet·access·points,·and·global·positioning·systems.¶

as soon as you press the SPACEBAR, Word detects the misspelling and corrects the misspelled word

rest of sentence entered

Figure 2–22

To Use the AutoCorrect Options Button

When you position the mouse pointer on text that Word automatically corrected, a small blue box appears below the text. If you point to the small blue box, Word displays the AutoCorrect Options button. When you click the **AutoCorrect Options button**, Word displays a menu that allows you to undo a correction or change how Word handles future automatic corrections of this type. The following steps illustrate the AutoCorrect Options button and menu.

1

- Position the mouse pointer in the text automatically corrected by Word (in this case, the word wireless) to display a small blue box below the automatically corrected word (Figure 2–23).

Wireless·commun...   ...ople·around·the·wor...

messages·wirelessly,·that·is,·transmitted·through·the·air.·Three·types·of·wireless·communications· include·wireless·messaging·services,·wireless·Internet·access·points,·and·global·positioning·systems.¶

clicking the small blue box will display the AutoCorrect Options button

mouse pointer is in automatically corrected text

Figure 2–23

2

- Point to the small blue box to display the AutoCorrect Options button.

- Click the AutoCorrect Options button to display the AutoCorrect Options menu (Figure 2–24).

- Press the ESCAPE key to remove the AutoCorrect Options menu from the screen.

messages·wirelessly,·that·is,·transmitted·through·the·air.·Three·types·of·wireless·communications· include·wireless·messaging·services,·wireless·Internet·access·points,·and·global·po...

AutoCorrect Options button

AutoCorrect Options menu

Change back to "wreless"

Stop Automatically Correcting "wreless"

Control AutoCorrect Options...

clicking this command will display the AutoCorrect dialog box

Figure 2–24

Q&A

Do I need to remove the AutoCorrect Options button from the screen?

No. When you move the mouse pointer, the AutoCorrect Options button will disappear from the screen. If, for some reason, you wanted to remove the AutoCorrect Options button from the screen, you could press the ESCAPE key a second time.

To Create an AutoCorrect Entry

In addition to the predefined list of AutoCorrect spelling, capitalization, and grammar errors, you can create your own AutoCorrect entries to add to the list. For example, if you tend to type the word mobile as moble, you should create an AutoCorrect entry for it. The following steps create an AutoCorrect entry.

• Click the Office Button to display the Office Button menu (Figure 2–25).

Figure 2–25

• Click the Word Options button on the Office Button menu to display the Word Options dialog box.

• Click Proofing in the left pane to display proofing options in the right pane.

• Click the AutoCorrect Options button in the right pane to display the AutoCorrect dialog box.

• When Word displays the AutoCorrect dialog box, type moble in the Replace text box.

• Press the TAB key and then type mobile in the With text box (Figure 2–26).

Figure 2–26

• Click the Add button in the AutoCorrect dialog box. (If your dialog box displays a Replace button instead, click it and then click the Yes button in the Microsoft Office Word dialog box.)

• Click the OK button to add the entry alphabetically to the list of words to correct automatically as you type.

• Click the OK button in the Word Options dialog box.

The AutoCorrect Dialog Box

In addition to creating AutoCorrect entries for words you commonly misspell or mistype, you can create entries for abbreviations, codes, and so on. For example, you could create an AutoCorrect entry for asap, indicating that Word should replace this text with the phrase, as soon as possible.

If, for some reason, you do not want Word to correct automatically as you type, you can turn off the Replace text as you type feature by clicking the Word Options button on the Office Button menu, clicking Proofing in the left pane of the Word Options dialog box, clicking the AutoCorrect Options button in the right pane of the Word Options dialog box (Figure 2–26 on the previous page), clicking the 'Replace text as you type' check box to remove the check mark, and then clicking the OK button in each open dialog box.

The AutoCorrect sheet in the AutoCorrect dialog box (Figure 2–26) contains other check boxes that correct capitalization errors if the check boxes are selected. If you type two capital letters in a row, such as TH, Word makes the second letter lowercase, Th. If you begin a sentence with a lowercase letter, Word capitalizes the first letter of the sentence. If you type the name of a day in lowercase, such as tuesday, Word capitalizes the first letter of the day, Tuesday. If you leave the CAPS LOCK key on and begin a new sentence, such as aFTER, Word corrects the typing, After, and turns off the CAPS LOCK key.

Sometimes you do not want Word to AutoCorrect a particular word or phrase. For example, you may use the code WD. in your documents. Because Word automatically capitalizes the first letter of a sentence, the character you enter following the period will be capitalized (in the previous sentence, it would capitalize the letter i in the word, in). To allow the code WD. to be entered into a document and still leave the AutoCorrect feature turned on, you should set an exception. To set an exception to an AutoCorrect rule, click the Word Options button on the Office Button menu, click Proofing in the left pane of the Word Options dialog box, click the AutoCorrect Options button in the right pane of the Word Options dialog box, click the Exceptions button (Figure 2–26), click the appropriate tab in the AutoCorrect Exceptions dialog box, type the exception entry in the text box, click the Add button, click the Close button in the AutoCorrect Exceptions dialog box, and then click the OK button in each of the remaining dialog boxes.

BTW

Automatic Corrections
If you do not want to keep a change automatically made by Word and you immediately notice the automatic correction, you can undo the change by clicking the Undo button on the Quick Access Toolbar or pressing CTRL+Z. You also can undo a correction through the AutoCorrect Options button, which was shown on page WD 92.

To Enter More Text

The next step is to continue typing text in the research paper up to the location of the citation.

1 Press the ENTER key, so that you can begin typing the text in the second paragraph.

2 Type `People use mobile phones, PDAs, and other mobile devices to access text messaging, instant messaging, and picture messaging services` and then press the SPACEBAR.

Citations

Both the MLA and APA guidelines suggest the use of in-text parenthetical citations (placed at the end of a sentence), instead of footnoting each source of material in a paper. These parenthetical acknowledgments guide the reader to the end of the paper for complete information about the source.

**Plan
Ahead**

Reference all sources.

During your research, be sure to record essential publication information about each of your sources. Following is a sample list of types of required information.

- Book: full name of author(s), complete title of book, edition (if available), volume (if available), publication city, publication year

- Magazine: full name of author(s), complete title of article, magazine title, date of magazine, page numbers of article

- Web site: full name of author(s), title of Web site, date viewed, Web address

Word provides tools to assist you with inserting citations in a paper and later generating a list of sources from the citations. With a documentation style selected, Word automatically formats the citations and list of sources. The process for adding citations in Word is as follows:

1. Modify the documentation style, if necessary.

2. Insert a citation placeholder.

3. Enter the source information for the citation.

You can combine Steps 2 and 3, where you insert the citation placeholder and enter the source information at once. Or, you can insert the citation placeholder as you write and then enter the source information for the citation at a later time. While entering the research paper in this chapter, you will use both methods.

To Change the Bibliography Style

The first step in inserting a citation is to be sure the citations and sources will be formatted using the correct documentation style, called the bibliography style in Word. The following steps change the specified documentation style.

1

- Click References on the Ribbon to display the References tab.

- Click the Bibliography Style box arrow on the References tab to display a gallery of predefined documentation styles (Figure 2–27).

2

- Click MLA in the Bibliography Style gallery to change the documentation style to MLA.

Figure 2–27

To Insert a Citation and Create Its Source

With the documentation style selected, the next task is to insert a citation placeholder and enter the source information. You can accomplish these steps at once by instructing Word to add a new source. The following steps add a new source for a magazine (periodical) article.

- Click the Insert Citation button on the References tab to display the Insert Citation menu (Figure 2–28).

Figure 2–28

- Click Add New Source on the Insert Citation menu to display the Create Source dialog box (Figure 2–29).

Q&A

What are the Bibliography Fields in the Create Source dialog box?

A **field** is a placeholder for data whose contents can change. You enter data in some fields; Word supplies data for others. In this case, you enter the contents of the fields for a particular source, for example, the author name in the Author field.

Experiment

- Click the Type of Source box arrow and then click one of the source types in the list, so that you can see how the list of fields changes to reflect the source type you selected.

Figure 2–29

- If necessary, click the Type of Source box arrow and then click Article in a Periodical, so that the list shows fields required for a magazine (periodical).

- Click the Author text box. Type `Davies, Habika` as the author.

- Click the Title text box. Type `Text Messaging, Instant Messaging, and Picture Messaging` as the article title.

- Press the TAB key and then type `Computing in Today's World` as the periodical title.

- Press the TAB key and then type `2008` as the year.

- Press the TAB key and then type `January` as the month.

- Press the TAB key twice and then type `34-42` as the pages (Figure 2–30).

Figure 2–30

- Click the OK button to close the dialog box, create the source, and insert the citation in the document at the location of the insertion point (Figure 2–31).

Figure 2–31

To Edit a Citation

In the MLA style, if a source has page numbers, you should include them in the citation. Thus, Word provides a means to enter the page numbers to be displayed in the citation. The following steps edit a citation, so that the page numbers appear in it.

- Click somewhere in the citation to be edited, in this case somewhere in (Davies), which selects the citation and displays the Citation Options box arrow.

- Click the Citation Options box arrow to display the Citation Options menu (Figure 2–32).

Q&A

What is the purpose of the tab to the left of the selected citation?

If, for some reason, you wanted to move a citation to a different location in the document, you would select it and then drag the citation tab to the desired location.

Figure 2–32

- Click Edit Citation on the Citation Options menu to display the Edit Citation dialog box.

- Type 34–42 in the Pages text box (Figure 2–33).

Figure 2–33

- Click the OK button to close the dialog box and add the page numbers to the citation in the document (Figure 2–34).

- Press the END key to move the insertion point to the end of the line, which also deselects the citation.

- Press the PERIOD key to end the sentence.

Figure 2–34

To Enter More Text

The next step is to continue typing text in the research paper up to the location of the footnote.

1 Press the SPACEBAR.

2 Type these three sentences (Figure 2–35): `Through text messaging services, users send and receive short text messages, which usually consist of fewer than 300 characters. Wireless instant messaging is an Internet communications service that allows a wireless mobile device to exchange instant messages with one or more mobile devices or online personal computers. Users send graphics, pictures, video clips, sound files, and short text messages with picture messaging services.`

BTW

Edit a Source
To edit a source, click somewhere in the citation, click the Citation Options box arrow, and then click Edit Source on the Citation Options menu to display the Edit Source dialog box (which resembles the Create Source dialog box). Make necessary changes and then click the OK button.

Figure 2–35

Footnotes

As discussed earlier in this chapter, explanatory notes are optional in the MLA documentation style. They are used primarily to elaborate on points discussed in the body of a research paper. The MLA style specifies that a superscript (raised number) be used for a **note reference mark** to signal that an explanatory note exists either at the bottom of the page as a **footnote** or at the end of the document as an **endnote**.

In Word, **note text** can be any length and format. Word automatically numbers notes sequentially by placing a note reference mark in the body of the document and also to the left of the note text. If you insert, rearrange, or remove notes, Word renumbers any subsequent note reference marks according to their new sequence in the document.

To Insert a Footnote Reference Mark

The following step inserts a footnote reference mark in the document at the location of the insertion point and also at the location where the footnote text will be typed.

1

- With the insertion point positioned as shown in Figure 2–35 on the previous page, click the Insert Footnote button on the References tab to display a note reference mark (a superscripted 1) in two places: (1) in the document window at the location of the insertion point and (2) at the bottom of the page where the footnote will be positioned, just below a separator line (Figure 2–36).

Q&A

What if I wanted explanatory notes to be positioned as endnotes instead of as footnotes?

You would click the Insert Endnote button on the References tab, which places the separator line and the endnote text at the end of the document, instead of the bottom of the page containing the reference.

Figure 2–36

Other Ways

1. Press CTRL+ALT+F

To Enter Footnote Text

The next step is to type the footnote text to the right of the note reference mark below the separator line.

1 Type the footnote text up to the citation: Podpora and Ruiz indicate that some messaging services use the term, video messaging, to refer separately to the capability of sending video clips **and then press the SPACEBAR.**

To Insert a Citation Placeholder

Earlier in this chapter, you inserted a citation and its source at once. Sometimes, you may not have the source information readily available and would prefer entering it at a later time.

In the footnote, you will insert a placeholder for the citation and enter the source information later. The following steps insert a citation placeholder.

- With the insertion point positioned as shown in Figure 2–37, click the Insert Citation button on the References tab to display the Insert Citation menu (Figure 2–37).

Figure 2–37

- Click Add New Placeholder on the Insert Citation menu to display the Placeholder Name dialog box.

- Type Podpora as the tag name for the source (Figure 2–38).

 What is a tag name?

A tag name is an identifier that links a citation to a source. Word automatically creates a tag name when you enter a source. When you create a citation placeholder, enter a meaningful tag name, which will appear in the citation placeholder until you edit the source.

- Click the OK button to close the dialog box and insert the tag name in the citation placeholder.

- Press the PERIOD key to end the sentence.

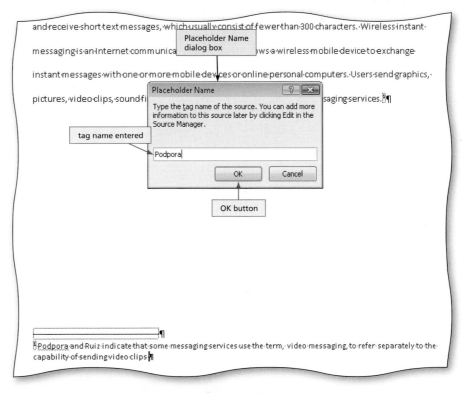

Figure 2–38

Footnote Text Style

When you insert a footnote, Word formats it using the Footnote Text style, which does not adhere to the MLA documentation style. For example, notice in Figure 2–38 on the previous page that the footnote text is single-spaced, left-aligned, and a smaller font size than the text in the research paper. According to the MLA style, notes should be formatted like all other paragraphs in the paper.

You could change the paragraph formatting of the footnote text to first-line indent and double-spacing and then change the font size from 10 to 11 point. If you use this technique, however, you will need to change the format of the footnote text for each footnote you enter into the document.

A more efficient technique is to modify the format of the Footnote Text style so that every footnote you enter in the document will use the formats defined in this style.

To Modify a Style Using a Shortcut Menu

The Footnote Text style should be based on the Research Paper Paragraphs style defined earlier in this chapter. Because the Footnote Text style specifically set paragraphs to single-spaced and the font size to 10 point, you will need to modify those formats to double-spaced paragraphs and 11-point font. The following steps modify the Footnote Text style.

- Right-click the note text in the footnote to display a shortcut menu related to footnotes (Figure 2–39).

Figure 2–39

2

- Click Style on the shortcut menu to display the Style dialog box. If necessary, click Footnote Text in the Styles list.

- Click the Modify button in the Style dialog box to display the Modify Style dialog box.

- Click the 'Style based on' box arrow and then click Research Paper Paragraphs so that the Footnote Text style is based on the Research Paper Paragraphs style.

- Click the 'Style for following paragraph' box arrow and then scroll to and click Research Paper Paragraphs so that the additional footnote paragraphs are based on the Research Paper Paragraphs style.

- Click the Font Size box arrow and then click 11 in the Font Size list to change the font size to 11.

- Click the Double Space button to set the line spacing to double (Figure 2–40).

Figure 2–40

3

- Click the OK button in the Modify Style dialog box to close the dialog box.

- Click the Apply button in the Style dialog box to apply the style changes to the footnote text (Figure 2–41).

Q&A Will all footnotes use this modified style?

Yes. Any future footnotes entered in the document will use an 11-point font with the paragraphs first-line indented and double-spaced.

Footnote Text style modified to match research paper paragraphs

Figure 2–41

Other Ways

1. Click Styles Dialog Box Launcher, click Footnote Text in list, click Footnote Text box arrow, click Modify, change settings, click OK button

2. Click Styles Dialog Box Launcher, click Manage Styles button, scroll to Footnote Text and then select it, click Modify button, change settings, click OK button in each dialog box

To Edit a Source

When you typed the footnote text for this research paper, you inserted a citation placeholder for the source. You now have the source information and are ready to enter it. The following steps edit the source.

- Click somewhere in the citation placeholder to be edited, in this case (Podpora), to select the citation placeholder.

- Click the Citation Options box arrow to display the Citation Options menu (Figure 2–42).

Figure 2–42

- Click Edit Source on the Citation Options menu to display the Edit Source dialog box.

- If necessary, click the Type of Source box arrow and then click Book, so that the list shows fields required for a book.

- Click the Author text box. Type Podpora, Maxine C., and Adelbert D. Ruiz as the author.

- Click the Title text box. Type Advances in Wireless Internet Access Point Technology as the book title.

- Press the TAB key and then type 2008 as the year.

- Press the TAB key and then type Dallas as the city.

- Press the TAB key and then type Wells Publishing as the publisher (Figure 2–43).

- Click the OK button to close the dialog box and create the source.

Figure 2–43

Other Ways

1. Click Manage Sources button on References tab, click placeholder source in Current List, click Edit button

To Edit a Citation

In the MLA style, if you reference the author's name in the text, you should not list it again in the parenthetical citation. Instead, just list the page number in the citation. The following steps edit the citation, suppressing the author but displaying the page numbers.

1 If necessary, click somewhere in the citation to be edited, in this case (Podpora), to select the citation and display the Citation Options box arrow.

2 Click the Citation Options box arrow to display the Citation Options menu.

3 Click Edit Citation on the Citation Options menu to display the Edit Citation dialog box.

4 Type 79-82 in the Pages text box.

5 Click the Author check box to place a check mark in it (Figure 2–44).

6 Click the OK button to close the dialog box, remove the author name from the citation in the footnote, and add page numbers to the citation.

Figure 2–44

Working with Footnotes and Endnotes

You edit footnote text just as you edit any other text in the document. To delete or move a note reference mark, however, you must be in the document text (not in the footnote text).

To delete a note, select the note reference mark in the document text (not in the footnote text) by dragging through the note reference mark and then click the Cut button on the Home tab. Another way to delete a note is to click immediately to the right of the note reference mark in the document text and then press the BACKSPACE key twice, or click immediately to the left of the note reference mark in the document text and then press the DELETE key twice.

To move a note to a different location in a document, select the note reference mark in the document text (not in the footnote text), click the Cut button on the Home tab, click the location where you want to move the note, and then click the Paste button on the Home tab. When you move or delete notes, Word automatically renumbers any remaining notes in the correct sequence.

If you position the mouse pointer on the note reference mark, the note text displays above the note reference mark as a ScreenTip. To remove the ScreenTip, move the mouse pointer.

If, for some reason, you wanted to change the format of note reference marks in footnotes or endnotes (i.e., from 1, 2, 3, to A, B, C), you would click the Footnotes Dialog Box Launcher to display the Footnote and Endnote dialog box, click the Number format box arrow, click the desired number format in the list, and then click the OK button.

If, for some reason, you wanted to convert footnotes to endnotes, you would click the Footnotes Dialog Box Launcher to display the Footnote and Endnote dialog box, click the Convert button, make sure the 'Convert all footnotes to endnotes' option button is selected, click the OK button, and then click the Close button in the Footnote and Endnote dialog box.

To Enter More Text

The next step is to continue typing text in the body of the research paper.

1. Position the insertion point after the note reference mark in the document, and then press the ENTER key.

2. Type the third paragraph of the research paper (Figure 2–45): In many public locations, people connect to the Internet through a wireless Internet access point using mobile computers and devices. Two types of wireless Internet access points are hot spots and 3-G networks. A 3-G network, which uses cellular radio technology, enables users to connect to the Internet through a mobile phone or computer equipped with an appropriate PC Card. A hot spot is a wireless network that allows mobile users to check e-mail, browse the Web, and access any Internet service - as long as their computers or devices have the proper wireless capability.

BTW

Spacing after Punctuation
Because word processing documents use variable character fonts, it often is difficult to determine in a printed document how many times someone has pressed the SPACEBAR between sentences. The rule is to press the SPACEBAR only once after periods, colons, and other punctuation marks.

To Count Words

Often when you write papers, you are required to compose the papers with a minimum number of words. The minimum requirement for the research paper in this chapter is 325 words. You can look on the status bar and see the total number of words thus far in a document. For example, Figure 2–45 shows the research paper has 250 words, but you are not sure if that count includes the words in your footnote. The following steps display the Word Count dialog box, so that you can verify whether the footnote text is included in the count.

1

• Click the Word Count indicator on the status bar to display the Word Count dialog box.

• If necessary, place a check mark in the 'Include textboxes, footnotes and endnotes' check box (Figure 2-45).

Q&A
Why do the statistics in my Word Count dialog box differ from Figure 2–45?
Depending on the accuracy of your typing, your statistics may differ.

2

• Click the Close button to close the dialog box.

Q&A
Can I display statistics for just a section of the document?
Yes. Select the section and then click the Word Count indicator on the status bar to display statistics about the selected text.

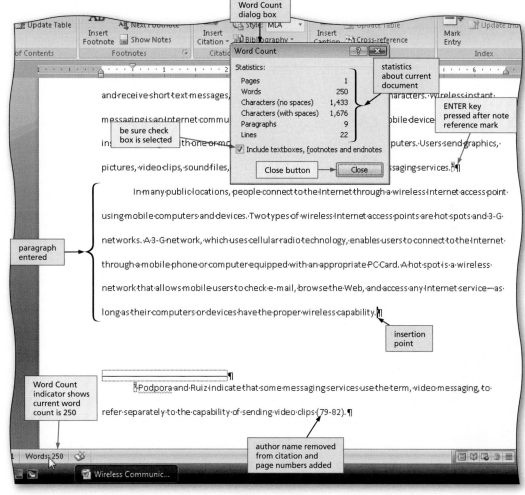

Figure 2–45

Other Ways

1. Click Word Count button on Review tab
2. Press CTRL+SHIFT+G

Automatic Page Breaks

As you type documents that exceed one page, Word automatically inserts page breaks, called **automatic page breaks** or **soft page breaks**, when it determines the text has filled one page according to paper size, margin settings, line spacing, and other settings. If you add text, delete text, or modify text on a page, Word recomputes the location of automatic page breaks and adjusts them accordingly.

Word performs page recomputation between the keystrokes, that is, in between the pauses in your typing. Thus, Word refers to the automatic page break task as **background repagination**. The steps on the next page illustrate Word's automatic page break feature.

To Enter More Text and Insert a Citation Placeholder

The next task is to type the fourth paragraph in the body of the research paper.

1 With the insertion point positioned at the end of the third paragraph as shown in Figure 2–45 on the previous page, press the ENTER key. Type the fourth paragraph of the research paper (Figure 2–46): A global positioning system (GPS) is a navigation system that consists of one or more earth-based receivers that accept and analyze signals sent by satellites in order to determine the receiver's geographic location, according to Shelly and Cashman **and then press the SPACEBAR.**

2 Click the Insert Citation button on the References tab to display the Insert Citation menu. Click Add New Placeholder on the Insert Citation menu to display the Placeholder Name dialog box.

3 Type Shelly as the tag name for the source.

4 Click the OK button to close the dialog box and insert the tag name in the citation placeholder.

5 Press the PERIOD key to end the sentence. Press the SPACEBAR. Type A GPS receiver is a handheld, mountable, or embedded device that contains an antenna, a radio receiver, and a processor. Many mobile devices, such as mobile phones and PDAs, have GPS capability built into the device.

6 Press the ENTER key.

BTW

Page Break Locations
As you type, your page break may occur at different locations depending on Word settings and the type of printer connected to the computer.

Figure 2–46

To Edit a Source

When you typed the fourth paragraph of the research paper, you inserted a citation placeholder, Shelly, for the source. You now have the source information, which is for a Web site, and are ready to enter it. The following steps edit the source for the Shelly citation placeholder.

1 Click somewhere in the citation placeholder to be edited, in this case (Shelly), to select the citation placeholder.

2 Click the Citation Options box arrow to display the Citation Options menu.

3 Click Edit Source on the Citation Options menu to display the Edit Source dialog box.

4 If necessary, click the Type of Source box arrow; scroll to and then click Web site, so that the list shows fields required for a Web site.

5 Place a check mark in the Show All Bibliography Fields check box to display more fields related to Web sites.

6 Click the Author text box. Type `Shelly, Gary B., and Thomas J. Cashman` as the author.

7 Click the Name of Web Page text box. Type `How a GPS Works` as the Web page title.

8 Click the Production Company text box. Type `Course Technology` as the production company.

9 Click the Year Accessed text box. Type `2008` as the year.

10 Press the TAB key and then type `March` as the month accessed.

Q&A What if some of the text boxes disappear as I enter the Web site fields?

With the Show All Bibliography Fields check box selected, all Web site fields may not be able to be displayed in the dialog box at the same time. In this case, some may scroll up.

11 Press the TAB key and then type `21` as the day accessed.

12 Press the TAB key and then type `www.scsite.com/wd2007/ pr2/wc.htm` as the URL (Figure 2–47).

13 Click the OK button to close the dialog box and create the source.

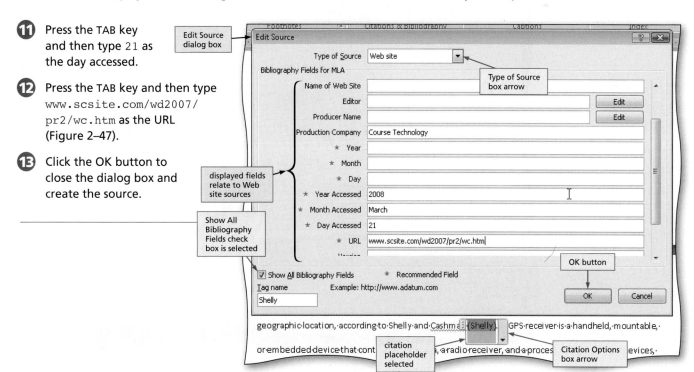

Figure 2–47

To Edit a Citation

As mentioned earlier, if you reference the author's name in the text, you should not list it again in the parenthetical citation. For Web site citations, when you suppress the author's name, the citation shows the Web site name because page numbers do not apply. The following steps edit the citation, suppressing the author and displaying the name of the Web site instead.

1 If necessary, click somewhere in the citation to be edited, in this case (Shelly), to select the citation and display the Citation Options box arrow.

2 Click the Citation Options box arrow and then click Edit Citation on the Citation Options menu to display the Edit Citation dialog box.

3 Click the Author check box to place a check mark in it (Figure 2–48).

4 Click the OK button to close the dialog box, remove the author name from the citation, and show the name of the Web site in the citation.

Figure 2–48

To Enter More Text

The next step is to type the last paragraph of text in the research paper.

1 Position the insertion point on the paragraph mark below the fourth paragraph in the research paper (Figure 2–48).

2 Type the last paragraph of the research paper (Figure 2–49): Mobile users communicate wirelessly through wireless

messaging services, wireless Internet access points, and global positioning systems. Anyone can take advantage of wireless communications using mobile computers and devices.

Figure 2–49

To Save an Existing Document with the Same File Name

You have made several edits to the research paper since you last saved it. Thus, you should save it again. The following step saves the document again.

1 Click the Save button on the Quick Access Toolbar to overwrite the previous Wireless Communications Paper file on the USB flash drive.

Creating an Alphabetical Works Cited Page

According to the MLA style, the **works cited page** is a list of sources that are referenced directly in a research paper. You place the list on a separate numbered page with the title, Works Cited, centered one inch from the top margin. The works are to be alphabetized by the author's last name or, if the work has no author, by the work's title. The first line of each entry begins at the left margin. Indent subsequent lines of the same entry one-half inch from the left margin.

Create the list of sources.
A **bibliography** is an alphabetical list of sources referenced in a paper. Whereas the text of the research paper contains brief references to the source (the citations), the bibliography lists all publication information about the source. Documentation styles differ significantly in their guidelines for preparing a bibliography. Each style identifies formats for various sources including books, magazines, pamphlets, newspapers, Web sites, television programs, paintings, maps, advertisements, letters, memos, and much more. You can find information about various styles and their guidelines in printed style guides and on the Web.

Plan Ahead

To Page Break Manually

The works cited are to be displayed on a separate numbered page. Thus, you must insert a manual page break following the body of the research paper so that the list of sources is displayed on a separate page. A **manual page break**, or **hard page break**, is one that you force into the document at a specific location.

Word never moves or adjusts manual page breaks; however, Word adjusts any automatic page breaks that follow a manual page break. Word inserts manual page breaks immediately above the location of the insertion point. The following step inserts a manual page break after the text of the research paper.

- With the insertion point at the end of the text of the research paper (Figure 2-49 on the previous page), press the ENTER key.

- Then, press CTRL+ENTER to insert a manual page break immediately above the insertion point and position the insertion point immediately below the manual page break (Figure 2–50).

- Scroll to position the top of the third page closer to the ruler.

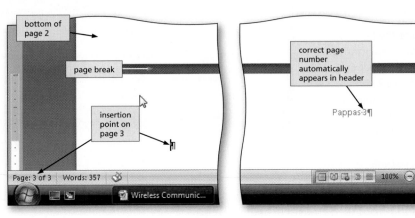

Figure 2–50

To Center the Title of the Works Cited Page

The works cited title is to be centered between the margins of the paper. If you simply issue the Center command, the title will not be centered properly. Instead, it will be one-half inch to the right of the center point because earlier you set first-line indent at one-half inch. Recall that Word is indenting the first line of every paragraph one-half inch.

To properly center the title of the works cited page, you must move the First Line Indent marker back to the left margin before centering the paragraph.

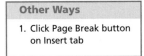

1 Drag the First Line Indent marker to the 0" mark on the ruler, which is at the left margin, to remove the first-line indent setting.

2 Press CTRL+E to center the paragraph mark.

3 Type Works Cited as the title.

4 Press the ENTER key.

5 Press CTRL+L to left-align the paragraph mark (Figure 2–51).

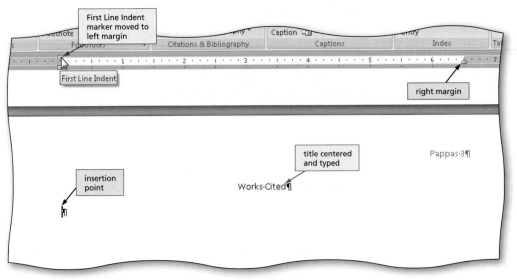

Figure 2–51

To Create the Bibliographical List

While typing the research paper, you created several citations and their sources. Word can format the list of sources and alphabetize them in a **bibliographical list**, saving you time looking up style guidelines. That is, Word will create a bibliographical list with each element of the source placed in its correct position with proper formatting and punctuation, according to the specified style. For example, in this research paper, the book source will list, in this order, the author name(s), book title, publisher city, publishing company name, and publication year with the book title underlined and the correct punctuation between each element according to the MLA style. The following steps create a MLA formatted bibliographical list from the sources previously entered.

1
- With the insertion point positioned as shown in Figure 2–52, click the Bibliography button on the References tab to display the Bibliography gallery (Figure 2–52).

Q&A

Will I select Works Cited from the Bibliography gallery?

No. The title it inserts is not formatted according to the MLA style. Thus, you will use the Insert Bibliography command instead.

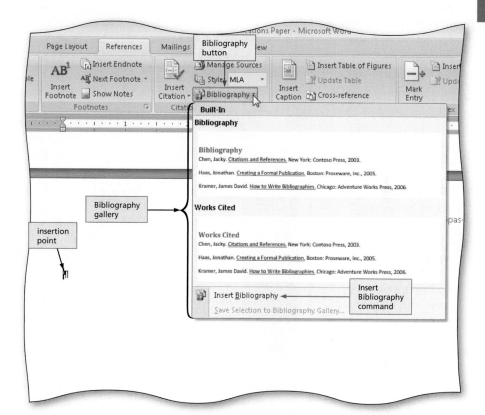

Figure 2–52

2
- Click Insert Bibliography in the Bibliography gallery to insert a list of sources at the location of the insertion point.

- If necessary, scroll to display the entire list of sources in the document window (Figure 2–53).

Figure 2–53

To Modify a Style Using the Styles Task Pane

Although the format within each entry in the bibliographical list meets the MLA style, the paragraph formatting does not. Currently, entries are based on the Normal style, which does not have the correct line or paragraph spacing. Thus, you will modify the style so that it is based on the No Spacing style (no blank space before or after a paragraph) and change its line spacing to double. The following steps modify the Bibliography style.

- Click somewhere in the list of sources to position the insertion point in a paragraph formatted with the Bibliography style.

Q&A

Why did the list of sources turn gray?

The entire list of sources is a field that Word automatically updates each time you make a change to one of the sources. Word, by default, shades fields gray on the screen to help you identify them. The gray shading, however, will not appear in the printed document.

- Click Home on the Ribbon to display the Home tab.

- Click the Styles Dialog Box Launcher to display the Styles task pane.

- If necessary, scroll to Bibliography in the Styles task pane. Click Bibliography to select it, if necessary, and then click its box arrow to display the Bibliography menu (Figure 2–54).

Figure 2–54

2

- Click Modify on the Bibliography menu to display the Modify Style dialog box.

- Click the 'Style based on' box arrow and then click No Spacing to base the Bibliography style on the No Spacing style.

- Click the 'Style for following paragraph' box arrow and then click No Spacing to base additional bibliographical paragraphs on the No Spacing style.

- Click the Double Space button to set the line spacing to double.

- Place a check mark in the Automatically update check box so that any future changes you make to the bibliographical paragraphs will update the Bibliography style automatically (Figure 2–55).

Figure 2–55

3

- Click the OK button in the Modify Style dialog box to close the dialog box and apply the style changes to the paragraphs in the document.

- Click the Close button on the Styles task pane title bar to close the task pane (Figure 2–56).

Figure 2–56

Other Ways

1. Click Styles Dialog Box Launcher, click Manage Styles button, scroll to style and then select it, click Modify button, change settings, click OK button in each dialog box

To Create a Hanging Indent

Currently, the first line of each source entry begins at the left margin. Subsequent lines in the same paragraph are to be indented one-half inch from the left margin. In essence, the first line hangs to the left of the rest of the paragraph; thus, this type of paragraph formatting is called a **hanging indent**.

One method of creating a hanging indent is to use the horizontal ruler. The **Hanging Indent marker** is the bottom triangle at the 0" mark on the ruler (Figure 2–57). The following steps create a hanging indent using the horizontal ruler.

- With the insertion point in the paragraph to format, point to the Hanging Indent marker on the ruler (Figure 2–57).

- Drag the Hanging Indent marker to the .5" mark on the ruler to set the hanging indent to one-half inch from the left margin (Figure 2–58).

Figure 2–57

 Q&A

Why were all three bibliographical paragraphs formatted with a hanging indent?

When you make a change to a paragraph based on the Bibliography style, the style is updated and all paragraphs based on that style also change because you selected the Automatically update check box in the Modify Style dialog box (shown in Figure 2–55 on the previous page).

Figure 2–58

Other Ways

1. Right-click paragraph, click Paragraph on shortcut menu, click Indents and Spacing tab, click Special box arrow, click Hanging, click OK button
2. Click Paragraph Dialog Box Launcher, click Indents and Spacing tab, click Special box arrow, click Hanging, click OK button
3. Press CTRL+T

To Modify a Source and Update the Bibliographical List

If you modify the contents of any source, the list of sources automatically updates because the list is a field. The following steps modify the title of the magazine article.

1
- Click References on the Ribbon to display the References tab.

- Click the Manage Sources button on the References tab to display the Source Manager dialog box.

- Click the source you wish to edit in the Current List.

- Click the Edit button to display the Edit Source dialog box.

- In the Title text box, add the word, Services, to the end of the title (Figure 2–59).

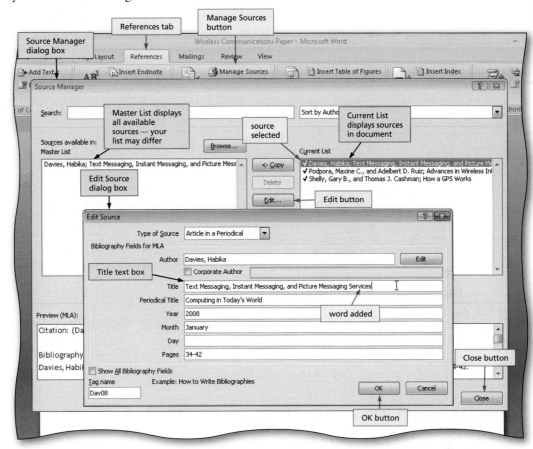

Figure 2–59

2
- Click the OK button to close the Edit Source dialog box.

- If a Microsoft Office Word dialog box appears, click its Yes button to update all occurrences of the source.

- Click the Close button in the Source Manager dialog box to update the list of sources in the document (Figure 2–60).

Q&A

What if the list of sources in the document does not update automatically?

Click in the list of sources and then press the F9 key, which is the shortcut key to update a field.

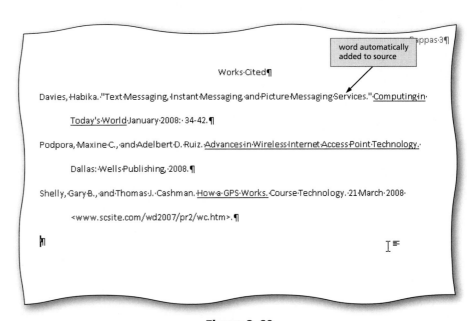

Figure 2–60

Proofing and Revising the Research Paper

As discussed in Chapter 1, once you complete a document, you might find it necessary to make changes to it. Before submitting a paper to be graded, you should proofread it. While **proofreading**, you look for grammatical errors and spelling errors. You want to be sure the transitions between sentences flow smoothly and the sentences themselves make sense.

<table>
<tr>
<td>Plan
Ahead</td>
<td>

Proofread and revise the paper.

As you proofread the paper, look for ways to improve it. Check all grammar, spelling, and punctuation. Be sure the text is logical and transitions are smooth. Where necessary, add text, delete text, reword text, and move text to different locations. Ask yourself these questions:

- Does the title suggest the topic?

- Is the thesis clear?

- Is the purpose of the paper clear?

- Does the paper have an introduction, body, and conclusion?

- Does each paragraph in the body relate to the thesis?

- Is the conclusion effective?

- Are all sources acknowledged?

</td>
</tr>
</table>

To assist you with the proofreading effort, Word provides several tools. You can go to a specific location in a document, move text, find and replace text, insert a synonym, check spelling and grammar, and look up information. The following pages discuss these tools.

To Use the Select Browse Object Menu

Often, you would like to bring a certain page, footnote, or other object into view in the document window. To accomplish this, you could scroll through the document to find a desired page, footnote, or item. Instead of scrolling through the document, however, you can use Word to go to a specific location via the Select Browse Object menu. The following steps display the footnote in the research paper using the Select Browse Object menu.

- Click the Select Browse Object button on the vertical scroll bar to display the Select Browse Object menu and then position the mouse pointer on the Browse by Footnote icon (Figure 2–61).

Figure 2–61

• Click the Browse by Footnote icon to set the browse object to footnotes.

• Position the mouse pointer on the Previous Footnote button on the vertical scroll bar (Figure 2–62).

Q&A

Did the function of the button change?

Yes. By default, it is the Previous Page button. Depending on the icon you click on the Select Browse Object menu, the function of the buttons above and below the Select Browse Object button on the vertical scroll bar changes.

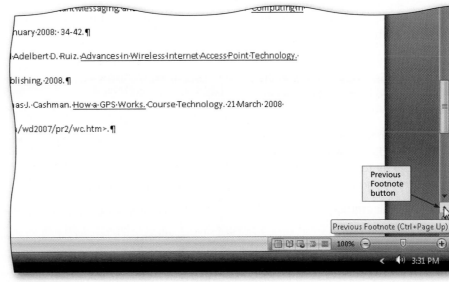

Figure 2–62

❸

• Click the Previous Footnote button to display the footnote reference mark in the document window (Figure 2–63).

Figure 2–63

Other Ways

1. Click Page Number indicator on status bar, click desired object in Go to what list, type desired object number in Enter object number text box, click Go To button
2. Press ALT+CTRL+HOME

Moving Text

While proofreading the research paper, you realize that text in the third paragraph would flow better if the third sentence were moved to the end of the paragraph.

To move text, such as words, characters, sentences, or paragraphs, you first select the text to be moved and then use drag-and-drop editing or the cut-and-paste technique to move the selected text. With **drag-and-drop editing**, you drag the selected item to the new location and then insert, or *drop*, it there. **Cutting** involves removing the selected item from the document and then placing it on the Clipboard. The **Clipboard** is a temporary Windows storage area. **Pasting** is the process of copying an item from the Clipboard into the document at the location of the insertion point.

When moving text a long distance or between application programs, use the Clipboard task pane to cut and paste. When moving text a short distance, the drag-and-drop technique is more efficient. Thus, the steps on the following pages demonstrate drag-and-drop editing.

To Select a Sentence

To drag-and-drop a sentence in the research paper, you first must select the sentence. The following step selects a sentence.

- Position the mouse pointer in the sentence to be moved (shown in Figure 2–64).

- Press and hold down the CTRL key. While holding down the CTRL key, click the sentence to select the entire sentence.

- Release the CTRL key.

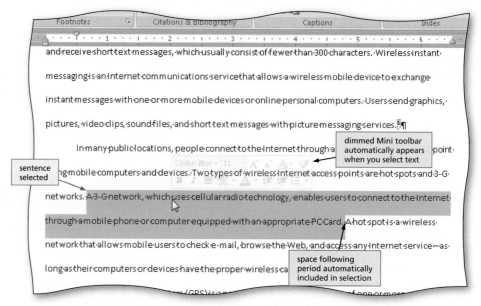

Figure 2–64

Other Ways

1. Drag through the sentence
2. With insertion point at beginning of sentence, press CTRL+SHIFT+RIGHT ARROW until sentence is selected

Selecting Text

In the previous steps and throughout Chapters 1 and 2, you have selected text. Table 2–3 summarizes the techniques used to select various items with the mouse.

Selecting Nonadjacent Items
In Word, you can select nonadjacent items, that is, items not next to each other. This is helpful when you are formatting multiple items the same way. To select nonadjacent items (text or graphics), do the following: select the first item, such as a word or paragraph, as usual. Press and hold down the CTRL key. While holding down the CTRL key, select any additional items.

Table 2–3 Techniques for Selecting Items with the Mouse	
Item To Select	**Mouse Action**
Block of text	Click at beginning of selection, scroll to end of selection, position mouse pointer at end of selection, hold down SHIFT key and then click; or drag through the text
Character(s)	Drag through character(s)
Document	Move mouse to left of text until mouse pointer changes to a right-pointing block arrow and then triple-click
Graphic	Click the graphic
Line	Move mouse to left of line until mouse pointer changes to a right-pointing block arrow and then click
Lines	Move mouse to left of first line until mouse pointer changes to a right-pointing block arrow and then drag up or down
Paragraph	Triple-click paragraph; or move mouse to left of paragraph until mouse pointer changes to a right-pointing block arrow and then double-click
Paragraphs	Move mouse to left of paragraph until mouse pointer changes to a right-pointing block arrow, double-click, and then drag up or down
Sentence	Press and hold down CTRL key and then click sentence
Word	Double-click the word
Words	Drag through words

To Move Selected Text

With the sentence to be moved selected, you can use drag-and-drop editing to move it. You should be sure that drag-and-drop editing is enabled by clicking the Word Options button on the Office Button menu, clicking Advanced in the left pane of the Word Options dialog box, verifying the 'Allow text to be dragged and dropped' check box is selected, and then clicking the OK button.

The following steps move the selected sentence so that it becomes the last sentence in the paragraph.

- With the mouse pointer in the selected text, press and hold down the mouse button (Figure 2–65).

Figure 2–65

- Drag the mouse pointer to the location where the selected text is to be moved, as shown in Figure 2–66.

- Release the mouse button to move the selected text to the location of the mouse pointer.

- Click outside the selected text to remove the selection (Figure 2–67).

Q&A What if I accidentally drag text to the wrong location?

Click the Undo button on the Quick Access Toolbar and try again.

Q&A Can I use drag-and-drop editing to move any selected item?

Yes, you can select words, sentences, phrases, and graphics and then use drag-and-drop editing to move them.

Figure 2–66

Figure 2–67

Other Ways
1. Click Cut button on Home tab, click where text is to be pasted, click Paste button on Home tab	2. Right-click selected text, click Cut on shortcut menu, right-click where text is to be pasted, click Paste on shortcut menu	3. Press CTRL+X, position insertion point where text is to be pasted, press CTRL+V

To Display the Paste Options Menu

When you drag-and-drop text, Word automatically displays a Paste Options button near the location of the drag-and-dropped text (Figure 2–67 on the previous page). If you click the **Paste Options button**, a menu appears that allows you to change the format of the item that was moved. The following steps display the Paste Options menu.

- Click the Paste Options button to display the Paste Options menu (Figure 2–68).

What is the purpose of the commands on the Paste Options menu?

In general, the first command indicates the pasted text should look the same as it did in its original location. The second command formats the pasted text to match the rest of the text where it was pasted. The third command removes all formatting from the pasted text. The last command displays the Word Options dialog box.

- Press the ESCAPE key to remove the Paste Options menu from the window.

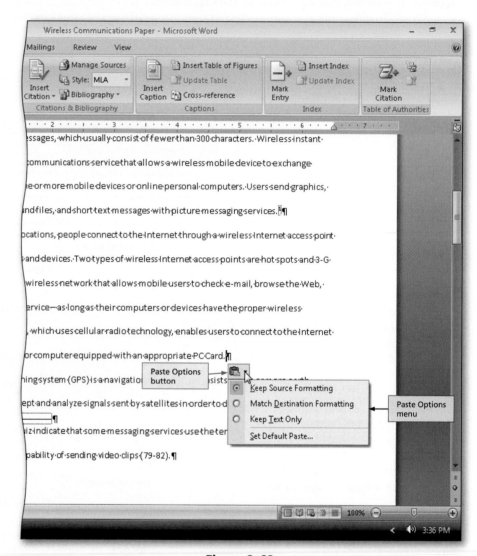

Figure 2–68

Dragging-and-Dropping
If you hold down the CTRL key while dragging a selected item, Word copies the item instead of moving it.

To Find and Replace Text

While proofreading the paper, you notice that you typed 3-G in the third paragraph (Figure 2–69). You prefer to use 3G, instead. Therefore, you need to change all occurrences of 3-G to 3G. To do this, you can use Word's find and replace feature, which automatically locates each occurrence of a word or phrase and then replaces it with specified text. The following steps use Find and Replace to replace all occurrences of 3-G with 3G.

1

- Click Home on the Ribbon to display the Home tab.

- Click the Replace button on the Home tab to display the Find and Replace dialog box.

- Type 3-G in the Find what text box.

- Press the TAB key. Type 3G in the Replace with text box (Figure 2–69).

Figure 2–69

2

- Click the Replace All button in the Find and Replace dialog box to instruct Word to replace all occurrences of the Find what text with the Replace with text (Figure 2–70).

3

- Click the OK button in the Microsoft Office Word dialog box.

- Click the Close button in the Find and Replace dialog box.

Other Ways

1. Click Select Browse Object button on vertical scroll bar, click Find icon, click Replace tab

2. Click Page Number indicator on status bar, click Replace tab in dialog box

3. Press CTRL+H

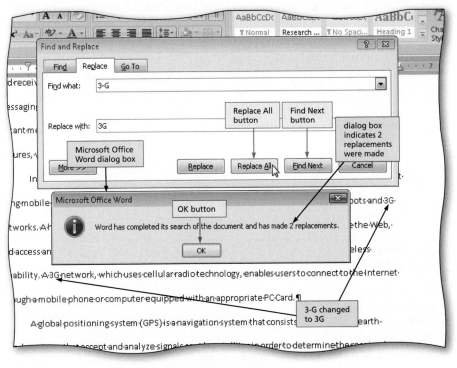

Figure 2–70

Find and Replace Dialog Box

The Replace All button in the Find and Replace dialog box replaces all occurrences of the Find what text with the Replace with text. In some cases, you may want to replace only certain occurrences of a word or phrase, not all of them. To instruct Word to confirm each change, click the Find Next button in the Find and Replace dialog box (Figure 2–70 on the previous page), instead of the Replace All button. When Word locates an occurrence of the text, it pauses and waits for you to click either the Replace button or the Find Next button. Clicking the Replace button changes the text; clicking the Find Next button instructs Word to disregard the replacement and look for the next occurrence of the Find what text.

If you accidentally replace the wrong text, you can undo a replacement by clicking the Undo button on the Standard toolbar. If you used the Replace All button, Word undoes all replacements. If you used the Replace button, Word undoes only the most recent replacement.

To Find Text

Sometimes, you may want only to find text, instead of finding and replacing text. To search for just a single occurrence of text, you would follow these steps.

1. Click the Find button on the Home tab; or click the Select Browse Object button on the vertical scroll bar and then click the Find icon on the Select Browse Object menu; or click the page indicator on the status bar and then click the Find tab; or press CTRL+F.

2. Type the text to locate in the Find what text box and then click the Find Next button. To edit the text, click the Cancel button in the Find and Replace dialog box; to find the next occurrence of the text, click the Find Next button.

To Find and Insert a Synonym

When writing, you may discover that you used the same word in multiple locations or that a word you used was not quite appropriate. In these instances, you will want to look up a **synonym**, or a word similar in meaning, to the duplicate or inappropriate word. A **thesaurus** is a book of synonyms. Word provides synonyms and a thesaurus for your convenience.

In this project, you would like a synonym for the word, proper, in the third paragraph of the research paper. The following steps show how to find a suitable synonym.

1

- Locate and then right-click the word for which you want to find a synonym (in this case, proper) to display a shortcut menu related to the word you right-clicked.

- Point to Synonyms on the shortcut menu to display a list of synonyms for the word you right-clicked (Figure 2–71).

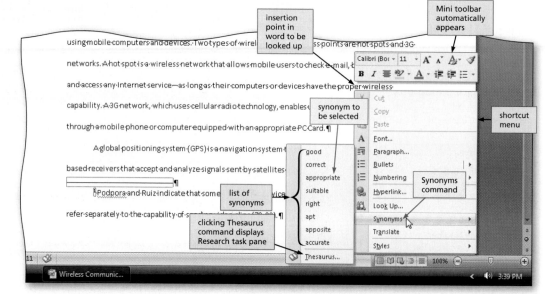

Figure 2–71

2
- Click the synonym you want (appropriate) on the Synonyms submenu to replace the word, proper, in the document with the word, appropriate (Figure 2–72).

Q&A

What if the synonyms list on the shortcut menu does not display a suitable word?

You can display the thesaurus in the Research task pane by clicking Thesaurus on the Synonyms submenu. The Research task pane displays a complete thesaurus, in which you can look up synonyms for various meanings of a word. You also can look up an **antonym**, or word with an opposite meaning. The Research task pane is discussed later in this chapter.

Figure 2–72

Other Ways	
1. Click Thesaurus on Review tab	2. Press SHIFT+F7

To Check Spelling and Grammar at Once

As discussed in Chapter 1, Word checks spelling and grammar as you type and places a wavy underline below possible spelling or grammar errors. Chapter 1 illustrated how to check these flagged words immediately. As an alternative, you can wait and check the entire document for spelling and grammar errors at once.

Note: In the following example the word, world, has been misspelled intentionally as wrld to illustrate the use of Word's check spelling and grammar at once feature. If you are completing this project on a personal computer, your research paper may contain different misspelled words, depending on the accuracy of your typing.

1
- Press CTRL+HOME because you want the spelling and grammar check to begin from the top of the document.

- Click Review on the Ribbon to display the Review tab.

- Click the Spelling & Grammar button on the Review tab to begin the spelling and grammar check at the location of the insertion point, which in this case, is at the beginning of the document (Figure 2–73).

Figure 2–73

• With the word, world, selected in the Suggestions list, click the Change button in the Spelling and Grammar dialog box to change the flagged word, wrld, to the selected suggestion, world, and then continue the spelling and grammar check until the next error is identified or the end of the document is reached (Figure 2–74).

• Click the Ignore All button in the Spelling and Grammar dialog box to ignore this and future occurrences of the flagged proper noun and then continue the spelling and grammar check until the next error is identified or the end of the document is reached.

4

• When Word flags the proper noun, Podpora, click the Ignore All button.

• When the spelling and grammar check is finished and Word displays a dialog box, click its OK button.

Q&A

Can I check spelling of just a section of a document?

Yes, select the text before starting the spelling and grammar check.

Figure 2–74

Other Ways

1. Click Spelling and Grammar Check icon on status bar, click Spelling on shortcut menu
2. Right-click flagged word, click Spelling on shortcut menu
3. Press F7

BTW

Contextual Spelling Errors

You can instruct Word to check for misuse of homophones and other types of contextual spelling errors. (Homophones are two or more words that are pronounced the same but that have different spellings or meanings, such as one and won.) With this feature, Word flags a contextual spelling error with a blue wavy underline. For example, Word would place a blue wavy underline below the words, one and knight, in this sentence: The team one the game last knight. (The correct sentence would be written as follows: The team won the game last night.) To view Word's suggested replacements for the flagged words, you could right-click each of the flagged words or start the spelling and grammar check by clicking the Spelling & Grammar button on the Review tab. On many installations of Word, the contextual spelling check is not activated by default. To activate it, click the Office Button, click Word Options on the Office Button menu, click Proofing in the left pane, place a check mark in the 'Use contextual spelling' check box, and then click the OK button.

The Main and Custom Dictionaries

As shown in the previous steps, Word may flag a proper noun as an error because the proper noun is not in its main dictionary. To prevent Word from flagging proper nouns as errors, you can add the proper nouns to the custom dictionary. To add a correctly spelled word to the custom dictionary, click the Add to Dictionary button in the Spelling and Grammar dialog box (Figure 2–74) or right-click the flagged word and then click Add to Dictionary on the shortcut menu. Once you have added a word to the custom dictionary, Word no longer will flag it as an error.

To View or Modify Entries in a Custom Dictionary

To view or modify the list of words in a custom dictionary, you would follow these steps.

1. Click the Office Button and then click the Word Options button.
2. Click Proofing in the left pane of the Word Options dialog box.
3. Click the Custom Dictionaries button.
4. When Word displays the Custom Dictionaries dialog box, place a check mark next to the dictionary name to view or modify. Click the Edit Word List button. (In this dialog box, you can add or delete entries to and from the selected custom dictionary.)
5. When finished viewing and/or modifying the list, click the OK button in the dialog box.
6. Click the OK button in the Custom Dictionaries dialog box.
7. If the 'Suggest from main dictionary only' check box is selected in the Word Options dialog box, remove the check mark. Click the OK button in the Word Options dialog box.

To Set the Default Custom Dictionary

If you have multiple custom dictionaries, you can specify which one Word should use when checking spelling. To set the default custom dictionary, you would follow these steps.

1. Click the Office Button and then click the Word Options button.
2. Click Proofing in the left pane of the Word Options dialog box.
3. Click the Custom Dictionaries button.
4. When the Custom Dictionaries dialog box is displayed, place a check mark next to the desired dictionary name. Click the Change Default button.
5. Click the OK button in the Custom Dictionaries dialog box.
6. If the 'Suggest from main dictionary only' check box is selected in the Word Options dialog box, remove the check mark. Click the OK button in the Word Options dialog box.

To Use the Research Task Pane to Look Up Information

From within Word, you can search through various forms of reference information. Earlier, this chapter discussed the Research task pane with respect to looking up a synonym in a thesaurus. Other services available in the Research task pane include a dictionary and if you are connected to the Web, an encyclopedia, a search engine, and other Web sites that provide information such as stock quotes, news articles, and company profiles.

Assume you want to know more about the acronym, PDA. The following steps use the Research task pane to look up information about a word.

- Locate the word you want to look up.

- While holding down the ALT key, click the word you want to look up (in this case, PDAs) to open the Research task pane and display a dictionary entry for the ALT+CLICKED word. Release the ALT key (Figure 2–75).

- If the Research task pane does not display a dictionary entry for the ALT+CLICKED word, click the Search for box arrow and then click All Reference Books.

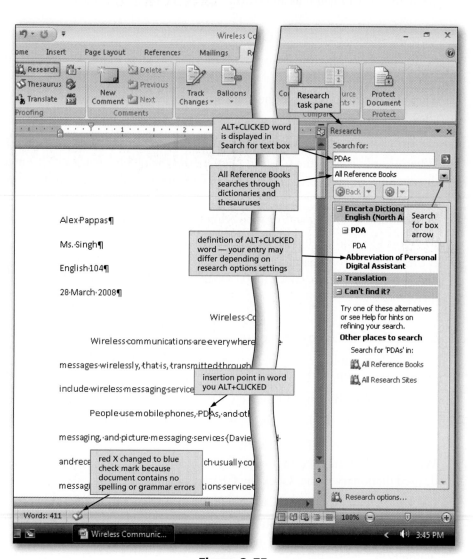

Figure 2–75

②

- Click the Search for box arrow and then click All Research Sites in the list to display Web sites with information about the ALT+CLICKED word (Figure 2–76).

Q&A

Can I copy information from the Research task pane into my document?

Yes, you can use the Copy and Paste commands. When using Word to insert material from the Research task pane or any other online reference, however, be very careful not to plagiarize.

③

- Click the Close button in the Research task pane.

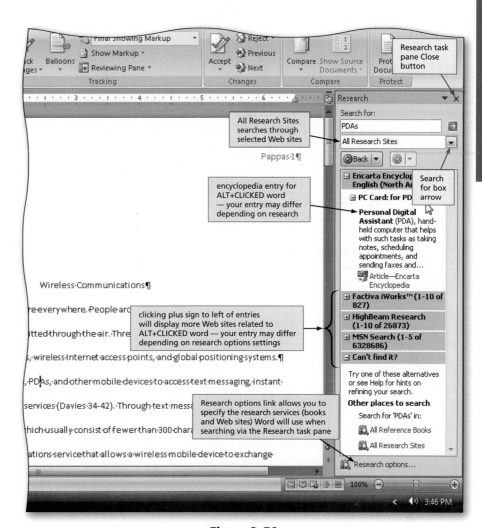

Figure 2–76

Other Ways

1. Click Research button on Review tab
2. Click Insert Citation button on References tab, click Search Libraries

Research Task Pane Options

When you install Word, it selects a series of services (reference books and Web sites) through which it searches when you use the Research task pane. You can view, modify, and update the list of services at any time.

Clicking the Research options link at the bottom of the Research task pane displays the Research Options dialog box, where you can view or modify the list of installed services. You can view information about any installed service by clicking the service in the list and then clicking the Properties button. To activate an installed service, click the check box to its left; likewise, to deactivate a service, remove the check mark. To add a particular Web site to the list, click the Add Services button, enter the Web address in the Address text box, and then click the Add button in the Add Services dialog box. To update or remove services, click the Update/Remove button, select the service in the list, click the Update (or Remove) button in the Update or Remove Services dialog box, and then click the Close button. You also can install parental controls through the Parental Control button in the Research Options dialog box, for example, if you want to restrict Web access from minor children who use Word.

To Change Document Properties

Before saving the research paper again, you want to add your name, course information, and some keywords as document properties. The following steps use the Document Information Panel to change document properties.

1 Click the Office Button to display the Office Button menu, point to Prepare on the Office Button menu, and then click Properties on the Prepare submenu to display the Document Information Panel.

2 Click the Author text box, if necessary, and then type your name as the Author property. If a name already is displayed in the Author text box, delete it before typing your name.

3 Click the Subject text box, if necessary delete any existing text, and then type your course and section as the Subject property.

4 Click the Keywords text box, if necessary delete any existing text, and then type `instant messaging, Internet access points, global positioning systems` as the Keywords property.

5 Click the Close the Document Information Panel button so that the Document Information Panel no longer is displayed.

To Save an Existing Document with the Same File Name

The document now is complete. You should save the research paper again. The following step saves the document again.

1 Click the Save button on the Quick Access Toolbar to overwrite the previous Wireless Communications Paper file on the USB flash drive.

To Print Document Properties and then the Document

With the document properties entered and the completed document saved, you may want to print the document properties along with the document. The following steps print the document properties, followed by the contents of the saved Wireless Communications Paper project.

1
• Click the Office Button to display the Office Button menu and then point to Print on the Office Button menu to display the Print submenu (Figure 2–77).

Figure 2–77

2

- Click Print on the Print submenu to display the Print dialog box.

- Click the Print what box arrow and then click Document properties to instruct Word to print the document properties instead of the document (Figure 2–78).

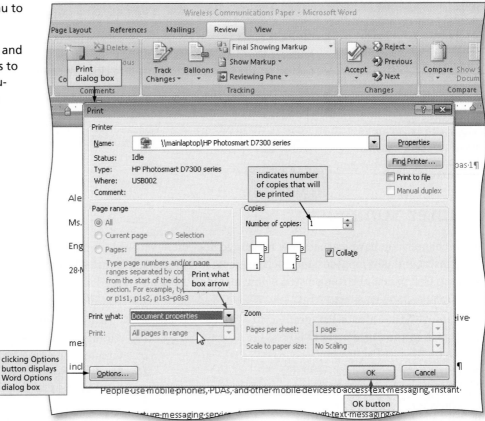

Figure 2–78

3

- Click the OK button to print the document properties (Figure 2–79).

4

- Click the Office Button again to display the Office Button menu, point to Print on the Office Button menu, and then click Quick Print on the Print submenu to print the research paper (shown in Figure 2–1 on page WD 75).

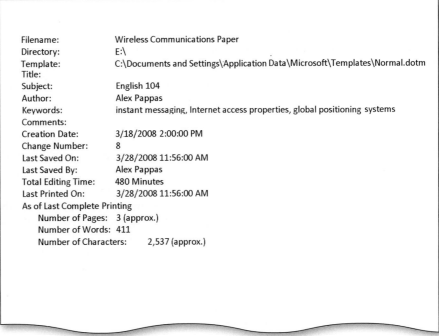

Filename:	Wireless Communications Paper
Directory:	E:\
Template:	C:\Documents and Settings\Application Data\Microsoft\Templates\Normal.dotm
Title:	
Subject:	English 104
Author:	Alex Pappas
Keywords:	instant messaging, Internet access properties, global positioning systems
Comments:	
Creation Date:	3/18/2008 2:00:00 PM
Change Number:	8
Last Saved On:	3/28/2008 11:56:00 AM
Last Saved By:	Alex Pappas
Total Editing Time:	480 Minutes
Last Printed On:	3/28/2008 11:56:00 AM

As of Last Complete Printing

Number of Pages: 3 (approx.)
Number of Words: 411
Number of Characters: 2,537 (approx.)

printed document properties — your properties may differ, depending on settings

Figure 2–79

BTW

Certification
The Microsoft Certified Application Specialist (MCAS) program provides an opportunity for you to obtain a valuable industry credential — proof that you have the Word 2007 skills required by employers. For more information, see Appendix G or visit the Word 2007 Certification Web page (scsite.com/wd2007/cert).

To Quit Word

This project is complete. The following steps quit Word.

1 Click the Close button on the right side of the title bar to quit Word; or if you have multiple Word documents open, click the Office Button and then click the Exit Word button on the Office Button menu to close all open documents and quit Word.

2 If necessary, click the Yes button in the Microsoft Office Word dialog box so that any changes you have made are saved.

Chapter Summary

In this chapter you have learned how to change document settings, use headers to number pages, create and modify styles, insert and edit citations and their sources, add footnotes, create a bibliographical list of sources, and use the Research task pane. The items listed below include all the new Word skills you have learned in this chapter.

1. Double-Space Text (WD 78)
2. Remove Space after a Paragraph (WD 79)
3. Switch to the Header (WD 80)
4. Right-Align a Paragraph (WD 81)
5. Insert a Page Number (WD 82)
6. Close the Header (WD 83)
7. Click and Type (WD 85)
8. Display the Rulers (WD 87)
9. First-Line Indent Paragraphs (WD 88)
10. Create a Quick Style (WD 90)
11. AutoCorrect as You Type (WD 91)
12. Use the AutoCorrect Options Button (WD 92)
13. Create an AutoCorrect Entry (WD 93)
14. Change the Bibliography Style (WD 95)
15. Insert a Citation and Create Its Source (WD 96)
16. Edit a Citation (WD 98)
17. Insert a Footnote Reference Mark (WD 100)
18. Insert a Citation Placeholder (WD 101)
19. Modify a Style Using a Shortcut Menu (WD 102)
20. Edit a Source (WD 104)
21. Count Words (WD 107)
22. Page Break Manually (WD 112)
23. Create the Bibliographical List (WD 113)
24. Modify a Style Using the Styles Task Pane (WD 114)
25. Create a Hanging Indent (WD 116)
26. Modify a Source and Update the Bibliographical List (WD 117)
27. Use the Select Browse Object Menu (WD 118)
28. Select a Sentence (WD 120)
29. Move Selected Text (WD 121)
30. Display the Paste Options Menu (WD 122)
31. Find and Replace Text (WD 123)
32. Find Text (WD 124)
33. Find and Insert a Synonym (WD 124)
34. Check Spelling and Grammar at Once (WD 125)
35. View or Modify Entries in a Custom Dictionary (WD 127)
36. Set the Default Custom Dictionary (WD 127)
37. Use the Research Task Pane to Look Up Information (WD 128)
38. Print Document Properties and then the Document (WD 130)

 If you have a SAM user profile, you may have access to hands-on instruction, practice, and assessment. Log in to your SAM account (http://sam2007.course.com) to launch any assigned training activities or exams that relate to the skills covered in this chapter.

BTW

Quick Reference
For a table that lists how to complete the tasks covered in this book using the mouse, Ribbon, shortcut menu, and keyboard, see the Quick Reference Summary at the back of this book, or visit the Word 2007 Quick Reference Web page (scsite.com/wd2007/qr).

Learn It Online

Test your knowledge of chapter content and key terms.

Instructions: To complete the Learn It Online exercises, start your browser, click the Address bar, and then enter the Web address `scsite.com/wd2007/learn`. When the Word 2007 Learn It Online page is displayed, click the link for the exercise you want to complete and then read the instructions.

Chapter Reinforcement TF, MC, and SA
A series of true/false, multiple choice, and short answer questions that test your knowledge of the chapter content.

Flash Cards
An interactive learning environment where you identify chapter key terms associated with displayed definitions.

Practice Test
A series of multiple choice questions that test your knowledge of chapter content and key terms.

Who Wants To Be a Computer Genius?
An interactive game that challenges your knowledge of chapter content in the style of a television quiz show.

Wheel of Terms
An interactive game that challenges your knowledge of chapter key terms in the style of the television show *Wheel of Fortune*.

Crossword Puzzle Challenge
A crossword puzzle that challenges your knowledge of key terms presented in the chapter.

Apply Your Knowledge

Reinforce the skills and apply the concepts you learned in this chapter.

Revising Text and Paragraphs in a Document
Instructions: Start Word. Open the document, Apply 2-1 Software Paragraphs Draft, from the Data Files for Students. See the inside back cover of this book for instructions on downloading the Data Files for Students, or contact your instructor for information about accessing the required files.

The document you open has a header and three paragraphs of text. You are to revise the document as follows: move a paragraph, move a word and change the format of the moved word, change paragraph indentation, change line spacing and paragraph spacing, replace all occurrences of a word with another word, and edit the header.

Perform the following tasks:
1. Select the last (third) paragraph. Use drag-and-drop editing to move this paragraph, so that it is the second paragraph in the document.
2. Select the underlined word, effectively, in the second sentence of the first paragraph. Use drag-and-drop editing to move the selected word, effectively, so that it follows the word, software, in the same sentence. Click the Paste Options button that displays to the right of the moved word, effectively. Remove the underline format from the moved sentence by clicking Keep Text Only on the shortcut menu.
3. Select the three paragraphs of text in the document.
4. Display the ruler, if necessary. With the paragraphs selected, use the ruler to indent the first line of the selected paragraphs one-half inch.
5. With the paragraphs still selected, change the line spacing of the selected paragraphs from single to double.

Continued >

Apply Your Knowledge *continued*

Figure 2–80

6. With the paragraphs still selected, use Line spacing box arrow to remove extra space below (after) the paragraphs. Click anywhere to remove the selection.

7. Use the Find and Replace dialog box to replace all occurrences of the word, Internet, with the word, Web. How many replacements were made?

8. Use the Find dialog box to locate the word, incorporated. Use Word's thesaurus to change the word, incorporated, to the word, integrated, in the first sentence of the second paragraph.

9. Switch to the header so that you can edit it. In the first line of the header, change the word, Draft, to the word, Modified, so that it reads: Software Paragraphs Modified. Change the first line of the header from the Normal style to the No Spacing style.

10. In the second line of the header, insert the page number (with no formatting) one space after the word, Page.

11. Change the alignment of both lines of text in the header from left-aligned to right-aligned. Switch back to the document text.

12. Change the document properties, as specified by your instructor.

13. Click the Office Button and then click Save As. Save the document using the file name, Apply 2-1 Software Paragraphs Modified.

14. Print the document properties and then print the revised document, shown in Figure 2–80.

15. Use the Research task pane to look up the definition of the word, online, in the first sentence of the second paragraph. Handwrite the COMPUTING definition of the word, online, on your printout.

16. Display the Research Options dialog box and on your printout, handwrite the currently active Reference Books, Research Sites, and Business and Financial Sites. If your instructor approves, activate one of the services.

Extend Your Knowledge

Extend the skills you learned in this chapter and experiment with new skills. You may need to use Help to complete the assignment.

Working with References and Proofing Tools

Instructions: Start Word. Open the document, Extend 2-1 Computing Options Paper Draft, from the Data Files for Students. See the inside back cover of this book for instructions on downloading the Data Files for Students, or contact your instructor for information on accessing the required files.

You will add another footnote to the paper, use the thesaurus, convert the document from MLA to APA style, convert the footnotes to endnotes, modify the Endnote Text style, change the format of the note reference marks, and translate the document to another language.

Perform the following tasks:

1. Insert a second footnote at an appropriate place in the research paper. Use the following footnote text: The Americans with Disabilities Act (ADA) requires any company with 15 or more employees to make reasonable attempts to accommodate the needs of physically challenged workers.

2. Use the Replace dialog box to find the word, imagine, in the document and then replace it with a word of your choice.

3. Save the document with a new file name and then print it. Select the entire document and then change the style of the citations and bibliography from MLA to APA. Save the APA version of the document with a new file name and then print it. Compare the two versions. Circle the differences between the two documents.

4. Convert the footnotes to endnotes.

5. Modify the Endnote Text style to 11-point Calibri font, double-spaced text with a first-line indent.

6. Change the format of the note reference marks to capital letters (A, B, etc.).

7. Save the revised document with endnotes with a new file name and then print it. On the printout with the endnotes, write the number of words, characters without spaces, characters with spaces, paragraphs, and lines in the document. Be sure to include endnote text in the statistics.

8. Translate the research paper into a language of your choice (Figure 2–81 on the next page) using the Translate button on the Review tab. Print the translated document.

Continued >

Extend Your Knowledge *continued*

Figure 2–81

Make It Right

Analyze a document and correct all errors and/or improve the design.

Inserting Missing Elements in an MLA Style Research Paper

Instructions: Start Word. Open the document, Make It Right 2-1 Certification Paper Draft, from the Data Files for Students. See the inside back cover of this book for instructions on downloading the Data Files for Students, or contact your instructor for information on accessing the required files.

The document is a research paper that is missing several elements. You are to insert these missing elements, all formatted according to the MLA documentation style: header with a page number, heading (name, course, and date information), paper title, footnote, and source information for the first citation and the citation in the footnote.

Perform the following tasks:

1. Insert a header with a page number, heading (use your own information: name, course information, and date), and an appropriate paper title, all formatted according to the MLA style.

2. Use the Select Browse Object button to go to page 2. How many bibliographical entries currently are on the Works Cited page? You will create additional source entries in Steps 3 and 4.

3. The Otoole placeholder (tag name) is missing its source information (Figure 2–82). Use the following source information to edit the source: magazine article titled "Career Builders and Boosts," written by Sarah W. O'Toole, magazine name is *IT World and Certifications*, publication date is March 2008, article is on pages 88-93. Edit the citation so that it displays the author name and the page numbers.

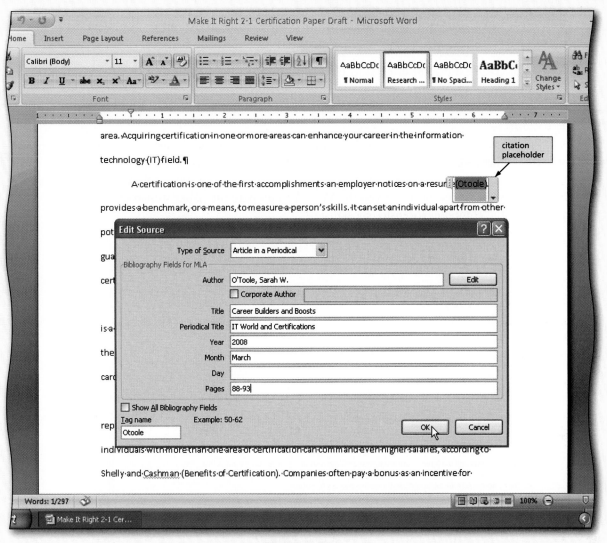

Figure 2–82

4. Insert the following footnote with the note reference at an appropriate place in the paper, formatted according to the MLA style: Debbins points out that, as an additional bonus, some certification training can be used for college credit. The citation for this footnote should be at the end of the footnote. The source information is as follows: book named *Preparing for the Future: IT Strategies*, authored by Floyd I. Debbins, published in 2008 at IT World Press in Chicago, pages 99-104. Edit the citation so that it displays only page numbers.

5. Use the Select Browse Object button to go to page 3. Be sure the bibliographical list on the Works Cited page contains all three entries. If necessary, use the F9 key to update the bibliographical list. Format the bibliographical paragraphs with a one-half inch hanging indent.

6. Modify the source of the book authored by Floyd I. Debbins, so that the publisher city is Boston instead of Chicago.

7. Use the Select Browse Object button to go to the footnote. Be sure the footnote is formatted properly.

8. Change the document properties, as specified by your instructor. Save the revised document with a new file name and then submit it in the format specified by your instructor.

In the Lab

Design and/or create a document using the guidelines, concepts, and skills presented in this chapter. Labs are listed in order of increasing difficulty.

Lab 1: Preparing a Short Research Paper

Problem: You are a college student currently enrolled in an introductory business class. Your assignment is to prepare a short research paper (300-350 words) about a computer-related job. The requirements are that the paper be presented according to the MLA documentation style and have three references. One of the three references must be from the Web. You prepare the paper shown in Figure 2–83, which discusses the computer forensics specialist.

Hankins 1

Mary Hankins

Mr. Habib

Business 102

14 March 2008

Computer Forensics Specialist

Computer forensics, also called digital forensics, network forensics, or cyberforensics, is a rapidly growing field that involves gathering and analyzing evidence from computers and networks. Because computers and the Internet are the fastest growing technology used for criminal activity, the need for computer forensics specialists will increase in years to come.

A computer forensics specialist examines computer media, programs, data, and log files on computers, servers, and networks. According to Shelly and Cashman (Computer Careers), many areas employ computer forensics specialists, including law enforcement, criminal prosecutors, military intelligence, insurance agencies, and information security departments in the private sector. A computer forensics specialist must have knowledge of the law, technical experience with many types of hardware and software products, superior communication skills, a willingness to learn and update skills, and a knack for problem solving.

When a problem occurs, it is the responsibility of the computer forensics specialist to carefully take several steps to identify and retrieve possible evidence that may exist on a suspect's computer. These steps include protecting the suspect's computer, discovering all files, recovering deleted files, revealing hidden files, accessing protected or encrypted files, analyzing all the data, and providing expert consultation and/or testimony as required (Reinman 52-58).

A computer forensics specialist must have knowledge of all aspects of the computer, from the operating system to computer architecture and hardware design. In the past, many computer forensics specialists were self-taught computer users. Today, extensive training, usually from several different

(a)

Figure 2–83

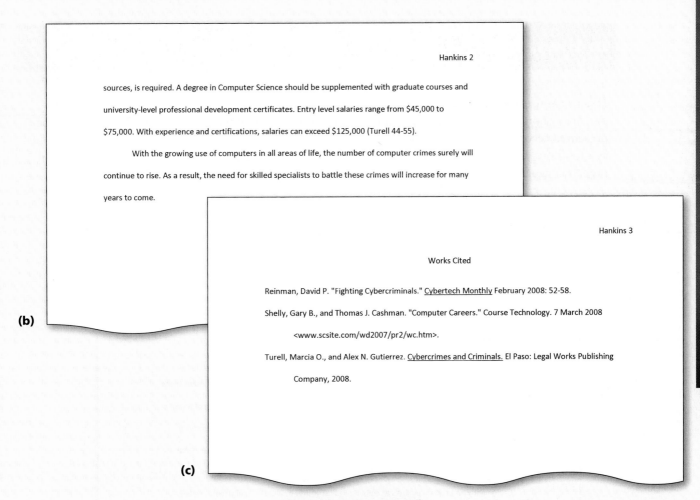

(b)

(c)

Figure 2–83 (continued)

Instructions: Perform the following tasks:

1. If necessary, display formatting marks on the screen.

2. Adjust line spacing to double.

3. Remove space below (after) paragraphs.

4. Create a header to number pages.

5. Type the name and course information at the left margin. Center and type the title.

6. Set first-line indent for paragraphs in the body of the research paper.

7. Create a Quick Style for the research paper paragraphs.

8. Type the research paper as shown in Figures 2–83a and 2–83b. Change the bibliography style to MLA. As you insert citations, enter their source information (shown in Figure 2–83c). Edit the citations so that they display according to Figures 2–83a and 2–83b.

9. At the end of the research paper text, press the ENTER key and then insert a manual page break so that the Works Cited page begins on a new page. Enter and format the works cited title (Figure 2–83c). Use Word to insert the bibliographical list (bibliography). Format the paragraphs in the list with a hanging indent.

10. Check the spelling and grammar of the paper at once.

11. Save the document on a USB flash drive using Lab 2-1 Computer Forensics Paper as the file name.

12. Print the research paper. Handwrite the number of words, paragraphs, and characters in the research paper above the title of your printed research paper.

In the Lab

Lab 2: Preparing a Research Report with a Footnote

Problem: You are a college student enrolled in an introductory English class. Your assignment is to prepare a short research paper in any area of interest to you. The requirements are that the paper be presented according to the MLA documentation style, contain at least one explanatory note positioned as a footnote, and have three references. One of the three references must be from the Internet. You prepare a paper about antivirus programs (Figure 2–84).

Yadav 1

Pahdi Yadav

Professor Milton

English 101

5 May 2008

Antivirus Programs

Today, people rely on computers to create, store, and manage critical information, many times via a home computer network. Information transmitted over networks has a higher degree of security risk than information kept in a user's home or company premises. Thus, it is crucial that they take measures to protect their computers and data from loss, damage, and misuse resulting from computer security risks. Antivirus programs are an effective way to protect a computer against viruses.

An antivirus program protects a computer against viruses by identifying and removing any computer viruses found in memory, on storage media, or on incoming files.[1] When you purchase a new computer, it often includes antivirus software. Antivirus programs work by scanning for programs that attempt to modify the boot program, the operating system, and other programs that normally are read from but not modified. In addition, many antivirus programs automatically scan files downloaded from the Web, e-mail attachments, opened files, and all types of removable media inserted in the computer (Karanos 201-205).

One technique that antivirus programs use to identify a virus is to look for virus signatures, or virus definitions, which are known specific patterns of virus code. According to Shelly and Cashman (Antivirus Programs), many vendors of antivirus programs allow registered users to update virus signature files automatically from the Web at no cost for a specified time. Updating the antivirus

---

[1] Bulowski points out that most antivirus programs also protect against worms and Trojan horses (55-61).

(a)

Figure 2–84

program's signature files regularly is important, because it will download any new virus definitions that

have been added since the last update.

Methods that guarantee a computer or network is safe from computer viruses simply do not

exist. Installing, updating, and using an antivirus program, though, is an effective technique to safeguard

your computer from loss.

(b)

Figure 2–84 (continued)

Instructions: Perform the following tasks:

1. Adjust line spacing to double and remove space below (after) paragraphs. Create a header to number pages. Type the name and course information at the left margin. Center and type the title. Set first-line indent for paragraphs in the body of the research paper. Create a Quick Style for the research paper paragraphs.

2. Type the research paper as shown in Figures 2–84a and 2–84b. Add the footnote as shown in Figure 2–84a. Change the Footnote Text style to the format specified in the MLA style. Change the bibliography style to MLA. As you insert citations, use the following source information:

   a. Type of Source: Periodical
      Author: Bulowski, Dana
      Title: Protection and Precaution: Keeping Your Computer Healthy
      Periodical Title: Computing Today
      Year: 2008
      Month: February
      Pages 55-61
   b. Type of Source: Book
      Author: Karanos, Hector
      Title: Internet Security
      Year: 2008
      City: Indianapolis
      Publisher: Citywide Cyber Press
   c. Type of Source: Web site
      Author: Shelly, Gary B., and Thomas J. Cashman
      Name of Web page: Antivirus Programs
      Production Company: Course Technology
      Year Accessed: 2008
      Month Accessed: February
      Day Accessed: 7
      URL: www.scsite.com/wd2007/pr2/wc.htm

3. At the end of the research paper text, press the ENTER key once and insert a manual page break so that the Works Cited page begins on a new page. Enter and format the works cited title. Use Word to insert the bibliographical list. Format the paragraphs in the list with a hanging indent.

4. Check the spelling and grammar of the paper.

5. Save the document on a USB flash drive using Lab 2-2 Antivirus Programs Paper as the file name.

6. Print the research paper. Handwrite the number of words, including the footnotes, in the research paper above the title of your printed research paper.

In the Lab

Lab 3: Composing a Research Paper from Notes

Problem: You have drafted the notes shown in Figure 2–85. Your assignment is to prepare a short research paper from these notes.

Home networks:
- Home users connect multiple computers and devices together in a home network.
- Home networking saves money and provides conveniences.
- Approximately 39 million homes have more than one computer.
- Many vendors offer home networking packages that include all the necessary hardware and software to network a home using wired or wireless techniques.

Three types of wired home networks: Ethernet, powerline cable, and phoneline (source: "Wired vs. Wireless Networks," an article on pages 24-29 in March 2008 issue of Modern Networking by Mark A. Travis).
- Traditional Ethernet networks require that each computer have built-in network capabilities or contain a network card, which connects to a central network hub or similar device with a physical cable. This may involve running cable through walls, ceilings, and floors in the house.
- The hardware and software of an Ethernet network can be difficult to configure for the average home user (source: a book called <u>Home Networking</u> by Frank A. Deakins, published at Current Press in New York in 2008).
- A phoneline network is an easy-to-install and inexpensive network that uses existing telephone lines in the home.
- A home powerline cable network is a network that uses the same lines that bring electricity into the house. This network requires no additional wiring.

Two types of wireless home networks: HomeRF and Wi-Fi (source: a Web site titled "Wired and Wireless Networks" by Gary B. Shelly and Thomas J. Cashman of Course Technology, viewed on April 23, 2008. Web address is www.scsite.com/wd2007/pr2/wc.htm).
- Wireless networks have the disadvantage of interference, because walls, ceilings, and other electrical devices such as cordless telephones and microwave ovens can disrupt wireless communications.
- A HomeRF (radio frequency) network uses radio waves, instead of cables, to transmit data.
- A Wi-Fi network sends signals over a wider distance than the Home RF network, which can be up to 1,500 feet in some configurations.

Figure 2–85

Instructions: Perform the following tasks:

1. Review the notes in Figure 2–85 and then rearrange and reword them. Embellish the paper as you deem necessary. Present the paper according to the MLA documentation style. Create an AutoCorrect entry that automatically corrects the spelling of the misspelled word, wird, to the correct spelling, wired. Add a footnote that refers the reader to the Web for more information. Enter citations and their sources as shown. Create the works cited page (bibliography) from the listed sources.

2. Check the spelling and grammar of the paper. Save the document on a USB flash drive using Lab 2-3 Home Networks Paper as the file name.

3. Use the Research task pane to look up a definition of a word in the paper. Copy and insert the definition into the document as a footnote. Be sure to quote the definition and cite the source.

4. Print the research paper. Handwrite the number of words, including the footnotes, in the research paper above the title of the printed research paper.

Cases and Places

Apply your creative thinking and problem solving skills to design and implement a solution.

• EASIER   •• MORE DIFFICULT

• 1: Create a Research Paper about Word Using the MLA Documentation Style

Chapter 1 of this book discussed the components of the Word window (pages WD 6 through 11). Using the material presented on those pages, write a short research paper (350–400 words) that describes the purpose and functionality of one or more of these components: document window, Ribbon, Mini toolbar and shortcut menus, Quick Access Toolbar, and Office Button. Use your textbook and Word Help as sources. Include at least two citations and one explanatory note positioned as a footnote. Add an AutoCorrect entry to correct a word you commonly mistype. Use the concepts and techniques presented in this chapter to format the paper according to the MLA documentation style. Check spelling and grammar of the finished paper.

•• 2: Create the Research Paper Presented in this Chapter Using the APA Documentation Style

As discussed in this chapter, two popular documentation styles for research papers are the Modern Language Association of America (MLA) and American Psychological Association (APA) styles. In this chapter, you created a research paper that followed guidelines of the MLA documentation style. Using the school library, this textbook, other textbooks, the Internet, magazines, or other sources, research the guidelines of the APA documentation style. Then, prepare the Wireless Communications Paper from this chapter following the guidelines of the APA documentation style. Use Figure 2–1 on page WD 75 as a starting point for the text and source information. Check spelling and grammar of the finished paper.

•• 3: Create a Research Paper that Compares Documentation Styles

This chapter discussed the requirements of the MLA documentation style. The American Psychological Association (APA) and the Chicago Manual of Style (CMS) are two other documentation styles supported by Word. Using the school library, this textbook, other textbooks, the Internet, magazines, or other sources, research the guidelines of the APA and CMS documentation styles to learn more about the differences among the MLA, APA, and CMS documentation styles. Using what you learn, write a short research paper (450-500 words) that compares the requirements and formats of the three documentation styles. Include at least two references and one explanatory note positioned as a footnote. Use the documentation style specified by your instructor to format the paper. Check spelling and grammar of the finished paper.

•• 4: Create a Research Paper about the Month You Were Born

Make It Personal

Did you ever wonder what world events took place during the month you were born (besides your birth)? For example, what happened with respect to politics, world affairs, and the economy? What made headline news? Were there any scientific breakthroughs? What was on television and at the box office? Were any famous people born? Did anyone famous die? What songs topped the charts? What was happening in the world of sports? Research the newsworthy events that took place during the month and year you were born (i.e., July 1981) by looking through newspapers, magazines, searching the Web, and/or interviewing family and friends. Write a short research paper (450-500 words) that summarizes your findings. Include at least two references and one explanatory note. Use the documentation style specified by your instructor to format the paper. Check spelling and grammar of the finished paper.

Continued >

STUDENT ASSIGNMENTS

Cases and Places *continued*

•• 5: Create a Research Paper about Spring Break Vacation Destinations

Working Together

With spring break just two months away, you and your fellow classmates are thinking about various spring break vacation destinations. Many options are available. Should you vacation close to home or travel across the country? Stay at a hotel, rent a condominium, or camp outdoors? Travel by car, train, or airplane? Book through a travel agent or the Web? Each team member is to research the attractions, accommodations, required transportation, and total cost of one spring break destination by looking through newspapers, magazines, searching the Web, and/or visiting a travel agency. Each team member is to write a minimum of 200 words summarizing his or her findings. Each team member also is to write at least one explanatory note and supply his or her source information for the citation and bibliography. Then, the team should meet as a group to compose a research paper that includes all team members' write-ups. Start by copying and pasting the text into a single document and then write an introduction and conclusion as a group. Use the documentation style specified by your instructor to format the paper. Check spelling and grammar of the finished paper. Set the default dictionary. If Word flags any of your last names as an error, add the name(s) to the custom dictionary. Hand in printouts of each team member's original write-up, as well as the final research paper.

3 | Creating a Cover Letter and a Resume

Objectives

You will have mastered the material in this chapter when you can:

- Format characters and paragraphs
- Insert and format clip art
- Set and use tab stops
- Identify the components of a business letter
- Insert the current date
- Create and insert a building block
- Insert a Word table, enter data in the table, and format the table
- Use a template to create a document

- Fill in a document template
- Copy and paste using the Office Clipboard
- Indent paragraphs
- Insert a Quick Part
- Sort a list
- Use print preview to view and print a document
- Address and print an envelope

3 | Creating a Cover Letter and a Resume

Introduction

In a business environment, people use documents to communicate with others. Business documents can include letters, memos, newsletters, proposals, and resumes. An effective business document clearly and concisely conveys its message and has a professional, organized appearance.

Some people prefer to use their own creative skills to design and compose business documents. Using Word, for example, you can develop the content and decide on the location of each item in a document. On occasion, however, you may have difficulty composing a particular type of document. To assist with the task of creating certain types of documents, such as resumes and fax cover letters, Word provides templates. A **template** is similar to a form with prewritten text; that is, Word prepares the requested document with text and/or formatting common to all documents of this nature. After Word creates a document from a template, you fill in the blanks or replace prewritten words in the document.

Project — Cover Letter and Resume

At some time in your professional life, you will prepare a cover letter along with a resume to send to prospective employers. In addition to some personal information, a **resume** usually contains the applicant's educational background and job experience. Employers review many resumes for each vacant position. Thus, you should design your resume carefully so that it presents you as the best candidate for the job. You also should attach a personalized cover letter to each resume you send. A **cover letter** enables you to elaborate on positive points in your resume; it also provides you with an opportunity to show a potential employer your writing skills.

The project in this chapter follows generally accepted guidelines for writing letters and resumes and uses Word to create the cover letter shown in Figure 3–1 and the resume shown in Figure 3–2 on page WD 148. The personalized cover letter to the prospective employer (Juniper Culinary Academy) includes a custom-made letterhead, as well as all essential business letter components. The resume for Lana Halima Canaan, a recent graduate of the culinary arts program, uses a Word template to present relevant information to a potential employer.

Overview

As you read through this chapter, you will learn how to create the cover letter and resume shown in Figures 3–1 and 3–2 by performing these general tasks:

- Design and compose a letterhead.
- Compose a cover letter.
- Print the cover letter.
- Use a template to create a resume.
- Print the resume.
- Address and print an envelope.

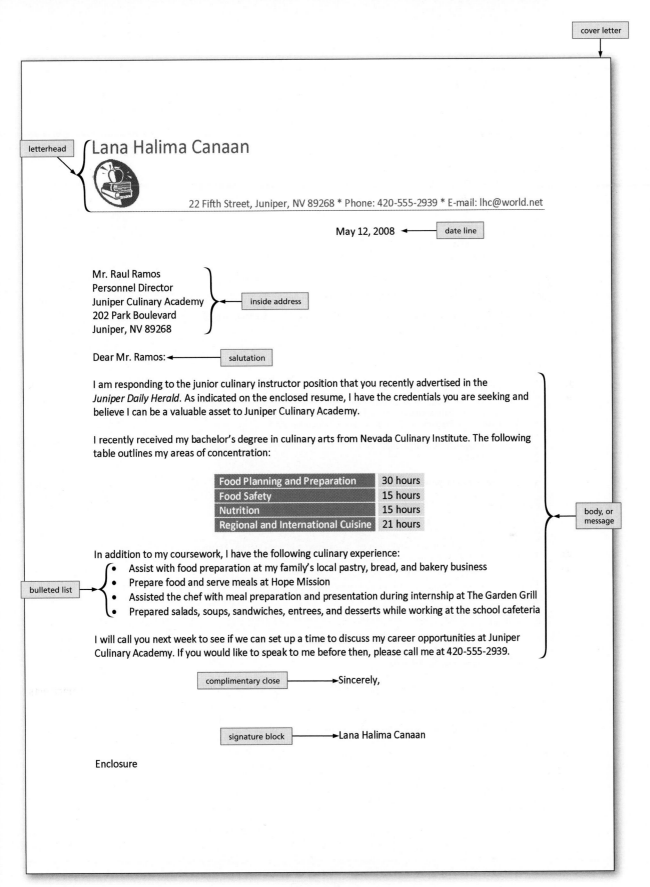

letterhead

Lana Halima Canaan

22 Fifth Street, Juniper, NV 89268 * Phone: 420-555-2939 * E-mail: lhc@world.net

May 12, 2008 ← date line

Mr. Raul Ramos
Personnel Director
Juniper Culinary Academy ← inside address
202 Park Boulevard
Juniper, NV 89268

Dear Mr. Ramos: ← salutation

I am responding to the junior culinary instructor position that you recently advertised in the *Juniper Daily Herald*. As indicated on the enclosed resume, I have the credentials you are seeking and believe I can be a valuable asset to Juniper Culinary Academy.

I recently received my bachelor's degree in culinary arts from Nevada Culinary Institute. The following table outlines my areas of concentration:

Food Planning and Preparation	30 hours
Food Safety	15 hours
Nutrition	15 hours
Regional and International Cuisine	21 hours

In addition to my coursework, I have the following culinary experience:

bulleted list

- Assist with food preparation at my family's local pastry, bread, and bakery business
- Prepare food and serve meals at Hope Mission
- Assisted the chef with meal preparation and presentation during internship at The Garden Grill
- Prepared salads, soups, sandwiches, entrees, and desserts while working at the school cafeteria

I will call you next week to see if we can set up a time to discuss my career opportunities at Juniper Culinary Academy. If you would like to speak to me before then, please call me at 420-555-2939.

complimentary close → Sincerely,

signature block → Lana Halima Canaan

Enclosure

body, or message

Figure 3–1

resume

▶Lana Halima Canaan

22 Fifth Street, Juniper, NV 89268
Phone: 420-555-2939
E-mail: lhc@world.net

Objectives

To obtain a full-time culinary instructor position with a culinary academy, school, or institute in the Juniper area.

Education

B.S. Culinary Arts (Nevada Culinary Institute, May 2008)

- Dean's List, six semesters
- Moeller Nutrition Award, January 2008
- Marge Rae Outstanding Student Scholarship, 2006 – 2008
- Baker Food Preparation Contest, 1st Place, November 2008
- Areas of concentration:
  Food Planning and Preparation
  Food Safety
  Nutrition
  Regional and International Cuisine

Experience

Chef Intern (September 2006 – May 2008)
 The Garden Grill (Juniper, NV)
 Assisted chef with meal selection, preparation, and presentation. Assumed chef responsibilities during last semester of school.

Assistant Cook (September 2004 – August 2006)
 Nevada Culinary Institute Cafeteria (Juniper, NV)
 Planned meals for staff and students. Prepared salads, soups, sandwiches, entrees, and desserts.

Skills

- Culinary Arts Association
- National Honor Society
- Nevada Restaurant Federation
- Nutrition Services of America
- Student Government Association, President

Community Service

Prepare food and serve meals at Hope Mission every week.

Figure 3–2

Plan
Ahead

General Project Guidelines

When creating a Word document, the actions you perform and decisions you make will affect the appearance and characteristics of the finished document. As you create a cover letter and resume, such as the project shown in Figure 3–1 on page WD 147 and Figure 3–2, you should follow these general guidelines:

1. **Design a creative letterhead.** Use text, graphics, formats, and colors that reflect your personality or employment goals. Include your name, postal mailing address, and telephone number. If you have an e-mail address and Web address, include those as well.

2. **Compose an effective cover letter.** A finished business letter (i.e., cover letter) should look like a symmetrically framed picture with evenly spaced margins, all balanced below an attractive letterhead. A well-written, properly formatted cover letter presents solid evidence of your writing skills and provides insight into your personality. The content of a letter should contain proper grammar, correct spelling, logically constructed sentences, flowing paragraphs, and sound ideas. Be sure to proofread it carefully.

3. **Craft a successful resume.** Your resume should present, at a minimum, your contact information, objective, educational background, and work experience to a potential employer. It should honestly present all your positive points. As with the cover letter, the resume should be error free. Ask someone else to proofread your resume and give you suggestions for improvements.

When necessary, more specific details concerning the above guidelines are presented at appropriate points in the chapter. The chapter also will identify the actions performed and decisions made regarding these guidelines during the creation of the cover letter shown in Figure 3–1 and the resume shown in Figure 3–2.

Creating a Letterhead

In many businesses, letterhead is preprinted on stationery that everyone in the company uses for correspondence. For personal letters, the cost of preprinted letterhead can be high. An alternative is to create your own letterhead and save it in a file. At a later time, when you want to create a letter using the letterhead, simply open the letterhead file and then save the file with a new name to preserve the original letterhead file. The letterhead in this project (Figure 3–1), follows this process; that is, you design and create a letterhead and then save it in a file.

Plan
Ahead

Design a creative letterhead.

A letterhead often is the first section a reader notices on a letter. Thus, it is important your letterhead appropriately reflect the essence of the individual or business (i.e., formal, youthful, technical, etc.). The letterhead should leave ample room for the contents of the letter. When designing a letterhead, consider its contents, placement, and appearance.

• **Contents of letterhead.** A letterhead should contain these elements:

• Complete legal name of the individual, group, or company

• Complete mailing address: street address including building, room, suite number, or post office box, along with city, state, and postal code

• Telephone number(s) and fax number, if one exists

Many letterheads also include a Web address, e-mail address, and a logo or other image. If you use an image, select one that expresses your personality or goals.

(continued)

Plan Ahead

(continued)

- **Placement of elements in the letterhead.** Some letterheads center their elements across the top of the page. Others align some or all of the elements with the left or right margins. Sometimes, the elements are split between the top and bottom of the page. For example, a name and logo may be at the top of the page with the address at the bottom of the page.

- **Appearance of letterhead elements.** Use fonts that are easy to read. Give your name impact by making its font size larger than the rest of the text in the letterhead. For additional emphasis, consider formatting the name in bold or italic. Choose colors that complement each other and convey your goals or personality.

  When finished designing the letterhead, determine if a divider line would help to visually separate the letterhead from the text of the letter.

The following pages start Word, enter and format the text and graphics in the letterhead, shown in Figure 3–1 on page WD 147, and then save the personal letterhead file.

To Start Word and Display Formatting Marks

Normal Style
If your screen settings differ from Figure 3–3, it is possible the default settings in your Normal style have been changed. Normal style settings are saved in the normal.dotm file. To restore the original Normal style settings, quit Word and use Windows Explorer to locate the normal.dotm file (be sure that hidden files and folders are displayed, and include system and hidden files in your search). Rename the normal.dotm file to oldnormal.dotm file. After renaming the normal.dotm file, it no longer will exist as normal.dotm. The next time you start Word, it will recreate a normal .dotm file using the original default settings.

If you are using a computer to step through the project in this chapter and you want your screens to match the figures in this book, you should change your computer's resolution to 1024×768. For information about how to change a computer's resolution, read Appendix D.

The following steps start Word and display formatting marks.

1 Start Word. If necessary, maximize the Word window.

2 If the Print Layout button is not selected, click it so that your screen layout matches Figure 3–3.

3 If your zoom level is not 100%, change it to 100%.

4 If the Show/Hide ¶ button on the Home tab is not selected already, click it to display formatting marks on the screen.

To Apply a Quick Style

When you press the ENTER key in the letterhead, you want the insertion point to advance to the next line, with no blank space between the lines. Recall that, by default, the Normal style in Word places 10 points of blank space after each paragraph and inserts a blank space equal to 1.15 lines between each line of text. The No Spacing style, however, does not put any extra blank space between lines when you press the ENTER key. The following step applies the No Spacing style to the current paragraph.

1 Click No Spacing in the Styles gallery to apply the No Spacing style to the current paragraph.

To Change Theme Colors

Recall that Word provides document themes that contain a variety of color schemes to assist you in selecting complementary colors in a document. In your own letterhead, you would select a color scheme that reflects your personality or goals. This letterhead uses the Urban color scheme. The following steps change theme colors.

1 Click the Change Styles button on the Home tab to display the Change Styles menu, and then point to Colors on the Change Styles menu to display the Colors gallery.

2 Click Urban in the Colors gallery to change the document theme colors to Urban.

To Type Text

To begin creating the personal letterhead file in this chapter, type your name in the document window. The following step types this first line of text in the document.

1 Type Lana Halima Canaan and then press the ENTER key.

Q&A Why not type the name in all capital letters?

Studies show that all capital letters can be more difficult to read.

Mini Toolbar

Recall from Chapter 1 that the Mini toolbar, which automatically appears based on certain tasks you perform, contains commands related to changing the appearance of text in a document. All commands on the Mini toolbar also exist on the Ribbon.

When the Mini toolbar appears, it initially is transparent. If you do not use the transparent Mini toolbar, it disappears from the screen. To use the Mini toolbar, move the mouse pointer into the toolbar, which causes the Mini toolbar to change from a transparent to a bright appearance. The following steps illustrate the use of the Mini toolbar.

To Use the Grow Font Button to Increase Font Size

You want the font size of the name to be larger than the rest of the text in the letterhead. In previous chapters, you used the Font Size box arrow on the Home tab to change the font size of text. Word also provides a Grow Font button, which increases the font size of selected text each time you click the button. The following steps use the Grow Font button on the Mini toolbar to increase the font size of the name.

1

- Move the mouse pointer to the left of the line to be selected (in this case, the line containing your name) until the mouse pointer changes to a right-pointing block arrow, and then click the mouse to select the line (Figure 3–3).

Figure 3–3

- Move the mouse pointer into the transparent Mini toolbar, so that it changes to a bright toolbar.

- Repeatedly click the Grow Font button on the Mini toolbar until the Font Size box displays 20, for 20 point (Figure 3–4).

Q&A

What if I click the Grow Font button too many times and make the font size too big?

Click the Shrink Font button until the desired font size is displayed.

Figure 3–4

 Experiment

- Repeatedly click the Grow Font and Shrink Font buttons on the Mini toolbar and watch the font size of the selected name change in the document window. When you have finished experimenting, set the font size to 20 point.

Other Ways
1. Click Grow Font button on Home tab
2. Press CTRL+>

To Color Text

The text in the letterhead is to be a shade of teal. The following steps change the color of the entered text.

1

- With the text still selected and the Mini toolbar still displaying, click the Font Color button arrow on the Mini toolbar to display the Font Color gallery (Figure 3–5).

Q&A

What if my Mini toolbar no longer is displayed?

Use the Font Color button arrow on the Home tab.

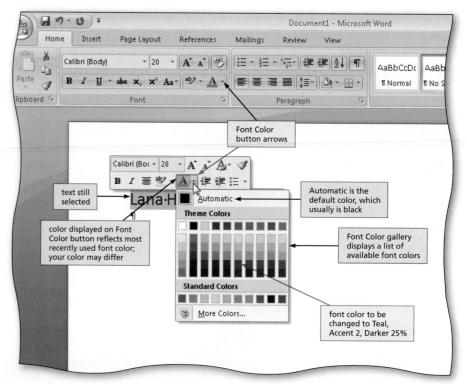

Figure 3–5

2

- Click Teal, Accent 2, Darker 25%, which is the sixth color in the fifth row in the Theme Colors area, to change the color of the selected text to a shade of teal.

- Click the paragraph mark below the name to deselect the text and position the insertion point on line 2 of the document (Figure 3–6).

Q&A How would I change the text color back to black?

If, for some reason, you wanted to change the text color back to black at this point, you would select the text, click the Font Color button arrow again, and then click Automatic in the Font Color gallery.

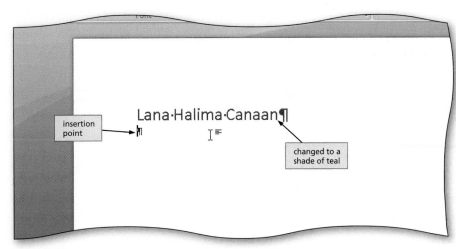

Figure 3–6

Other Ways		
1. Click the Font Color button arrow on Home tab, click desired color	2. Click Font Dialog Box Launcher, click Font tab, click Font color box arrow,	click desired color, click OK button

To Insert Clip Art

Files containing graphical images, or **graphics**, are available from a variety of sources. In Chapter 1, you inserted a digital picture taken with a digital camera in a document. In this project, you insert **clip art**, which is a predefined graphic. In the Microsoft Office programs, clip art is located in the **Clip Organizer**, which contains a collection of clip art, photographs, sounds, and videos.

The letterhead in this project contains clip art of an apple on a stack of books (Figure 3–1 on page WD 147), which represents Lana's desire to be an instructor. Thus, the next steps insert clip art on line 2 of the letterhead below the job seeker's name.

1

- With the insertion point on line 2 below the name, click Insert on the Ribbon to display the Insert tab.

- Click the Clip Art button on the Insert tab to display the Clip Art task pane.

Q&A What is a task pane?

A **task pane** is a separate window that enables you to carry out some Word tasks more efficiently.

- If the Search for text box displays text, drag through the text to select it.

- Type teacher in the Search for text box (Figure 3–7).

Figure 3–7

• Click the Go button to display a list of clips that match the description, teacher (Figure 3–8).

Why is my list of clips different from Figure 3–8?

If you are connected to the Internet, the Clip Art task pane displays clips from the Web as well as those installed on your hard disk.

Go button

list of clips that matches description

globe icon indicates clip art from the Web

Figure 3–8

3

• Click the clip art of the apple on the stack of books to insert it in the document at the location of the insertion point (Figure 3–9).

4

• Click the Close button on the Clip Art task pane title bar to close the task pane.

inserted clip art is selected automatically

Picture Tools tab automatically appears because a graphic is selected in the document window

Close button

clip art selected

box arrow is displayed when you click or point to clip art; clicking box arrow displays a menu

Figure 3–9

To Resize a Graphic Using the Size Dialog Box

In this project, the graphic is 35 percent of its original size. Instead of dragging the sizing handle to change the graphic's size, as you learned how to do in Chapter 1, you can use the Size dialog box to set exact size percentages. The following steps resize a graphic using the Size dialog box.

- With the graphic still selected, click the Size Dialog Box Launcher on the Format tab to display the Size dialog box (Figure 3–10).

Q&A

What if the Format tab is not the active tab on my Ribbon?

Double-click the graphic or click Format on the Ribbon to display the Format tab.

Figure 3–10

- In the Scale area, triple-click the Height text box to select it.

- Type 35 and then press the TAB key to display 35% in the Height and Width text boxes and resize the selected graphic to 35 percent of its original size (Figure 3–11).

Q&A

How do I know to use 35 percent for the resized graphic?

The larger graphic consumed too much room on the page. Try various percentages to determine the size that works best in the letterhead design.

❸

- Click the Close button in the Size dialog box to close the dialog box.

Figure 3–11

Other Ways
1. Right-click graphic, click Size on shortcut menu, click Size tab, enter Height and Width values, click Close button

To Recolor a Graphic

The clip art currently is bright red and black, which does not blend well with the current color scheme. In Word, you can change the color of a graphic. The following steps change the color of the graphic to a shade in the current color scheme.

1

- With the graphic still selected, click the Recolor button on the Format tab to display the Recolor gallery (Figure 3–12).

Figure 3–12

2

- Click Accent color 2 Light in the Recolor gallery (third color in Light Variations area) to change the color of the selected graphic in the document window (Figure 3–13).

Q&A

How would I change a graphic back to its original colors?

With the graphic selected, you would click the Reset Picture button on the Format tab or click No Recolor in the Recolor gallery.

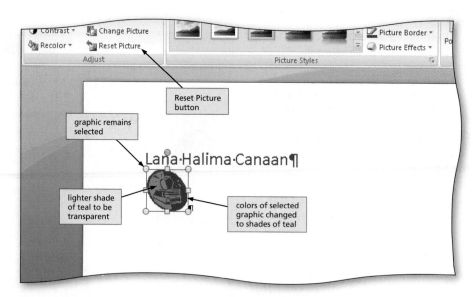

Figure 3–13

Other Ways

1. Right-click graphic, click Format Picture on shortcut menu, click Picture in left pane, click Recolor button, select color, click Close button

To Set a Transparent Color in a Graphic

Although the graphic now is the right color scheme, it is difficult to distinguish the objects in the graphic because they use shades of the same color. In Word, you can make one color in a graphic transparent, that is, remove the color. In this project, you make the lighter shades of teal in the graphic transparent, which results in a graphic that is teal and white — making the image easier to identify. The following steps set a transparent color in a graphic.

- With the graphic still selected, click the Recolor button on the Format tab to display the Recolor gallery (Figure 3–14).

Figure 3–14

- Click Set Transparent Color in the Recolor gallery to display a pen mouse pointer in the document window.

- Position the pen mouse pointer in the graphic where you want to make the color transparent (Figure 3–15).

Figure 3–15

3

- Click the location in the graphic where you want the color to be transparent (Figure 3–16).

- Press the END key to deselect the graphic and move the insertion point to the end of the line, which is between the graphic and the paragraph mark.

Figure 3–16

Using Tab Stops to Align Text

In the letterhead, the graphic of the apple and the stack of books is left-aligned. The address, phone, and e-mail information in the letterhead is to be positioned at the right margin on the same line. In Word, a paragraph cannot be both left-aligned and right-aligned. If you click the Align Text Right button on the Ribbon, for example, the graphic will be right-aligned. To place text at the right margin of a left-aligned paragraph, you set a tab stop at the right margin. A **tab stop** is a location on the horizontal ruler that tells Word where to position the insertion point when you press the TAB key on the keyboard.

Leader Characters
You also can use the Tabs dialog box to place leader characters in the empty space occupied by a tab character. Leader characters, such as a series of dots, often are used in a table of contents to precede page numbers.

To Display the Ruler

You want to see the location of tab stops on the horizontal ruler. The following step displays the ruler in the document window.

 If the rulers are not displayed already, click the View Ruler button on the vertical scroll bar.

To Set Custom Tab Stops Using the Tabs Dialog Box

Word, by default, places a tab stop at every .5" mark on the ruler (shown in Figure 3–17). These default tab stops are indicated at the bottom of the horizontal ruler by small vertical tick marks. You also can set your own custom tab stops.

The next step in creating the letterhead for this project is to set a custom tab stop at the right margin, that is, at the 6.5" mark on the ruler, because you want the address, phone, and e-mail information at the right margin. One method of setting custom tab stops is to click the ruler at the desired location of the tab stop. You cannot click, however, at the right margin location. Thus, the following steps use the Tabs dialog box to set a custom tab stop.

1

- With the insertion point positioned between the paragraph mark and the graphic, click the Paragraph Dialog Box Launcher to display the Paragraph dialog box (Figure 3–17).

Figure 3–17

2

- Click the Tabs button in the Paragraph dialog box to display the Tabs dialog box.

- Type 6.5 in the Tab stop position text box.

- Click Right in the Alignment area to specify alignment for text at the tab stop (Figure 3–18).

Figure 3–18

3

- Click the Set button in the Tabs dialog box to set a right-aligned custom tab stop.

- Click the OK button to place a right tab marker at the 6.5" mark on the ruler (Figure 3–19).

 What happened to all the default tab stops on the ruler?

When you set a custom tab stop, Word clears all default tab stops to the left of the newly set custom tab stop on the ruler.

Figure 3–19

Tab Stops

Tab settings are a paragraph format. Thus, each time you press the ENTER key, any custom tab stops are carried forward to the next paragraph.

To move the insertion point from one tab stop to another, press the TAB key on the keyboard. When you press the TAB key, a **tab character** formatting mark appears in the empty space between the tab stops.

When you set a custom tab stop, you specify how the text will align at a tab stop. The tab marker on the ruler reflects the alignment of the characters at the location of the tab stop. Table 3–1 shows types of tab stop alignments in Word and their corresponding tab markers. To change an existing tab stop's alignment, double-click the tab marker on the ruler to display the Tabs dialog box (or display the Tabs dialog box as described in the steps on the previous page), click the tab stop position you wish to change, click the new alignment, and then click the OK button. You can remove an existing tab stop by clicking the tab stop position in the Tabs dialog box and then clicking the Clear button in the dialog box. To remove all tab stops, click the Clear All button in the Tabs dialog box.

Table 3–1 Types of Tab Stop Alignments			
Tab Stop	**Tab Marker**	**Result of Pressing TAB Key**	**Example**
Left Tab	∟	Left-aligns text at the location of the tab stop	toolbar ruler
Center Tab	⊥	Centers text at location of the tab stop	toolbar ruler
Right Tab	⌐	Right-aligns text at location of the tab stop	toolbar ruler
Decimal Tab	⊥·	Aligns text on decimal point at location of the tab stop	45.72 223.75
Bar Tab	|	Aligns text at a bar character at the location of the tab stop	toolbar ruler

To Specify Font Color before Typing

The address, phone, and e-mail information should be the same color as the name. The following steps enter text using the most recently defined color.

1 Click the Font Color button on the Home tab so that the text you type will be the color displayed on the face of the button.

Q&A What if the color I want is not displayed on the face of the Font Color button?
Click the Font Color button arrow and then click the desired color in the Font Color gallery.

2 With the insertion point positioned between the graphic and the paragraph mark (as shown in Figure 3–19 on the previous page), press the TAB key to move the insertion point to the 6.5" mark on the ruler.

3 Type `22 Fifth Street, Juniper, NV 89268 * Phone: 420-555-2939 * E-mail: lhc@world.net` in the letterhead (Figure 3–20).

Font Color button

right tab marker at 6.5" mark on ruler

most recently used color, which displays on button face, is the desired color for the text to be typed

text aligned with right tab marker on ruler

Lana·Ha[...]

formatting mark indicates TAB key was pressed

text entered in same color as name

→ 22·Fifth·Street,·Juniper,·NV·89268·*·Phone:·420-555-2939·*·E-mail:·lhc@world.net¶

paragraph mark color changes to color displayed on Font Color button

Figure 3–20

To Bottom Border a Paragraph

The letterhead in this project has a horizontal line that extends from the left margin to the right margin immediately below the address, phone, and e-mail information. In Word, you can draw a solid line, called a **border**, at any edge of a paragraph. That is, borders may be added above or below a paragraph, to the left or right of a paragraph, or in any combination of these sides. The following steps add a bottom border to the paragraph containing address, phone, and e-mail information.

• With the insertion point in the paragraph to border, click the Border button arrow on the Home tab to display the Border gallery (Figure 3–21).

Figure 3–21

• Click Bottom Border in the Border gallery to place a border below the paragraph containing the insertion point (Figure 3–22).

Q&A If the face of the Border button displays the border icon I want to use, can I click the Border button instead of using the Border button arrow?

Yes.

Figure 3–22

Q&A How would I remove an existing border from a paragraph?

If, for some reason, you wanted to remove a border from a paragraph, you would position the insertion point in the paragraph, click the Border button arrow on the Home tab, and then click No Border (Figure 3–21) in the Border gallery.

Other Ways
1. Click Page Borders on Page Layout tab, click Borders tab in Borders and Shading
dialog box, select desired border, click OK button

To Clear Formatting

The next step is to position the insertion point below the letterhead, so that you can type the content of the letter. When you press the ENTER key at the end of a paragraph containing a border, Word moves the border forward to the next paragraph. It also retains all current settings. That is, the paragraph text will be teal and will have a bottom border. Instead, you want the paragraph and characters on the new line to use the Normal style: black font with no border. In Word, the term, **clear formatting**, refers to returning the formatting to the Normal style. The following steps clear formatting at the location of the insertion point.

- With the insertion point between the e-mail address and paragraph mark (as shown in Figure 3–22 on the previous page), press the ENTER key (Figure 3–23).

Figure 3–23

- Click the Clear Formatting button on the Home tab to apply the Normal style to the location of the insertion point (Figure 3–24).

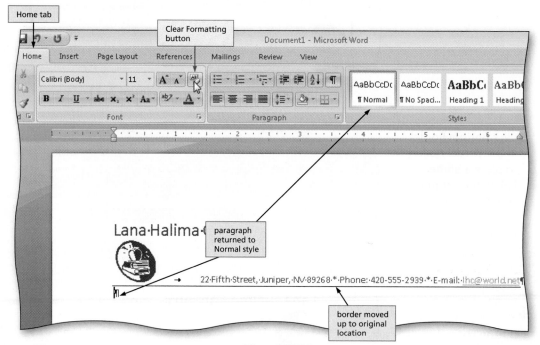

Figure 3–24

Other Ways

1. Click More button in Styles gallery on Home tab, click Clear Formatting
2. Click Styles Dialog Box Launcher, click Clear All in Styles task pane
3. Press CTRL+SPACEBAR, press CTRL+Q

AutoFormat As You Type

As you type text in a document, Word automatically formats it for you. For example, when you press the ENTER key or SPACEBAR after typing an e-mail address or Web address, Word automatically formats the address as a hyperlink, that is, colored blue and underlined. In Figure 3–23, Word formatted the e-mail address as a hyperlink because you pressed the ENTER key at the end of the line. Table 3–2 outlines commonly used AutoFormat As You Type options and their results.

Table 3–2 Commonly Used AutoFormat As You Type Options

Typed Text	AutoFormat Feature	Example
Quotation marks or apostrophes	Changes straight quotation marks or apostrophes to curly ones	"the" becomes "the"
Text, a space, one hyphen, one or no spaces, text, space	Changes the hyphen to an en dash	ages 20 - 45 becomes ages 20 – 45
Text, two hyphens, text, space	Changes the two hyphens to an em dash	Two types--yellow and red becomes Two types—yellow and red
Web or e-mail address followed by SPACEBAR or ENTER key	Formats Web or e-mail address as a hyperlink	www.scsite.com becomes www.scsite.com
Three hyphens, underscores, equal signs, asterisks, tildes, or number signs and then ENTER key	Places a border above a paragraph	--- This line becomes ⎯⎯⎯⎯⎯⎯⎯ This line
Number followed by a period, hyphen, right parenthesis, or greater than sign and then a space or tab followed by text	Creates a numbered list when you press the SPACEBAR or TAB key	1. Word 2. Excel becomes 1. Word 2. Excel
Asterisk, hyphen, or greater than sign and then a space or tab followed by text	Creates a bulleted list when you press the SPACEBAR or TAB key	* Home tab * Insert tab becomes • Home tab • Insert tab
Fraction and then a space or hyphen	Condenses the fraction entry so that it consumes one space instead of three	1/2 becomes ½
Ordinal and then a space or hyphen	Makes part of the ordinal a superscript	3rd becomes 3rd

AutoFormat Settings
For an AutoFormat option to work as expected, it must be enabled. To check if an AutoFormat option is enabled, click the Office Button, click the Word Options button, click Proofing in the left pane, click the AutoCorrect Options button, click the AutoFormat As You Type tab, select the appropriate check boxes, and then click the OK button in each open dialog box.

To Convert a Hyperlink to Regular Text

The e-mail address in the letterhead should be formatted as regular text; that is, it should not be blue or underlined. Thus, the next step is to remove the hyperlink format from the e-mail address in the letterhead.

1
- Right-click the hyperlink (in this case, the e-mail address) to display the Mini toolbar and a shortcut menu (Figure 3–25).

Figure 3–25

2

- Click Remove Hyperlink on the shortcut menu to remove the hyperlink format from the e-mail address.

- Position the insertion point on the paragraph mark below the border (Figure 3–26).

Q&A

Could I have used the AutoCorrect Options button instead of the Remove Hyperlink command?

Yes. Alternatively, you could have pointed to the small blue box at the beginning of the hyperlink, clicked the AutoCorrect Options button, and then clicked Undo Hyperlink on the AutoCorrect Options menu.

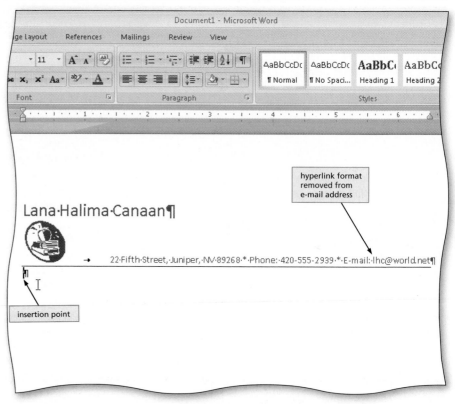

Figure 3–26

Other Ways

1. With insertion point in hyperlink, click Hyperlink button on Insert tab, click Remove Link button

To Save the Letterhead

The letterhead now is complete. Thus, you should save it in a file. For a detailed example of the procedure summarized below, refer to pages WD 19 through WD 21 in Chapter 1.

Note: If you are using Windows XP, see Appendix F for alternate steps.

BTW

Saving a Template
As an alternative to saving the letterhead as a Word document, you could save it as a template by clicking the Office Button, pointing to Save As, clicking Word Template, clicking Templates in the Favorite Links section, entering the template name, and then clicking the Save button. To use the template, click the Office Button, click New, click My templates in the left pane, and then double-click the template icon or name.

1 With a USB flash drive connected to one of the computer's USB ports, click the Save button on the Quick Access Toolbar to display the Save As dialog box.

2 Type `Canaan Letterhead` in the File name text box to change the file name.

3 If Computer is not displayed in the Favorite Links section, drag the top or bottom edge of the Save As dialog box until Computer is displayed. Click Computer in the Favorite Links section and then select the USB flash drive.

4 Click the Save button in the Save As dialog box to save the document on the USB flash drive with the file name, Canaan Letterhead.

Q&A

How can I keep reusing this same letterhead file for every letter I create?

If the letterhead file is not yet opened, you can instruct Word to create a new document window that contains the contents of an existing document. If the letterhead file is already opened, you can save the file with a new file name.

TO CREATE A NEW FILE FROM AN EXISTING FILE

If you wish to open a new document window that contains the contents of an existing file, you would follow these steps.

1. Click the Office Button and then click New to display the New Document dialog box.

2. Click 'New from existing' in the Templates area to display the New from Existing Document dialog box.

3. Locate and select the file from which you wish to create a new file.

4. Click the Create New button in the dialog box.

Creating a Cover Letter

You have created a letterhead for the cover letter. The next step is to compose the cover letter. The following pages use Word to compose a cover letter that contains a table and a bulleted list.

Plan Ahead

> **Compose an effective cover letter.**
> You always should send a personalized cover letter with a resume. The cover letter should highlight aspects of your background relevant to the position. To help you recall past achievements and activities, keep a personal file containing documents that outline your accomplishments.
>
> A cover letter is a type of business letter. When composing a business letter, you need to be sure to include all essential elements and to decide which letter style to use.
>
> • **Include all essential letter elements.** All business letters, including cover letters, contain the same basic elements. Essential business letter elements include the date line, inside address, message, and signature block (shown in Figure 3–1 on page WD 147).
>
> • **Determine which letter style to use.** You can follow many different styles when creating business letters. A letter style specifies guidelines for the alignment and spacing of elements in the business letter.

To Save the Document with a New File Name

The current open file has the name Canaan Letterhead, which is the name of the personal letterhead. You want the letterhead to remain intact. Thus, the following steps save the document with a new file name.

1 With a USB flash drive connected to one of the computer's USB ports, click the Office Button to display the Office Button menu and then click Save As on the Office Button menu to display the Save As dialog box.

2 Type Canaan Cover Letter in the File name text box to change the file name.

3 If necessary, select the USB flash drive as the save location.

4 Click the Save button in the Save As dialog box to save the document on the USB flash drive with the file name, Canaan Cover Letter.

To Apply a Quick Style

When you press the ENTER key in the letter, you want the insertion point to advance to the next line, with no blank space between the lines. Recall that, by default, the Normal style in Word places 10 points of blank space after each paragraph and inserts a blank space equal to 1.15 lines between each line of text. The No Spacing style, however, does not put any blank space between lines when you press the ENTER key. Thus, the following step applies the No Spacing style to the current paragraph.

 With the insertion point on the paragraph mark below the border, click No Spacing in the Styles gallery to apply the No Spacing style to the current paragraph.

Plan Ahead

> **Include all essential letter elements.**
> Be sure to include all essential business letter elements, properly spaced, in your cover letter.
>
> * The **date line**, which consists of the month, day, and year, is positioned two to six lines below the letterhead.
>
> * The **inside address**, placed three to eight lines below the date line, usually contains the addressee's courtesy title plus full name, job title, business affiliation, and full geographical address.
>
> * The **salutation**, if present, begins two lines below the last line of the inside address. If you do not know the recipient's name, avoid using the salutation "To whom it may concern" — it is impersonal. Instead, use the recipient's title in the salutation, e.g., Dear Personnel Director.
>
> * The body of the letter, the **message**, begins two lines below the salutation. Within the message, paragraphs are single-spaced with one blank line between paragraphs.
>
> * Two lines below the last line of the message, the **complimentary close** is displayed. Capitalize only the first word in a complimentary close.
>
> * Type the **signature block** at least four blank lines below the complimentary close, allowing room for the author to sign his or her name.

Plan Ahead

> **Determine which letter style to use.**
> Three common business letter styles are the block, the modified block, and the modified semi-block. Each style specifies different alignments and indentations.
>
> * In the block letter style, all components of the letter begin flush with the left margin.
>
> * In the modified block letter style, the date, complimentary close, and signature block are positioned approximately one-half inch to the right of center or at the right margin. All other components of the letter begin flush with the left margin.
>
> * In the modified semi-block letter style, the date, complimentary close, and signature block are centered, positioned approximately one-half inch to the right of center or at the right margin. The first line of each paragraph in the body of the letter is indented one-half to one inch from the left margin. All other components of the letter begin flush with the left margin.
>
> The cover letter in this project follows the modified block style.

To Set Custom Tab Stops Using the Ruler

The first required element of the cover letter is the date line, which in this letter is to be positioned two lines below the letterhead. The date line contains the month, day, and year, and begins 3.5 inches from the left margin, which is approximately one-half inch to the right of center. Thus, you should set a custom tab stop at the 3.5" mark on the ruler. Earlier you used the Tabs dialog box to set a tab stop because you could not use the ruler to set a tab stop at the right margin. The following steps set a left-aligned tab stop using the ruler.

1

- With the insertion point on the paragraph mark below the border, press the ENTER key so that a blank line appears between the letterhead and the date line.

- If necessary, click the tab selector at the left edge of the horizontal ruler until it displays the Left Tab icon.

- Position the mouse pointer on the 3.5" mark on the ruler (Figure 3–27).

 What is the purpose of the tab selector?

Before using the ruler to set a tab stop, you must ensure the correct tab stop icon appears in the tab selector. Each time you click the tab selector, its icon changes. For a list of the types of tab stops, see Table 3–1 on page WD 160.

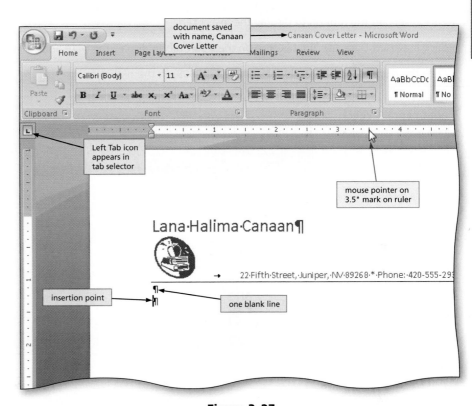

Figure 3–27

2

- Click the 3.5" mark on the ruler to place a left tab marker at that location on the ruler (Figure 3–28).

What if I click the wrong location on the ruler?

You can move a custom tab stop by dragging the tab marker to the desired location on the ruler. Or, you can remove a custom tab stop by pointing to the tab marker on the ruler and then dragging the tab marker down and out of the ruler.

Figure 3–28

To Insert the Current Date in a Document

The next step is to enter the current date at the 3.5" tab stop in the document, as specified in the guidelines for a modified block style letter. Word provides a method of inserting a computer's system date in a document. The following steps insert the current date in the cover letter.

- Press the TAB key.

- Click Insert on the Ribbon to display the Insert tab.

- Click the Insert Date and Time button on the Insert tab to display the Date and Time dialog box.

- Click the desired format (in this case, May 12, 2008) in the dialog box.

- If the Update automatically check box is selected, click the check box to remove the check mark (Figure 3–29).

Q&A

Why should the Update automatically check box not be selected?

In this project, the date at the top of the letter should always show today's date. If, however, you wanted the date always to change to reflect the current computer date, for example showing the date you open or print the letter, then you would put a check mark in this check box.

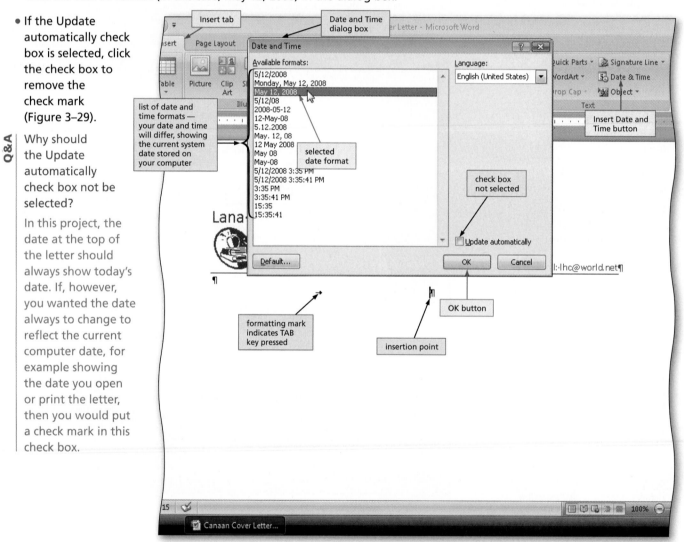

Figure 3–29

2
- Click the OK button to insert the current date at the location of the insertion point (Figure 3–30).

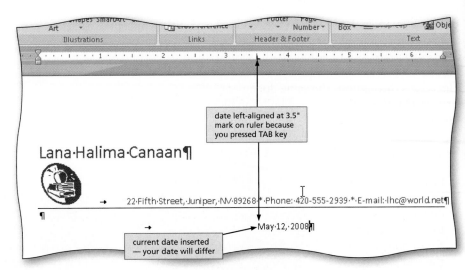

date left-aligned at 3.5" mark on ruler because you pressed TAB key

current date inserted — your date will differ

Figure 3–30

To Enter the Inside Address and Salutation

The next step in composing the cover letter is to type the inside address and salutation.

1 With the insertion point at the end of the date, press the ENTER key three times.

2 Type `Mr. Raul Ramos` and then press the ENTER key.

3 Type `Personnel Director` and then press the ENTER key.

4 Type `Juniper Culinary Academy` and then press the ENTER key.

5 Type `202 Park Boulevard` and then press the ENTER key.

6 Type `Juniper, NV 89268` and then press the ENTER key twice.

7 Type `Dear Mr. Ramos` and then press the COLON key (:) to complete the entries of the inside address and salutation (Figure 3–31).

inside address entered

salutation entered

Figure 3–31

To Create a Building Block

If you use the same text or graphic frequently, you can store the text or graphic in a **building block** and then use the stored building block entry in the open document, as well as in future documents. That is, you can create the entry once as a building block, and for all future occurrences of the text or graphic, you can insert the building block as you need it. In this way, you avoid entering the text or graphics inconsistently or incorrectly in different locations throughout the same document.

The next steps create a building block for the prospective employer's name, Juniper Culinary Academy. Later in the chapter, you will insert the building block in the document instead of typing the employer's name.

1

- Select the text to be a building block, in this case, Juniper Culinary Academy. Do not select the paragraph mark at the end of the text.

Q&A

Why is the paragraph mark not part of the building block?

Only select the paragraph mark if you want to store paragraph formatting, such as indentation and line spacing, as part of the building block.

- Click the Quick Parts button on the Insert tab to display the Quick Parts menu (Figure 3–32).

Figure 3–32

2

- Click Save Selection to Quick Part Gallery on the Quick Parts menu to display the Create New Building Block dialog box.

- Type jca in the Name text box to replace the proposed building block name (Juniper Culinary) with a shorter building block name (Figure 3–33).

3

- Click the OK button to store the building block entry and close the dialog box.

- If Word displays another dialog box, click the Yes button.

Figure 3–33

Other Ways

1. Select text, press ALT+F3

To Insert a Nonbreaking Space

Some compound words, such as proper nouns, dates, units of time and measure, abbreviations, and geographic destinations, should not be divided at the end of a line. These words either should fit as a unit at the end of a line or be wrapped together to the next line.

Word provides two special characters to assist with this task: nonbreaking space and nonbreaking hyphen. A **nonbreaking space** is a special space character that prevents two words from splitting if the first word falls at the end of a line. Similarly, a **nonbreaking hyphen** is a special type of hyphen that prevents two words separated by a hyphen from splitting at the end of a line.

The following steps insert a nonbreaking space between the words in the newspaper name.

1

- Click to the right of the colon in the salutation and then press the ENTER key twice to position the insertion point one blank line below the salutation.

- Type I am responding to the junior culinary instructor position that you recently advertised in the and then press the SPACEBAR.

- Press CTRL+I to turn on italics. Type Juniper as the first word in the newspaper name and then press CTRL+SHIFT+SPACEBAR to insert a nonbreaking space after the word, Juniper (Figure 3–34).

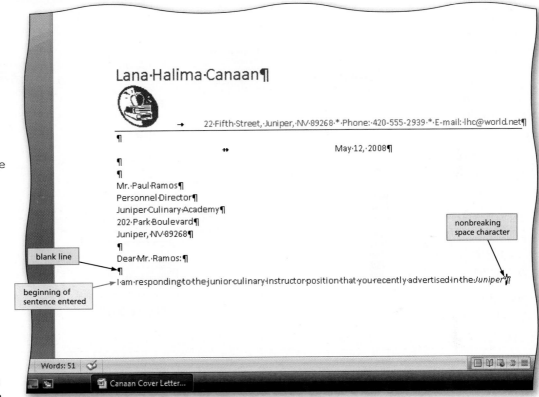

Figure 3–34

2

- Type Daily and then press CTRL+SHIFT+SPACEBAR to insert another nonbreaking space after the word, Daily.

- Type Herald and then press CTRL+I to turn off italics. Press the PERIOD key (Figure 3–35).

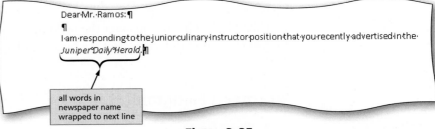

Figure 3–35

Other Ways
1. Click Symbol button on Insert tab, click More Symbols, click Special Characters tab, click   Nonbreaking Space in Character list, click Insert button, click Close button

To Insert a Building Block

At the end of the next sentence in the body of the cover letter, you want the prospective employer name, Juniper Culinary Academy, to be displayed. Recall that earlier in this chapter, you created a building block name of jca for Juniper Culinary Academy. Thus, you will type the building block name and then instruct Word to replace the building block name with the stored building block entry of Juniper Culinary Academy. The following steps insert a building block.

- Press the SPACEBAR. Type As indicated on the enclosed resume, I have the credentials you are seeking and believe I can be a valuable asset to jca as shown in Figure 3–36.

Figure 3–36

- Press the F3 key to instruct word to replace the building block name (jca) with the stored building block entry (Juniper Culinary Academy).

- Press the PERIOD key (Figure 3–37).

Figure 3–37

Other Ways

1. Click Quick Parts button on Insert tab, click desired building block

Building Blocks vs. AutoCorrect

In Project 2, you learned how to use the AutoCorrect feature, which enables you to insert and create AutoCorrect entries, similarly to how you created and inserted building blocks in this chapter. The difference between an AutoCorrect entry and a building block entry is that the AutoCorrect feature makes corrections for you automatically as soon as you press the SPACEBAR or type a punctuation mark, whereas you must instruct Word to insert a building block. That is, you enter the building block name and then press the F3 key, or click the Quick Parts button and select the building block from the list.

To Enter a Paragraph

The next step in creating the cover letter is to enter a paragraph of text.

Press the ENTER key twice to place a blank line between paragraphs, according to the guidelines of the modified block letter style.

BTW

Nonbreaking Hyphen
If you wanted to insert a nonbreaking hyphen, you would press CTRL+SHIFT+HYPHEN.

2 **Type** I recently received my bachelor's degree in culinary arts from Nevada Culinary Institute. The following table outlines my areas of concentration:

3 Press the ENTER key twice.

Tables

The next step in composing the cover letter is to place a table listing the number of credit hours for areas of concentration (shown in Figure 3–1 on page WD 147). A Word **table** is a collection of rows and columns. The intersection of a row and a column is called a **cell**, and cells are filled with text.

The first step in creating a table is to insert an empty table into the document. When inserting a table, you must specify the total number of rows and columns required, which is called the **dimension** of the table. The table in this project has two columns. You often do not know the total number of rows in a table. Thus, many Word users create one row initially and then add more rows as needed. In Word, the first number in a dimension is the number of columns, and the second is the number of rows. For example, in Word, a 2 × 1 (pronounced "two by one") table consists of two columns and one row.

To Insert an Empty Table

The next step is to insert an empty table in the cover letter. The following steps insert a table with two columns and one row at the location of the insertion point.

1

- Click the Table button on the Insert tab to display the Table gallery.

  🔎 **Experiment**

- Point to various cells on the grid to see a preview of the table in the document window.

2

- Position the mouse pointer on the cell in the first row and second column of the grid to preview the desired table dimension (Figure 3–38).

Figure 3–38

3

- Click the cell in the first row and second column of the grid to insert an empty table with one row and two columns in the document (Figure 3–39).

Q&A

What are the small circles in the table cells?

Each table cell has an **end-of-cell mark**, which is a formatting mark that assists you with selecting and formatting cells. Similarly, each row has an **end-of-row mark**, which you can use to add columns to the right of a table. Recall that formatting marks do not print on a hard copy. The end-of-cell marks currently are left-aligned, that is, positioned at the left edge of each cell.

Figure 3–39

Other Ways

1. Click Table on Insert tab, click Insert Table on Table gallery, enter number of columns and rows, click OK button

To Enter Data in a Table

The next step is to enter data in the cells of the empty table. The data you enter in a cell wordwraps just as text wordwraps between the margins of a document. To place data in a cell, you click the cell and then type.

To advance rightward from one cell to the next, press the TAB key. When you are at the rightmost cell in a row, press the TAB key to move to the first cell in the next row; do not press the ENTER key. The ENTER key is used to begin a new paragraph within a cell. One way to add new rows to a table is to press the TAB key when the insertion point is positioned in the bottom-right corner cell of the table. The next steps enter data in the table, adding rows as necessary.

1

- If necessary, scroll the table up in the document window.

- With the insertion point in the left cell of the table, type `Food Planning and Preparation` and then press the TAB key to advance the insertion point to the next cell.

- Type `30 hours` and then press the TAB key to add a second row to the table and position the insertion point in the first column of the new row (Figure 3–40).

Q&A How do I edit cell contents if I make a mistake?

Click in the cell and then correct the entry.

Figure 3–40

2

- Type `Food Safety` and then press the TAB key. Type `15 hours` and then press the TAB key.

- Type `Nutrition` and then press the TAB key. Type `15 hours` and then press the TAB key.

- Type `Regional and International Cuisine` and then press the TAB key. Type `21 hours` to complete the entries in the table (Figure 3–41).

Figure 3–41

To Apply a Table Style

The next step is to apply a table style to the table. Word provides a Table Styles gallery, allowing you to change the basic table format to a more visually appealing style. Word provides a gallery of more than 90 table styles, which include a variety of colors and shading. In this project, you do not want the heading rows or alternating rows to use a different format; that is, you want the formatting applied to the rows in the table to be the same. The following steps apply a table style to the table in the cover letter.

1

- With the insertion point in the table, remove the check marks from the Header Row and Banded Rows check boxes on the Design tab so that all rows in the table will be formatted the same.

Q&A

What if the Design tab in the Table Tools tab no longer is the active tab?

Click in the table and then click Design on the Ribbon.

2

- Click the More button in the Table Styles gallery (shown in Figure 3–41 on the previous page) to expand the Table Styles gallery.

- Scroll and then point to Medium Grid 3 - Accent 2 in the Table Styles gallery to display a live preview of that style applied to the table in the document (Figure 3–42).

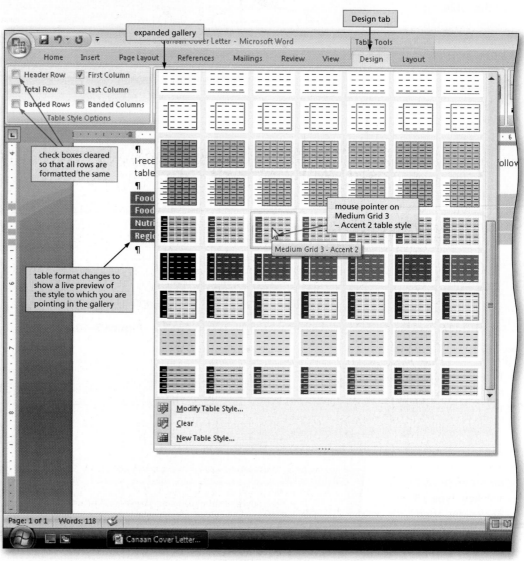

Figure 3–42

Experiment

- Point to various table styles in the Table Styles gallery and watch the format of the table change in the document window.

3

- Click Medium Grid 3 - Accent 2 in the Table Styles gallery to apply the selected style to the table (Figure 3–43).

Figure 3–43

To Resize Table Columns to Fit Table Contents

The table in this project currently extends from the left margin to the right margin of the document. You want each column only to be as wide as the longest entry in the table. That is, the first column must be wide enough to accommodate the words, Regional and International Cuisine, and the second column should be only as wide as the hours entered. The following steps instruct Word to fit the width of the columns to the contents of the table automatically.

1

- With the insertion point in the table, click Layout on the Ribbon to display the Layout tab.

- Click the AutoFit button on the Layout tab to display the AutoFit menu (Figure 3–44).

Figure 3–44

2

• Click AutoFit Contents on the AutoFit menu, so that Word automatically adjusts the widths of the columns based on the text in the table (Figure 3–45).

Q&A

Can I resize columns manually?

Yes, you can drag a **column boundary**, the border to the right of a column, until the column is the desired width. Similarly, you can resize a row by dragging the **row boundary**, the border at the bottom of a row, until the row is the desired height. You also can resize the entire table by dragging the **table resize handle**, which is a small square that appears when you point to a corner of the table (shown in Figure 3–46).

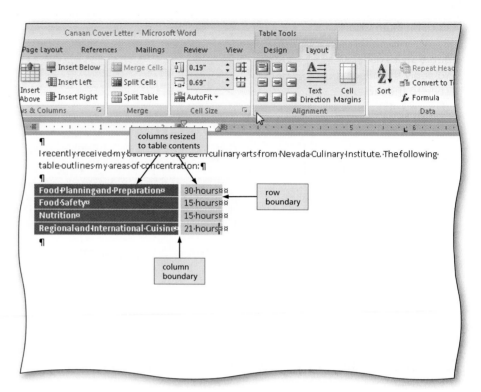

Figure 3–45

Other Ways

1. Right-click table, point to AutoFit on shortcut menu, click AutoFit to Contents

2. Double-click column boundary

Selecting Table Contents

When working with tables, you may need to select the contents of cells, rows, columns, or the entire table. Table 3–3 identifies ways to select various items in a table.

Table 3–3 Selecting Items in a Table

Item to Select	Action
Cell	Click left edge of cell
Column	Click border at top of column
Multiple cells, rows, or columns adjacent to one another	Drag through cells, rows, or columns
Multiple cells, rows, or columns not adjacent to one another	Select first cell, row, or column and then hold down CTRL key while selecting next cell, row, or column
Next cell	Press TAB key
Previous cell	Press SHIFT+TAB
Row	Click to left of row
Table	Click table move handle

To Select a Table

When you first create a table, it is left-aligned, that is, flush with the left margin. In this cover letter, the table should be centered. To center a table, you first select the entire table.

1

• Position the mouse pointer in the table so that the table move handle appears.

• Click the table move handle to select the entire table (Figure 3–46).

Figure 3–46

To Center a Selected Table

The following steps center the selected table between the margins.

1 Move the mouse pointer into the Mini toolbar, so that the toolbar changes to a bright toolbar.

2 Click the Center button on the Mini toolbar to center the selected table between the left and right margins (Figure 3–47).

Q&A When should I use the Mini toolbar versus the Ribbon?

If the command you want to use is not on the currently displayed tab on the Ribbon and it is available on the Mini toolbar, use the Mini toolbar instead of switching to a different tab. This technique minimizes mouse movement.

Q&A How would I center the contents of the table cells instead of the entire table?

If you wanted to center the contents of the cells, you would select the cells by dragging through them and then click the Center button.

BTW

Tables
For simple tables, such as the one just created, Word users often select the table dimension in the grid to create the table. For more complex tables, such as one with a varying number of columns per row, Word has a Draw Table feature that allows users to draw a table in the document using a pencil pointer. To use this feature, click Table on the Insert tab and then click Draw Table.

Figure 3–47

Adding and Deleting Table Rows

As discussed in the previous steps, you can add a row to the end of a table by positioning the insertion point in the bottom-right corner cell and then pressing the TAB key. You also can add rows to a table by clicking the Insert Rows Above button or Insert Rows Below button on the Layout tab to insert a row above or below the location of the insertion point in the table. Similarly, you can right-click the table, point to Insert on the shortcut menu, and then click Insert Rows Above or Insert Rows Below.

To add columns to a table, click the Insert Columns to the Left button or Insert Columns to the Right button on the Layout tab to insert a column to the left or right of the location of the insertion point in the table. Similarly, you can right-click the table, point to Insert on the shortcut menu, and then click Insert Columns to the Left or Insert Columns to the Right.

If you want to delete row(s) or delete column(s) from a table, position the insertion point in the row(s) or column(s) to delete, click the Delete button on the Layout tab, and then click Delete Rows or Delete Columns. Or, select the row or column to delete, right-click the selection, and then click Delete Rows or Delete Columns on the shortcut menu.

To delete the contents of a cell, select the cell contents by pointing to the left edge of a cell and clicking when the mouse pointer changes direction, and then press the DELETE key. You also can drag and drop or cut and paste the contents of cells.

BTW

Table Rows and Columns
To change the width of a column to an exact measurement, hold down the ALT key while dragging markers on the ruler. Or, enter values in the Table Row Height and Table Column Width text boxes on the Layout tab.

To Add More Text

The next step is to add more text below the table.

1 Position the insertion point on the paragraph mark below the table and then press the ENTER key.

2 Type In addition to my coursework, I have the following culinary experience: and then press the ENTER key.

To Bullet a List as You Type

In Chapter 1, you learned how to apply bullets to existing paragraphs. If you know before you type that a list should be bulleted, you can use Word's AutoFormat As You Type feature to bullet the paragraphs as you type them (Table 3–2 on page WD 163). The following steps add bullets to a list as you type.

1
- Press the ASTERISK key (*) as the first character on the line (Figure 3–48).

Figure 3–48

2

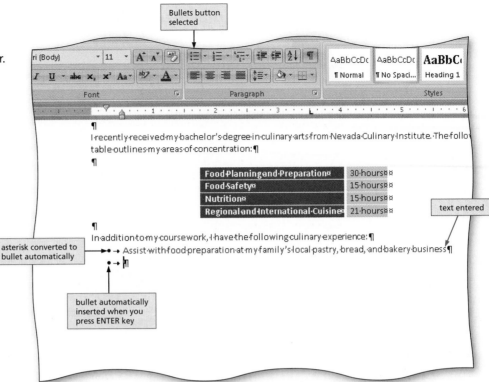

- Press the SPACEBAR to convert the asterisk to a bullet character.

 What if I did not want the asterisk converted to a bullet character?

You would undo the AutoFormat by clicking the Undo button, or by clicking the AutoCorrect Options button and then clicking Undo Automatic Bullets on the AutoCorrect Options menu, or by clicking the Bullets button on the Home tab.

- **Type** Assist with food preparation at my family's local pastry, bread, and bakery business **as the first bulleted item.**

- Press the ENTER key to place another bullet character at the beginning of the next line (Figure 3–49).

Figure 3–49

3

- **Type** Prepare food and serve meals at Hope Mission **and then press the ENTER key.**

- **Type** Assisted the chef with meal preparation and presentation during internship at The Garden Grill **and then press the ENTER key.**

- **Type** Prepared salads, soups, sandwiches, entrees, and desserts while working at the school cafeteria **and then press the ENTER key.**

- Press the ENTER key to turn off automatic bullets as you type (Figure 3–50).

Figure 3–50

 Why did automatic bullets stop?

When you press the ENTER key without entering any text after the automatic bullet character, Word turns off the automatic bullets feature.

Other Ways

1. Click Bullets button on Home tab

2. Right-click paragraph to be bulleted, click bullets button on Mini toolbar

3. Right-click paragraph to be bulleted, point to Bullets on shortcut menu, click desired bullet style

To Enter the Remainder of the Cover Letter

The next step is to enter the remainder of the cover letter.

1 Press the ENTER key and then type the paragraph shown in Figure 3–51, making certain you use the building block name, jca, to insert the employer name.

2 Press the ENTER key twice. Press the TAB key. Type Sincerely and then press the COMMA key.

3 Press the ENTER key four times. Press the TAB key. Type Lana Halima Canaan and then press the ENTER key twice. Type Enclosure as the final text in the cover letter (Figure 3–51).

I·will·call·you·next·week·to·see·if·we·can·set·up·a·time·to·discuss·my·career·opportunities·at·Juniper·Culinary·Academy.·If·you·would·like·to·speak·to·me·before·then,·please·call·me·at·420-555-2939.·¶

paragraph entered

→   Sincerely,¶

→   Lana·Halima·Canaan¶

remainder of cover letter entered

Enclosure¶

Figure 3–51

To Change Document Properties

Before saving the research paper again, you want to add your name, course and section, and some keywords as document properties. The following steps use the Document Information Panel to change document properties.

1 Display the Office Button menu, point to Prepare on the Office Button menu, and then click Properties on the Prepare submenu to display the Document Information Panel.

2 Click the Author text box, if necessary, and then type your name as the Author property. If a name already is displayed in the Author text box, delete it before typing your name. Click the Subject text box, if necessary delete any existing text, and then type your course and section as the Subject property. Click the Keywords text box, if necessary delete any existing text, and then type Cover Letter as the Keywords property.

3 Close the Document Information Panel.

To Save an Existing Document and Print It

The document now is complete. You should save the cover letter again. The following steps save the document again and then print it. Do not close the Canaan Cover Letter file. You will use it again later in this chapter to copy the address, phone, and e-mail information to the resume.

1 Click the Save button on the Quick Access Toolbar to overwrite the previous Canaan Cover Letter file on the USB flash drive.

2 Display the Office Button menu, point to Print, and then click Quick Print to print the cover letter (shown in Figure 3–1 on page WD 147).

Using a Template to Create a Resume

The next step in this project is to create the resume (Figure 3–2 on page WD 148). Although you could compose a resume in a blank document window, this chapter shows instead how to use a template, where Word formats the resume with appropriate headings and spacing. You customize the resume created by the template by filling in blanks and by selecting and replacing text.

Plan Ahead

Craft a successful resume.

Two types of resumes are the chronological resume and the functional resume. A chronological resume sequences information by time, with the most recent listed first. This type of resume highlights a job seeker's job continuity and growth. A functional resume groups information by skills and accomplishments. This resume emphasizes a job seeker's experience and qualifications in specialized areas. Some resumes use a combination of the two formats. For an entry-level job search, experts recommend a chronological resume or a combination of the two types of resumes.

When creating your resume, be sure to include necessary information and present it appropriately. Keep descriptions short and concise, using action words and bulleted lists.

- **Include necessary information.** Your resume should include contact information, a clearly written objective, educational background, and experience. Use your complete legal name and mailing address, along with phone number and e-mail address, if one exists. Other sections you might consider including are organizations, recognitions and awards, and skills. Do not include your social security number, marital status, age, height, weight, gender, physical appearance, health, citizenship, previous pay rates, reasons for leaving a prior job, current date, high-school information (if you are a college graduate), and references. Employers assume you will give references, if asked, and this information simply clutters a resume.

- **Present your resume appropriately.** For printed resumes, use a high-quality ink-jet or laser printer to print your resume (and cover letter) on standard letter-size white or ivory paper. Consider using paper that contains cotton fibers for a professional look. Select envelopes that are the same quality and grade as the paper. If you e-mail the resume, consider that the potential employer may not have the same software you used to create the resume and thus may not be able to open it up. As an alternative, you could save the file in a format, such as a PDF, that can be viewed with a reader program. Many job seekers also post their resume on the Web.

BTW

Saving in the PDF Format
To save a Word document in the PDF format, you need to install the Save as PDF add-in from Microsoft. Use Help to search for the term, PDF, to assist with this process. Once installed, the PDF or XPS command will appear when you point to Save As on the Office Button menu. Both the PDF and XPS formats are intended to enable users to share documents easily with other users.

To Use a Template

Word installs a variety of templates for letters, fax cover sheets, reports, and resumes on your hard disk. The templates are grouped in five styles: Equity, Median, Oriel, Origin, and Urban. The templates in each style use similar formatting, themes, etc., enabling users to create a set of documents that complement one another. In this chapter, you will create a resume from the template in the Origin style. The following steps create a new document based on a template.

1
- Display the Office Button menu (Figure 3–52).

Office Button

cover letter file remains open

Canaan Cover Letter - Microsoft Word

Office Button menu

New

New command to be selected

Recent Documents

Open

Save

Figure 3–52

2

- Click New on the Office Button menu to display the New Document dialog box.

- Click Installed Templates in the Templates area to display the list of templates on the hard disk.

🔍 **Experiment**

- Click various installed templates in the Installed Templates list and watch the preview of the template display at the right edge of the dialog box.

3

- Scroll through the Installed Templates list and then click Origin Resume to select it (Figure 3–53).

Figure 3–53

Q&A | How do I access a template on the Web?

If you are connected to the Internet when you click the desired template in the Microsoft Office Online area of the New Document dialog box, Word automatically displays templates from the Microsoft Office Online Web page that you can download.

4

- Click the Create button to create a new document based on the selected template (Figure 3–54).

Figure 3–54

To Print the Resume

To see the entire resume created by the resume template, print the document shown in the Word window.

1 Ready the printer. Display the Office Button menu, point to Print, and then click Quick Print to print the resume created from the template (Figure 3–55).

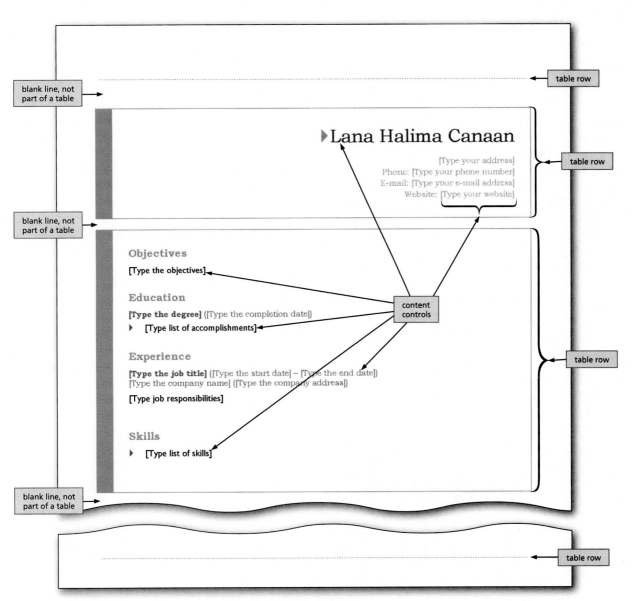

Figure 3–55

Resume Template

The resume created from the template, shown in Figure 3–55, consists of four individual tables, each with one row and one column. The first and last tables contain a decorative blue line; the second table contains the labels and content controls for the job seeker's contact information; and the third table contains labels and content controls for the Objectives, Education, Experience, and Skills sections of the resume. A **content control** contains instructions for filling areas of the template. To select a content control, you click it. As soon as you begin typing in the selected content control, your typing replaces the instruction in the control. Thus, you do not need to delete the selection before you begin typing.

The next step is to personalize the resume. The following pages personalize the resume created by the resume template.

To Delete Rows

The first and last rows of the resume created from the template contain a decorative line. The resume in this project deletes those rows to provide more space for the contents of the resume. The following steps delete the first and last rows on the resume.

- With the insertion point at the top of the document, click Layout on the Ribbon to display the Layout tab.

- Click the Delete button on the Layout tab to display the Delete menu (Figure 3–56).

Figure 3–56

- Click Delete Rows on the Delete menu to delete the row containing the insertion point (Figure 3–57).

What happened to the Table Tools tab on the Ribbon?

It is a contextual tab that appears only when the insertion point is in a table. With the row deleted, the insertion point is above the table row containing contact information.

Figure 3–57

- Press CTRL+END and then press the DOWN ARROW key to position the insertion point at the bottom of the document in the last row.

- Click Layout on the Ribbon to display the Layout tab.

- Click the Delete button on the Layout tab to display the Delete menu (Figure 3–58).

- Click Delete Rows on the Delete menu to delete the row containing the insertion point.

Figure 3–58

Other Ways
1. Right-click selected rows, click Delete Rows on shortcut menu

To Modify Text in a Content Control

The next step is to select text that the template inserted in the resume and replace it with personal information. The name area on your resume may contain a name, which Word copied from the Word Options dialog box, or it may contain the instruction, Type your name. This content control should contain your name. In this project, the name is bold to give it more emphasis on the resume. It also uses the same color as the name on the cover letter.

The following steps modify the text in the content control that contains the job seeker's name.

①

- Press CTRL+HOME to position the insertion point at the top of the document.

- Click the name content control to select it (if it already contains a name, instead of the instruction, Type name here, drag through the name to select it). Then, type Lana Halima Canaan as the name.

- Triple-click the name content control to select its contents, so that you can format the name (Figure 3–59).

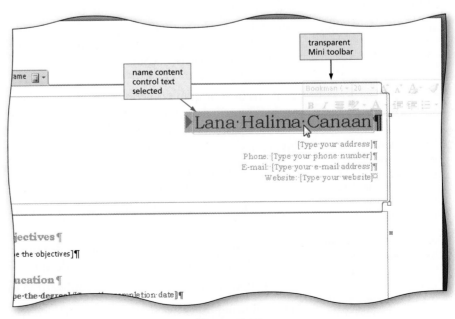

Figure 3–59

2

- Move the mouse pointer into the transparent Mini toolbar, so that it changes to a bright toolbar.

- Click the Bold button on the Mini toolbar to bold the selected name.

- Click the Font Color button on the Mini toolbar to change the font color of the selected name to the most recently used font color, which was the color of the name in the cover letter (Figure 3–60).

Q&A
Instead of using buttons on the Mini toolbar, can I use the Bold and Font Color buttons on the Home tab?

Yes.

Figure 3–60

BTW

Windows Vista Taskbar
If your Windows Vista taskbar does not display a separate program button for each open Word document (as shown in Figure 3–61), click the Office Button, click the Word Options button, click Advanced in the left pane, scroll to the Display area in the right pane, place a check mark in the Show all windows in the Taskbar check box, and then click the OK button.

To Save the Resume

You have completed several tasks on the resume. Thus, you should save it in a file.

1 Click the Save button on the Quick Access Toolbar.

2 Save the file on your USB flash drive using `Canaan Resume` as the file name.

Copying and Pasting

The next step in personalizing the resume is to enter the address, phone, and e-mail information in the content controls. One way to enter this information in the resume is to type it. Recall, however, that you already typed this information in the cover letter. Thus, a timesaving alternative would be to use the Office Clipboard to copy it from the cover letter to the resume. The **Office Clipboard** is a temporary storage area that holds up to 24 items (text or graphics) copied from any Office program.

Through the Office Clipboard, you can copy multiple items from any Office document and then paste them into the same or another Office document by following these general guidelines:

BTW

Clipboard
The Windows Clipboard, which can hold only one item at a time, is not the same as the Office Clipboard. When you collect multiple items on the Office Clipboard, however, the last copied item is copied to the Windows Clipboard as well. When you clear the Office Clipboard, the Windows Clipboard also is cleared.

1. Items are copied *from* a **source document**. If the source document is not the active document, display it in the document window.

2. Display the Office Clipboard task pane and then copy items from the source document to the Office Clipboard.

3. Items are copied *to* a **destination document**. If the destination document is not the active document, display the destination document in the document window.

4. Paste items from the Office Clipboard to the destination document.

The following pages use these guidelines to copy the address, phone, and e-mail information from the letterhead to the resume.

To Switch from One Open Document to Another

The step below switches from the open resume document to the open cover letter document, which is the source document in this case.

1

- Click the Canaan Cover Letter - Microsoft Word program button on the Windows Vista taskbar to switch from the resume document to the cover letter document (Figure 3–61).

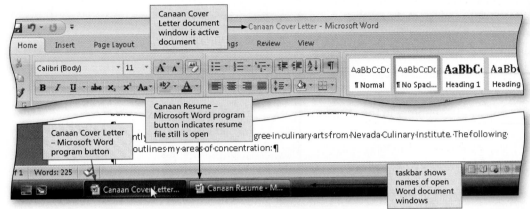

Figure 3–61

Other Ways	
1. Click Switch Windows button on View tab, click document name	2. Press ALT+TAB

To Copy Items to the Office Clipboard

You can copy multiple items to the Office Clipboard through the Clipboard task pane and then paste them later. The following steps copy three items from the source document, the Canaan Cover Letter document, to the Office Clipboard.

1

- If necessary, scroll to the top of the cover letter, so that the items to be copied are visible in the document window.

- Click the Clipboard Dialog Box Launcher on the Home tab to display the Clipboard task pane.

- If the Office Clipboard in the Clipboard task pane is not empty, click the Clear All button in the Clipboard task pane (Figure 3–62).

Figure 3–62

- In the cover letter, select the address, 22 Fifth Street, Juniper, NV 89268, which is the first item to be copied. Do not include the spaces to the right and left of the address.

- Click the Copy button on the Home tab to copy the selection to the Office Clipboard (Figure 3–63).

Q&A Does the copied item always display in its entirety in the Office Clipboard?

No. If the entry is too long, only the first portion is displayed.

Q&A What appears in the Office Clipboard if I copy a graphic instead of text?

A thumbnail of the copied graphic is displayed.

Figure 3–63

- Select the phone number (just the number, not the word Phone: and no spaces before or after the number) and then click the Copy button on the Home tab to copy the selection to the Office Clipboard.

- Select the e-mail address (just the e-mail address, not the word E-mail: and no spaces before or after the address) and then click the Copy button on the Home tab to copy the selection to the Office Clipboard (Figure 3–64).

Q&A What if I copy more than the maximum 24 items allowed in the Office Clipboard?

When you copy a 25th item, Word deletes the first item to make room for the new item.

Q&A Can I delete an item from the Office Clipboard?

Yes. Point to the item in the gallery, click the box arrow to the right of the item, and then click Delete.

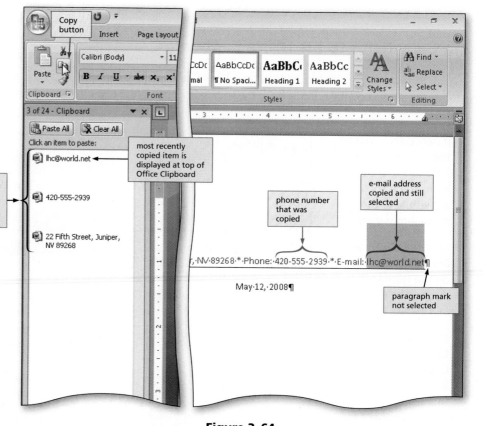

Figure 3–64

Other Ways

1. With Clipboard task pane displayed, right-click selected item, click Copy on shortcut menu

2. With Clipboard task pane displayed and item to copy selected, press CTRL+C

To Paste from the Office Clipboard

The next step is to paste the copied items (the address, phone, and e-mail information) into the destination document, in this case, the resume document. Recall that the address, phone, and e-mail address are part of content controls in the resume.

The following steps paste the address, phone, and e-mail information from the Office Clipboard into the resume.

1

- Click the Canaan Resume - Microsoft Word program button on the Windows Vista taskbar to display the resume document.

Q&A Does the destination document have to be a different document?

No. The source and destination documents can be the same document.

- If the Clipboard task pane is not displayed on the screen, click the Clipboard Dialog Box Launcher on the Home tab to display the Clipboard task pane.

- Click the content control in the resume with the instruction, Type your address, to select it (Figure 3–65).

Q&A What is the function of the Paste All button?

It pastes all items in a row, without any characters between them, at the location of the insertion point or selection.

Figure 3–65

BTW

Clipboard Task Pane
The Clipboard task pane may appear on the screen if you click the Copy button or the Cut button twice in succession, or if you copy and paste an item and then copy another item. You can display the Clipboard task pane by clicking the Office Clipboard icon, if it appears in the notification area on the Windows Vista taskbar. If the Office Clipboard icon does not appear, click the Options button at the bottom of the Clipboard task pane and then click Show Office Clipboard Icon on Taskbar.

● Click the address entry in the Office Clipboard to paste it in the document at the location of the selected content control (Figure 3–66).

Q&A

Are the contents of the Office Clipboard erased when you paste?

No.

Figure 3–66

● Click the content control in the resume with the instruction, Type your phone number, to select it.

● Click the phone entry in the Office Clipboard to paste it in the document at the location of the selected content control.

● Click the content control in the resume with the instruction, Type your e-mail address, to select it.

● Click the e-mail entry in the Office Clipboard to paste it in the document at the location of the selected content control (Figure 3–67).

● Click the Close button on the Clipboard task pane title bar.

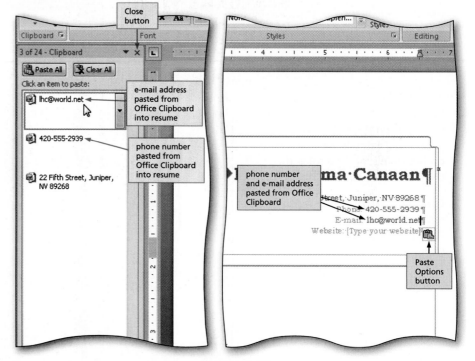

Figure 3–67

Other Ways

1. With Clipboard task pane displayed, right-click selected item, click Paste on shortcut menu

2. With Clipboard task pane displayed, press CTRL+V

Paste Options Button

When you paste items into a document, Word automatically displays the Paste Options button on the screen. The Paste Options button allows you to change the format of pasted items. For example, you can instruct Word to format the pasted text the same as the text from where it was copied or format it the same as the text to where it was pasted. You also can have Word remove all extra non-text characters that were pasted. For example, if you included a paragraph mark when copying at the end of a line in the address of the resume, the Paste Options button allows you to remove the paragraph mark from the pasted text.

To Change Font Color

The phone and e-mail labels should be the same color as the other contact information. Currently, they are a shade different from each other. The following steps change text color to the most recently used color.

1 Drag through the text, Phone:, to select it. Move the mouse pointer into the transparent Mini toolbar, so that it changes to a bright toolbar. Click the Font Color button on the Mini toolbar to change the color of the Phone: label to the color displayed on the button.

2 Drag through the text, E-mail:, to select it. Move the mouse pointer into the transparent Mini toolbar, so that it changes to a bright toolbar. Click the Font Color button on the Mini toolbar to change the color of the E-mail: label.

To Delete Text and Lines

You do not have a Web address. Thus, the Website content control, its corresponding label, and the line should be deleted. The following steps delete text.

1
- Drag through the text to be deleted, as shown in Figure 3–68.

2
- Press the DELETE key to delete the label and content control.

- Press the UP ARROW key to position the insertion point at the end of the e-mail address.

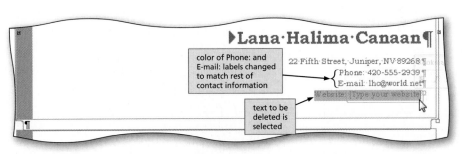

Figure 3–68

- Press the DELETE key to delete the extra paragraph mark and line below the e-mail address.

Other Ways
1. With text selected, click Cut button on Home tab   2. Right-click selected text, click Cut on shortcut menu   3. With text selected, press CTRL+X

To Zoom the Document

The text in the resume is a little small for you to read. The following step changes the zoom to 110 percent.

1 Use the Zoom slider to change the zoom to 110% (Figure 3–69).

Figure 3–69

To Enter More Text in Content Controls

The next step is to select content controls in the resume and replace their instructions with personal information. The following steps enter text in the Objectives and some of the Education sections of the resume.

1 Scroll to position the Objectives section near the top of the document window. In the Objectives section of the resume, click the content control with the instruction, Type the objectives. Type `To obtain a full-time culinary instructor position with a culinary academy, school, or institute in the Juniper area.`

2 In the Education section of the resume, click the content control with the instruction, Type the degree. Type `B.S. Culinary Arts` and then click the content control with the instruction, Type the completion date.

3 Type `Nevada Culinary Institute, May 2008` and then click the content control with the instruction, Type list of accomplishments. Type `Dean's List, six semesters` and then press the ENTER key. Type `Moeller Nutrition Award, January 2008` and then press the ENTER key. Type `Marge Rae Outstanding Student Scholarship, 2006 - 2008` and then press the ENTER key. Type `Baker Food Preparation Contest, 1st Place, November 2008` (Figure 3–70).

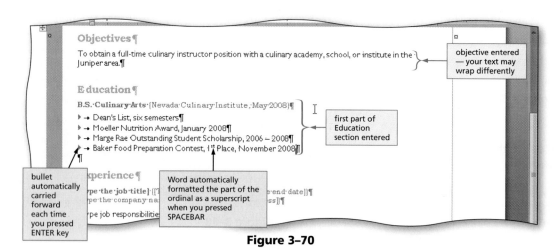

Figure 3–70

To Enter a Line Break

The next step in personalizing the resume is to enter the areas of concentration in the education section. You want only the first line that says, Areas of concentration:, to begin with a bullet. If you press the ENTER key on subsequent lines, Word automatically will carry forward the paragraph formatting, which includes the bullet. Thus, you will not press the ENTER key between each line. Instead, you will create a **line break**, which advances the insertion point to the beginning of the next physical line, ignoring any paragraph formatting. The following steps enter the areas of concentration using a line break, instead of a paragraph break, between each line.

• Press the ENTER key.

• Type `Areas of concentration:` and then press SHIFT+ENTER to insert a line break character and move the insertion point to the beginning of the next physical line (Figure 3–71).

Figure 3–71

2

- Type Food Planning and Preparation and then press SHIFT+ENTER.

- Type Food Safety and then press SHIFT+ENTER.

- Type Nutrition and then press SHIFT+ENTER.

- Type Regional and International Cuisine as the last entry. Do not press SHIFT+ENTER at the end of this line (Figure 3–72).

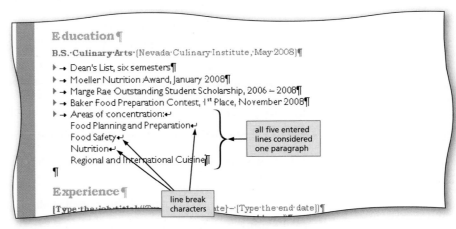

Figure 3–72

BTW

Line Break Character
Line break characters do not print. A line break character is a formatting mark that indicates a line break at the end of the line.

To Change Spacing Below Paragraphs

The blank paragraph below the Education section has spacing after (below) of 6 point. You do not want space below this paragraph because you want enough room for all the resume text. The following steps change the spacing after to 0 point.

1 Position the insertion point in the paragraph to be adjusted, in this case, the paragraph mark below the Education section on the resume.

2 Display the Page Layout tab.

3 Click the Spacing After box down arrow on the Page Layout tab as many times as necessary until 0 pt is displayed in the Spacing After text box (Figure 3–73).

Figure 3–73

To Enter More Text in Content Controls

The next step is to select content controls in the Experience section of the resume and replace their instructions with personalized information.

1 In the Experience section of the resume, click the content control with the instruction, Type the job title.

2 Type `Chef Intern` and then bold the text, Chef Intern.

3 Click the content control with the instruction, Type the start date.

4 Type `September 2006` and then click the content control with the instruction, Type the end date.

5 Type `May 2008` and then click the content control with the instruction, Type the company name.

6 Type `The Garden Grill` and then click the content control with the instruction, Type the company address.

7 Type `Juniper, NV` as the company address.

To Indent a Paragraph

In the resume, the lines below the job title that contain the company name and job responsibilities are to be indented, so that the job titles are easier to see. The following step indents the left edge of a paragraph.

1

- Display the Home tab.

- With the insertion point in the paragraph to indent, click the Increase Indent button on the Home tab to indent the paragraph one-half inch (Figure 3–74).

 Q&A

Why did the paragraph indent one-half inch?

Each time you click the Increase Indent button, the current paragraph indents one-half inch. Similarly, when you click the Decrease Indent button, the paragraph decreases the indent by one-half inch.

Figure 3–74

 Experiment

- Repeatedly click the Increase Indent and Decrease Indent buttons on the Home tab and watch the left indent of the current paragraph change. When you have finished experimenting, use the Increase Indent and Decrease Indent buttons to set the left margin to the one-inch mark on the ruler.

Other Ways		
1. Drag Left Indent marker on ruler	Indents and Spacing sheet, set indentation in Left text box, click OK button	and Spacing sheet, set indentation in Left text box, click OK button
2. Enter value in Indent Left text box on Page Layout tab		
3. Click Paragraph Dialog Box Launcher on Home tab, click	4. Right-click text, click Paragraph on shortcut menu, click Indents	5. Press CTRL+M

To Change Spacing Below Paragraphs

The next step is to remove the blank space below the company name paragraph, so that the company name and job description paragraphs are closer together. The following steps change the spacing after to 0 point.

1 Display the Page Layout tab.

2 With the insertion point in the paragraph to be adjusted, as shown in Figure 3–74, click the Spacing After box down arrow on the Page Layout tab as many times as necessary until 0 pt is displayed in the Spacing After text box.

To Enter and Format More Text in Content Controls

The next step is to select the job responsibilities content control in the Experience section of the resume and replace its instructions with personal information.

1 In the Experience section of the resume, click the content control with the instruction, Type job responsibilities.

2 Type Assisted chef with meal selection, preparation, and presentation. Assumed chef responsibilities during last semester of school.

3 With the insertion point in the paragraph to be adjusted, in this case, the job responsibilities paragraph, click the Spacing After box down arrow on the Page Layout tab as many times as necessary until 6 pt is displayed in the Spacing After text box.

4 Display the Home tab.

5 Click the Increase Indent button on the Home tab to indent the paragraph one-half inch (Figure 3–75).

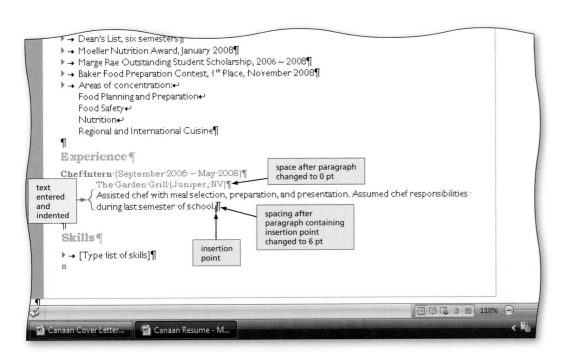

Figure 3–75

To Insert a Building Block Using the Quick Parts Gallery

In this resume, the Experience section contains two jobs. The template, however, inserted content controls for only one job. Word has defined the sections and subsections of the resume in the building blocks, which you can insert in the document. In this case, you want to insert the Experience Subsection building block. The following steps insert a building block.

- Scroll to display the Experience section at the top of the document window.

- Position the insertion point on the paragraph mark below the first job entry.

- Display the Insert tab.

- Click the Quick Parts button on the Insert tab and then scroll through the Quick Parts gallery until Experience Subsection is displayed (Figure 3–76).

Figure 3–76

- Click Experience Subsection in the Quick Parts gallery to insert the building block in the document at the location of the insertion point.

- Press the DELETE key to remove the extra paragraph mark inserted with the building block (Figure 3–77).

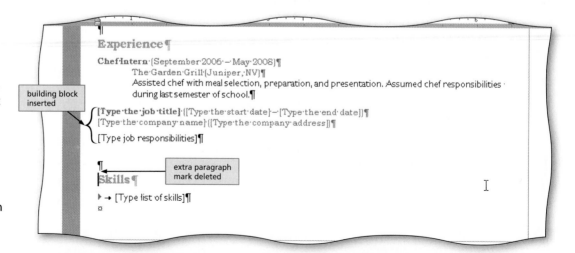

Figure 3–77

To Enter and Format the Experience Subsection and the Skills Section

The next step is to select content controls in the Experience Subsection building block just inserted and the Skills section in the resume and replace the instructions with personal information.

1 Enter Assistant Cook as the job title and then bold the job title. Enter September 2004 as the start date. Enter August 2006 as the end date. Enter Nevada Culinary Institute Cafeteria as the company name. Enter Juniper, NV as the company address.

2 Display the Home tab. With the insertion point in the paragraph to indent (company address line), click the Increase Indent button on the Home tab to indent the paragraph one-half inch.

3 Display the Page Layout tab. With the insertion point in the paragraph to be adjusted (company address line), change the Spacing After to 0 point.

4 Enter this text for the job responsibilities: Planned meals for staff and students. Prepared salads, soups, sandwiches, entrees, and desserts.

5 With the insertion point in the paragraph to be adjusted, in this case, the job responsibilities paragraph, change Spacing After to 0 point.

6 Display the Home tab. Click the Increase Indent button on the Home tab to indent the paragraph one-half inch.

7 In the Skills section, click the content control with the instruction, Type list of skills, to select it. Type National Honor Society and then press the ENTER key. Type Culinary Arts Association and then press the ENTER key. Type Nutrition Services of America and then press the ENTER key. Type Student Government Association, President and then press the ENTER key. Enter Nevada Restaurant Federation as the last skill (Figure 3–78).

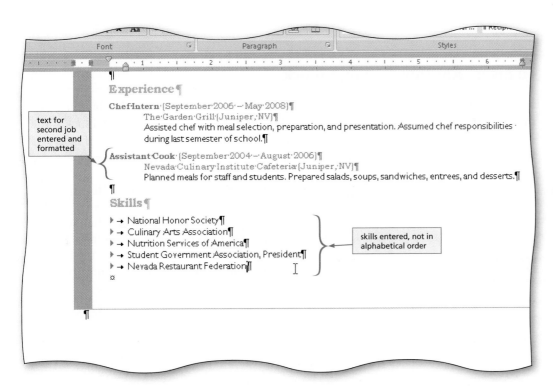

Figure 3–78

To Sort Paragraphs

The next step is to alphabetize the paragraphs in the Skills section of the resume. In Word, you can arrange paragraphs in alphabetic, numeric, or date order based on the first character in each paragraph. Ordering characters in this manner is called **sorting**. The following steps sort paragraphs.

1

- Drag through the paragraphs to be sorted, in this case, the list of skills.

- Click the Sort button on the Home tab to display the Sort Text dialog box (Figure 3–79).

Q&A

What does ascending mean?

Ascending means to sort in alphabetic, numeric or earliest-to-latest date order.

Figure 3–79

2

- Click the OK button to close the dialog box and instruct Word to alphabetize the selected paragraphs.

To Insert Another Building Block

The last section of the resume is the Community Service section. No building block exists for this section; however, the format of the Reference Section building block is the same format you would like for the Community Service section. Thus, you will insert the Reference Section building block and modify its text. The following steps insert a building block.

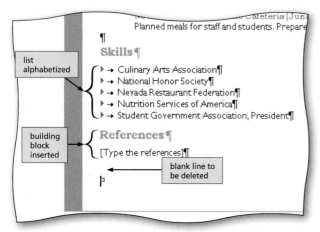

Figure 3–80

1 Position the insertion point on the line below the Skills section on the resume. Display the Insert tab. Click the Quick Parts button on the Insert tab and then scroll through the Quick Parts gallery until Reference Section is displayed. Click Reference Section to insert the building block in the document at the location of the insertion point (Figure 3–80).

2 Press the BACKSPACE key to remove the extra blank line inserted with the building block.

To Enter and Format the Community Service Section

The next step is to select content controls in the section just inserted in the resume and replace its instructions with community service information.

1 Change the title, References, to Community Service.

2 Display the Page Layout tab. With the insertion point in the paragraph to be adjusted (Community Service heading), change the Spacing Before to 12 point.

3 In the last content control, type Prepare food and serve meals at Hope Mission every week.

4 With the insertion point in the paragraph to be adjusted, in this case, the community services paragraph, change Spacing After to 0 point (Figure 3–81).

5 If the document flows to a second page, reduce the space after internal paragraphs so that it fits on a single page.

Figure 3–81

To Change Theme Colors

The cover letter created earlier in this chapter used the Urban color scheme. Because you will be mailing the resume along with the cover letter, you decide also to use the Urban color scheme for the resume. The following step changes theme colors.

1 Display the Home tab. Click the Change Styles button on the Home tab, point to Colors on the Change Styles menu, and then click Urban in the Colors gallery to change the document theme colors to Urban.

To Print Preview a Document

To see exactly how a document will look when you print it, you could display it in print preview. **Print preview** displays the entire document in reduced size on the Word screen. In print preview, you can edit and format text, adjust margins, view multiple pages, reduce the document to fit on a single page, and print the document. The following steps view and print the resume in print preview.

1

- Click the Office Button and then point to Print on the Office Button menu (Figure 3–82).

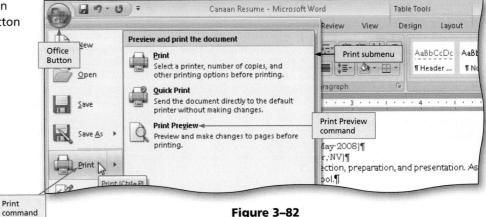

Figure 3–82

2

- Click Print Preview on the Print submenu to display the document in print preview (Figure 3–83).

- If necessary, click the One Page button on the Print Preview tab to display the document as one readable page in the window.

- Click the Print button on the Print Preview tab and then click the OK button in the Print dialog box to print the resume, as shown in Figure 3–2 on page WD 148.

- Click the Close Print Preview button on the Print Preview tab to redisplay the resume in the document window.

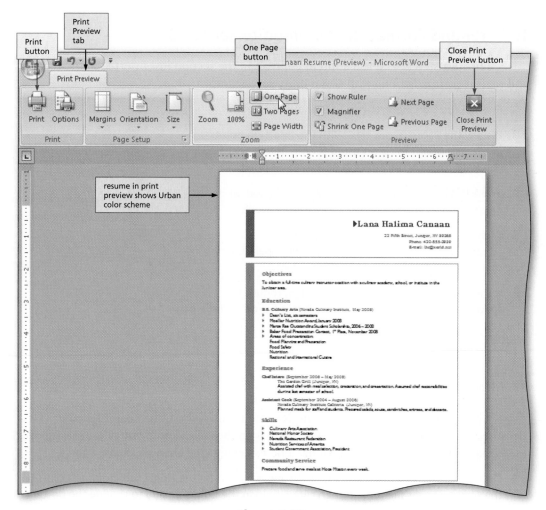

Figure 3–83

Print Preview

If you want to display two pages in print preview, click the Two Pages button on the Print Preview tab. With the Magnifier check box on the Print Preview tab selected, you can click in the document to zoom in or out. Magnifying a page does not affect the printed document. To edit a document, remove the check mark from the Magnifier check box and then edit the text. If a document spills onto a second page by a line or two, click the Shrink One Page button and Word will try to fit all content on a single page.

To Change Document Properties and Save Again

Before saving the resume a final time, you want to add your name, course and section, and some keywords as document properties. The following steps use the Document Information Panel to change document properties and then save the document again.

1 Display the Office Button menu, point to Prepare on the Office Button menu, and then click Properties on the Prepare submenu to display the Document Information Panel.

2 Enter your name in the Author text box. Enter your course and section in the Subject text box. Enter the text, Resume, in the Keywords text box.

3 Close the Document Information Panel.

4 Click the Save button on the Quick Access Toolbar to overwrite the previous Canaan Resume file on the USB flash drive.

Addressing and Printing Envelopes and Mailing Labels

With Word, you can print address information on an envelope or on a mailing label. Computer-printed addresses look more professional than handwritten ones. Thus, the following steps address and print an envelope.

To Address and Print an Envelope

 1

- Switch to the cover letter by clicking its program button on the Windows Vista taskbar.

- Close the Clipboard task pane.

- Scroll through the cover letter to display the inside address in the document window.

- Drag through the inside address to select it (Figure 3–84).

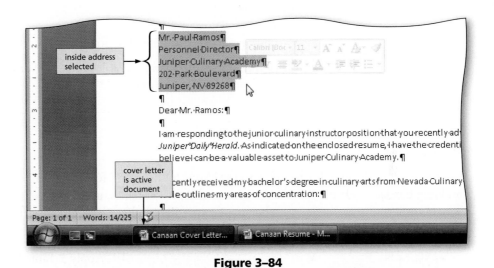

Figure 3–84

2

- Click Mailings on the Ribbon to display the Mailings tab.

- Click the Create Envelopes button on the Mailings tab to display the Envelopes and Labels dialog box.

- If necessary, click the Envelopes tab in the dialog box.

- Click the Return address text box.

- Type Lana Halima Canaan and then press the ENTER key.

- Type 22 Fifth Street and then press the ENTER key.

- Type Juniper, NV 89268 (Figure 3–85).

- Insert an envelope in your printer, as shown in the Feed area of the dialog box (your Feed area may be different depending on your printer).

- Click the Print button in the Envelopes and Labels dialog box to print the envelope.

- If a dialog box is displayed, click the No button.

Figure 3–85

BTW

Certification
The Microsoft Certified Application Specialist (MCAS) program provides an opportunity for you to obtain a valuable industry credential — proof that you have the Word 2007 skills required by employers. For more information, see Appendix G or visit the Word 2007 Certification Web page (scsite.com/wd2007/cert).

Envelopes and Labels

Instead of printing the envelope immediately, you can add it to the document by clicking the Add to Document button in the Envelopes and Labels dialog box. To specify a different envelope or label type (identified by a number on the box of envelopes or labels), click the Options button in the Envelopes and Labels dialog box.

Instead of printing an envelope, you can print a mailing label. To do this, click the Labels tab in the Envelopes and Labels dialog box (Figure 3–85 on the previous page). Type the delivery address in the Address box. To print the same address on all labels on the page, click Full page of the same label. Click the Print button in the dialog box.

To Quit Word

This project is complete. The following step quits Word.

 Click the Office Button and then click the Exit Word button on the Office Button menu to close all open documents and quit Word.

Chapter Summary

In this chapter, you have learned how to use Word to insert and format clip art, set and use tab stops, create and insert building blocks, insert the current date, insert and format tables, use print preview, copy and paste, and use templates. The items listed below include all the new Word skills you have learned in this chapter.

1. Use the Grow Font Button to Increase Font Size (WD 151)
2. Color Text (WD 152)
3. Insert Clip Art (WD 153)
4. Resize a Graphic Using the Size Dialog Box (WD 155)
5. Recolor a Graphic (WD 156)
6. Set a Transparent Color in a Graphic (WD 157)
7. Set Custom Tab Stops Using the Tabs Dialog Box (WD 158)
8. Bottom Border a Paragraph (WD 161)
9. Clear Formatting (WD 162)
10. Convert a Hyperlink to Regular Text (WD 163)
11. Create a New File from an Existing File (WD 165)
12. Set Custom Tab Stops Using the Ruler (WD 167)
13. Insert the Current Date in a Document (WD 168)
14. Create a Building Block (WD 170)
15. Insert a Nonbreaking Space (WD 171)
16. Insert a Building Block (WD 172)
17. Insert an Empty Table (WD 173)
18. Enter Data in a Table (WD 175)
19. Apply a Table Style (WD 176)
20. Resize Table Columns to Fit Table Contents (WD 177)
21. Bullet a List as You Type (WD 180)
22. Use a Template (WD 183)
23. Delete Rows (WD 186)
24. Modify Text in a Content Control (WD 187)
25. Switch from One Open Document to Another (WD 189)
26. Copy Items to the Office Clipboard (WD 189)
27. Paste from the Office Clipboard (WD 191)
28. Delete Text and Lines (WD 193)
29. Enter a Line Break (WD 194)
30. Indent a Paragraph (WD 196)
31. Insert a Building Block Using the Quick Parts Gallery (WD 198)
32. Sort Paragraphs (WD 200)
33. Print Preview a Document (WD 201)
34. Address and Print an Envelope (WD 203)

 If you have a SAM user profile, you may have access to hands-on instruction, practice, and assessment. Log in to your SAM account (http://sam2007.course.com) to launch any assigned training activities or exams that relate to the skills covered in this chapter.

Learn It Online

Test your knowledge of chapter content and key terms.

Instructions: To complete the Learn It Online exercises, start your browser, click the Address bar, and then enter the Web address scsite.com/wd2007/learn. When the Word 2007 Learn It Online page is displayed, click the link for the exercise you want to complete and then read the instructions.

Chapter Reinforcement TF, MC, and SA
A series of true/false, multiple choice, and short answer questions that test your knowledge of the chapter content.

Flash Cards
An interactive learning environment where you identify chapter key terms associated with displayed definitions.

Practice Test
A series of multiple choice questions that test your knowledge of chapter content and key terms.

Who Wants To Be a Computer Genius?
An interactive game that challenges your knowledge of chapter content in the style of a television quiz show.

Wheel of Terms
An interactive game that challenges your knowledge of chapter key terms in the style of the television show *Wheel of Fortune*.

Crossword Puzzle Challenge
A crossword puzzle that challenges your knowledge of key terms presented in the chapter.

Apply Your Knowledge

Reinforce the skills and apply the concepts you learned in this chapter.

Working with Tabs and a Table
Instructions: Start Word. Open the document, Apply 3-1 Expenses Table Draft, from the Data Files for Students. See the inside back cover of this book for instructions on downloading the Data Files for Students, or contact your instructor for information about accessing the required files.

The document is a Word table that you are to edit and format. The revised table is shown in Figure 3–86.

Monthly Club Expenses

	January	February	March	April
Decorations	170.88	129.72	74.43	167.85
Postage	65.90	62.90	40.19	69.91
Computer Supplies	17.29	18.50	72.50	19.12
Paper Supplies	46.57	41.67	38.82	48.70
Food/Beverages	122.04	99.88	55.43	100.00
Hall Rental	120.00	120.00	120.00	120.00
Total	542.68	472.67	401.37	525.58

Figure 3–86

Continued >

STUDENT ASSIGNMENTS

Apply Your Knowledge *continued*

Perform the following tasks:

1. In the line containing the table title, Monthly Club Expenses, remove the tab stop at the 1" mark on the ruler.

2. Set a centered tab at the 3.25" mark on the ruler.

3. Bold the characters in the title. Increase their font size to 14. Change their color to Red, Accent 2, Darker 25%.

4. Add a new row to the bottom of the table. In the first cell of the new row, type Total as the entry. Enter these values in the next three cells: January – 542.68; February – 472.67; April – 525.58.

5. Delete the row containing the Duplicating Fees expenses.

6. Insert a column between the February and April columns. Fill in the column as follows: Column Title – March; Decorations – 74.43; Postage – 40.19; Computer Supplies – 72.50; Paper Supplies – 38.82; Food/Beverages – 55.43; Hall Rental – 120.00; Total – 401.37.

7. In the Design tab, remove the check mark from the Banded Rows check box. Place a check mark in the Total Row check box. The three check boxes that should have check marks are Header Row, Total Row, and First Column. Apply the Medium Grid 3 - Accent 1 style to the table.

8. Make all columns as wide as their contents (AutoFit Contents).

9. Center the table between the left and right margins of the page.

10. Change the document properties, as specified by your instructor.

11. Click the Office Button and then click Save As. Save the document using the file name, Apply 3-1 Expenses Table Modified.

12. Print the document properties.

13. Print the revised table, shown in Figure 3–86.

Extend Your Knowledge

Extend the skills you learned in this chapter and experiment with new skills. You may need to use Help to complete the assignment.

Working with Pictures, Symbols, Borders, and Tables

Instructions: Start Word. Open the document, Extend 3-1 Club Letter Draft, from the Data Files for Students. See the inside back cover of this book for instructions on downloading the Data Files for Students, or contact your instructor for information about accessing the required files.

You will flip the clip art, insert symbols, add a decorative border, add totals to the table, modify the table style, and print mailing labels.

Perform the following tasks:

1. Use Help to learn about rotating objects, inserting symbols, working with borders, entering formulas, and printing mailing labels.

2. Flip the image in the letterhead horizontally so that the fruit faces toward the middle of the letter instead of toward the margin.

3. In the letterhead, replace the asterisk characters that separate the address, phone, and e-mail information with a symbol in one of the Wingdings fonts (Figure 3–87).

4. Remove the bottom border in the letterhead. Add a new bottom border that has a color and style different from the default Word border.

5. Add a row to the bottom of the table with a label indicating it contains totals. For each of the columns, use the Formula button on the Layout tab to sum the contents of the column. Write down the formula that Word uses to sum the contents of a column. Add a column to the right of the table with a label indicating it contains totals. For each of the rows, use a formula to sum the row. Write down the formula that Word uses to sum the contents of a row.

6. Change the table style. One at a time, select and deselect each check box in the Table Style Options group. Write down the function of each check box: Header Row, Total Row, Banded Rows, First Column, Last Column, and Banded Columns. Select the check boxes you prefer for the table.

7. Change the document properties, as specified by your instructor. Save the revised document using a new file name and then submit it in the format specified by your instructor.

8. Print a single mailing label for the letter.

9. Print a full page of mailing labels, each containing the address shown in Figure 3-87.

Figure 3-87

Make It Right

Analyze a document and correct all errors and/or improve the design.

Formatting a Business Letter

Instructions: Start Word. Open the document, Make It Right 3-1 Cover Letter Draft, from the Data Files for Students. See the inside back cover of this book for instructions about downloading the Data Files for Students, or contact your instructor for information on accessing the required files.

The document is a cover letter that is missing elements and formatted incorrectly (Figure 3–88). You are to insert and format clip art in the letterhead, change the color of the text and graphic, change the letter style from block to modified block, sort a list, and format the table.

Figure 3–88

Perform the following tasks:

1. Locate and insert an appropriate clip art image. If you have access to the Internet, use one from the Web. Resize the graphic, if necessary.

2. Change the color of the text in the letterhead. Recolor the graphic to match the color of the text. Format one color in the graphic as transparent.

3. The letter currently is the block letter style. It should be the modified block letter style. Format the appropriate paragraphs by setting custom tab stops and then positioning those paragraphs at the tab stops. Be sure to position the insertion point in the paragraph before setting the tab stop.

4. Sort the paragraphs in the bulleted list.

5. Center the table. Apply a table style of your choice. Resize the table columns to fit the contents of the cells.

6. Change the document properties, as specified by your instructor. Save the revised document using a new file name and then submit it in the format specified by your instructor.

In the Lab

Design and/or create a document using the guidelines, concepts, and skills presented in this chapter. Labs are listed in order of increasing difficulty.

Lab 1: Creating a Cover Letter with a Table

Problem: You are a student at Norson Central College. Graduation is approaching quickly and you would like a part-time job while furthering your studies. Thus, you prepare the cover letter shown in Figure 3–89.

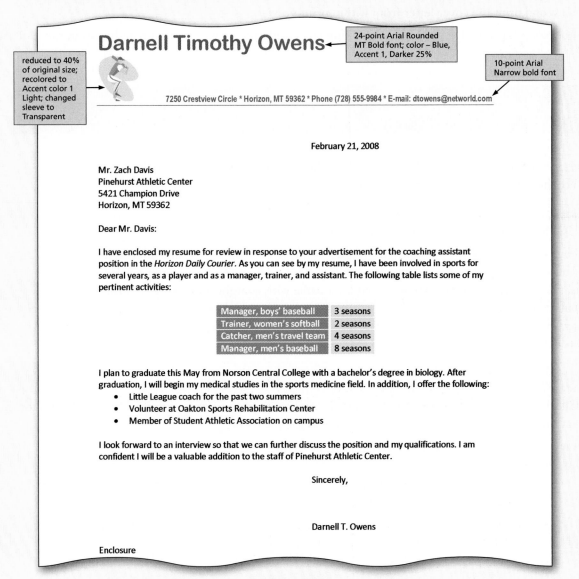

Figure 3–89

Continued >

In the Lab *continued*

Perform the following tasks:

1. Create the letterhead shown at the top of Figure 3–89 on the previous page. Insert the clip art image and then resize and format it as indicated in the figure. Remove the hyperlink format from the e-mail address. If necessary, clear formatting after entering the bottom border. Save the letterhead with the file name, Lab 3-1 Owens Letterhead.

2. Create the letter shown in Figure 3–89. Set a tab stop at the 3.5" mark on the ruler for the date line, complimentary close, and signature block. Insert the current date. After entering the inside address, create a building block for Pinehurst Athletic Center and insert the building block whenever you have to enter the company name. Insert nonbreaking space characters in the newspaper name. Insert and center the table. Format the table using the Medium Grid 3 - Accent 1 table style. Select only the First Column check box in the Table Style Options group. Adjust the column widths so that they are as wide as the contents of the cells. Bullet the list as you type it.

3. Check the spelling of the letter. Change the document properties, as specified by your instructor. Save the letter with Lab 3-1 Owens Cover Letter as the file name.

4. View and print the cover letter from within print preview.

5. Address and print an envelope and a mailing label using the inside and return addresses in the cover letter.

In the Lab

Lab 2: Creating a Resume from a Template

Problem: You are a nursing student at Ferrell College. As graduation is approaching quickly, you prepare the resume shown in Figure 3–90 using one of Word's resume templates.

Perform the following tasks:

1. Use the Equity Resume template to create a resume.

2. Personalize the resume as shown in Figure 3–90. Use your own name and address information when you personalize the resume. If necessary, drag the blue-dotted column border to the right of the name to the right, to make room for a name with a larger font size. Insert the Experience Subsection building block, so that you can enter the second job. Indent the text in the Experience section as shown. Enter line break characters between the job responsibility lines. Adjust line spacing in the Experience section, so that it matches Figure 3–90. Change the title, Skills, to the word, Activities.

3. Change the theme fonts to Aspect.

4. Check the spelling of the resume. Change the document properties, as specified by your instructor. Save the resume with Lab 3-2 Marsh Resume as the file name.

5. View and print the resume from within print preview.

Constance Leah Marsh

Phone: 504-555-8272

322 East Center Street
Apollo, WY 83163
E-mail: clmarsh@world.net

Objectives

To secure a nursing position at a primary care facility.

Education

May 2008 | Ferrell College, Apollo, Wyoming
- B.S., Nursing
- Certified Nursing Assistant

Experience

January 2007 – May 2008 | Health Care Assistant
Prime Assisted Living | Apollo, Wyoming
Organized daily activities and events for patients
Acted as receptionist at front desk as needed
Assisted patients with personal care, grooming, and medical needs

September 2005 – December 2006 |Nursing Assistant
Clearview Hospital | Apollo, Wyoming
Assisted nursing staff with patient care
Directed calls and patient visitors
Updated files and charts

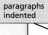
paragraphs indented

Activities

- Volunteer at a local hospital reading to patients
- Teach Pilates class for seniors at Halwell Physical Therapy Center
- Member of local women's outreach group promoting literacy
- Volunteer at Women's Health Center twice a month

Figure 3–90

In the Lab

Lab 3: Creating a Letter

Problem: You are a president of the Parents Educational Organization for the local high school. The organization currently is taking nominations for outstanding teacher award and you write thank-you letters to nominators, also asking them for donations.

Instructions: Prepare the letter shown in Figure 3–91. Follow the guidelines in the modified semi-block letter style. Use proper spacing between elements of the letter. Check the spelling of the letter. Change the document properties, as specified by your instructor. Save the letter with Lab 3-3 Ling Letter as the file name.

Kim S. Ling
Parents Educational Organization
99 Ohio Avenue, Harrust, NH 03891
(317) 555-1865 * E-mail: ksling@net.com

February 14, 2008

Ms. Laura Ennis
74 MacEnroe Court
Fairview, IN 46142

Dear Ms. Ennis:

Thank you for your recent nomination of Mr. Serensi from Bakersville North High School for our outstanding teacher award. He will be pleased that you believe he was a great influence in your decision to become a teacher.

In addition to the honor of being selected outstanding teacher, we present our candidates with a monetary gift. They use the funds for future classroom needs, including:
- Reading materials to be kept in the classroom
- Emergency funds to assist students in need of supplies
- Supplies for additional projects to be determined by teacher
- Guest author and speaker visits

If you are interested in donating to this worthy cause, please contact me via e-mail or telephone. All donors' names are engraved on a plaque on display in the school auditorium. Listed in the table below are the donation levels.

Donation Level	Donation Amount
Gold	$500
Silver	$250
Bronze	$100

Again, we thank you for your interest in our project.

Yours truly,

Kim Ling
President

Figure 3–91

Cases and Places

Apply your creative thinking and problem solving skills to design and implement a solution.

● EASIER ●● MORE DIFFICULT

● 1: Create a Fax Cover Sheet from a Template

Your boss has asked you to send a fax that includes a fax cover sheet. In the New Document dialog box, click Installed Templates in the Templates pane and then click Equity Fax in the Installed Templates list. Click in each area to enter the following information in the fax cover sheet: the fax is from your boss, Max Henreich; the fax should go to Shirelle Bradley; her fax number is (317) 555-0922; the fax contains three pages; and the phone is (317) 555-1350. Use today's date for the date. The Re: area should contain the following text: Site visit materials. Leave the CC: field blank. The For Review check box should be checked, and your boss wants the following comment on the cover sheet: Here are the notes for tomorrow's site visit.

● 2: Create this Chapter's Resume Using a Different Template

Information can look and be perceived completely differently simply by virtue of the way it is presented. Take the resume created in this chapter and create it using a different template. For example, try the Equity, Median, Oreil, or Urban Resume template in the Installed Templates list. Make sure each section of the resume in this chapter is presented in the new document. You may need to rename or delete sections and add building blocks. Open the resume you created in this chapter and use the copy and paste commands to simplify entering the text. Select a theme you like best for the finished resume.

●● 3: Create a Memo Using a Template from the Web

As assistant director of programs at a local park, you are responsible for soliciting ideas from employees regarding future programs and activities. In the New Document dialog box, click Memos in the Microsoft Office Online area to create a memo. Select a template you like. Use the following information to complete the memo: the memo should go to all staff members; the meeting will be held in room A42 on March 14, 2008 at 3:00 p.m.; attendees should be prepared to discuss their ideas for spring and summer activities; and attendance is mandatory. Mention that if anyone is to be on vacation or unavailable, he or she should contact you prior to the meeting to arrange for submission of activities lists.

●● 4: Create Your Resume and Cover Letter for a Potential Job

Make It Personal

Assume you are graduating this semester and need to find a job immediately after graduation. Check a local newspaper or online employment source to find an advertisement for a job relating to your major or a job for which you believe you are qualified. Use the techniques you learned in this chapter to create your resume and a cover letter. Tailor your cover letter and your resume to fit the job description. Make sure you include an objective, education, and work experience section. Also include any other pertinent sections. Use the copy and paste commands on the Office Clipboard to copy your name and address information from one document to the other.

Continued >

Cases and Places *continued*

•• 5: Create Documents Using Templates from the Web

Working Together

As active members of your school's Travel and Leisure Club, you have been assigned the task of publicizing the club's upcoming activities and soliciting new memberships. Assign each team member one of the following tasks: create a calendar listing various club activities for a three-month period, including any scheduled trips, parties, or meetings; design an award or certificate for excellence or other recognition presented to your club by another campus group; compose a letter of thanks from a past member; and create an invitation to join the Travel and Leisure Club. Visit Microsoft Office Online to obtain templates for awards and certificates, calendars, and invitations. Then, as a group, write a cover letter soliciting memberships and listing the reasons why students should join the club. Include a table or bulleted list similar to those used in this chapter. Make the package attractive and eye-catching.

Web Feature

Creating a Web Page Using Word

Objectives

You will have mastered the material in this feature when you can:

- Save a Word document as a Web page
- Insert a hyperlink

- Add a background color with a pattern
- Use Windows Explorer to view a Web page

Web Feature Introduction

Many people have personal Web pages, allowing them to share personal information with users around the world. Job seekers often post their resume on the Web so that potential employers can search for and view their resumes online. With Word, you easily can save any existing document as a Web page. You then can post your Web page to a Web server.

Project — Web Page

Personal Web pages contain text, documents, images, links, videos, and audio. If you have created a document using an Office program, such as Word, you can save it in a format that can be opened by a Web browser.

The project in this feature illustrates how to save the resume created in Chapter 3 as a Web page (Figure 1a). The resume itself contains an e-mail address formatted as a hyperlink. When you click the e-mail address, Word starts your e-mail program automatically with the recipient's address (lhc@world.net) already filled in. You simply type a subject and message (Figure 1b) and then click the Send button. Clicking the Send button places the message in the Outbox or sends it if you are connected to an e-mail server.

Overview

As you read through this feature, you will learn how to create the resume Web page shown in Figure 1a by performing these general tasks:

- Save a Word document as a Web page.
- Format the Web page.
- Use Windows Explorer to view a Web page.

Plan Ahead

> **General Project Guidelines**
> When creating a resume Web page, the actions you perform and decisions you make will affect the appearance and characteristics of the finished document. As you create a resume Web page, such as the project shown in Figure 1a, you should follow these general guidelines:
>
> 1. **Craft a successful resume.** Your resume should present, at a minimum, your contact information, objective, educational background, and work experience to a potential employer. It should honestly present all your positive points. Ask someone else to proofread your resume and give you suggestions for improvements.
>
> 2. **Create a resume Web page from your resume Word document.** Save the Word document as a Web page. Improve the usability of the resume Web page by making your e-mail address a link to an e-mail program. Enhance the look of the Web page by adding, for example, a background color. Be sure to test your finished Web page document in at least one browser program to be sure it looks and works as you intended.
>
> 3. **Publish your resume Web page.** Once you have created a Web page, you can publish it. **Publishing** is the process of making a Web page available to others on a network, such as the Internet or a company's intranet. In Word, you can publish a Web page by saving it to a Web server or to an FTP site. Many Internet access providers offer storage space on their Web servers at no cost to their subscribers. The procedures for using Microsoft Office to publish a Web page are discussed in Appendix D.
>
> This Web Feature focuses on the second guideline, identifying the actions you perform and the decisions you make during the creation of the resume Web page shown in Figure 1a.

browser window

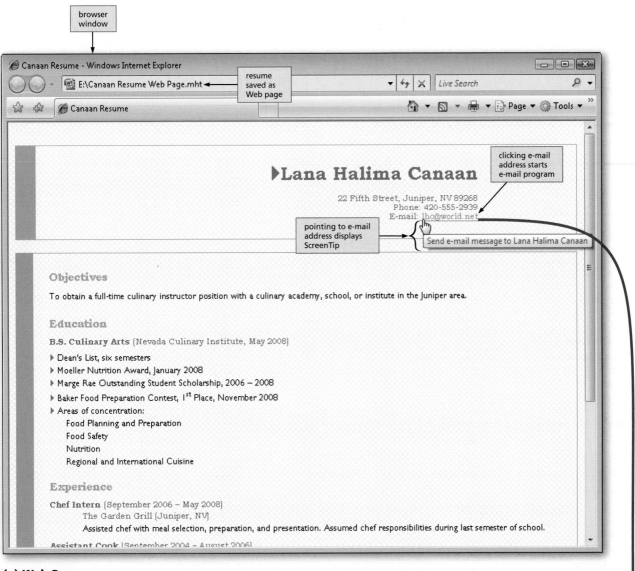

(a) Web Page Displaying Resume

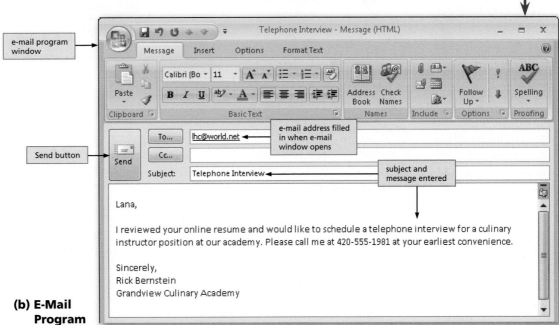

(b) E-Mail Program

Figure 1

Saving a Word Document as a Web Page

Once you have created a Word document, you can save it as a Web page so that it can be published and then viewed in a Web browser, such as Internet Explorer. When you save a file as a Web page, Word converts the contents of the document into **HTML** (hypertext markup language), which is a language that browsers can interpret. Some of Word's formatting features are not supported by Web pages. Thus, your Web page may look slightly different from the original Word document.

When saving a document as a Web page, you have three choices in Word:

- The **single file Web page format** saves all of the components of the Web page in a single file that has an .mht extension. This format is particularly useful for e-mailing documents in HTML format.

- The **Web Page format** saves some of the components of the Web page in a folder, separate from the Web page. This format is useful if you need access to the individual components, such as images, that make up the Web page.

- The **filtered Web Page format** saves the file in Web page format and then reduces the size of the file by removing specific Microsoft Office formats. This format is useful if you want to speed up the time it takes to download a Web page that contains many graphics, video, audio, or animations.

The Web page in this feature uses the single file Web page format.

BTW

Saving as a Web Page
Because you might not have access to a Web server, the Web page you create in this feature is saved on a USB flash drive rather than to a Web server.

To Save a Word Document as a Web Page

The following steps save the resume created in Chapter 3 as a Web page. If you are stepping through this feature on a computer, you will need the resume document named Canaan Resume that was created in Chapter 3. (If you did not create the resume, see your instructor for a copy of it.)

1
- Start Word and then open the file named Canaan Resume created in Chapter 3.

2
- With the resume file open in the document window, click the Office Button and then point to Save As on the Office Button menu to display the Save As submenu (Figure 2).

Figure 2

- Click Other Formats on the Save As sub-menu to display the Save As dialog box.

- Type `Canaan Resume Web Page` in the File name text box to change the file name. If necessary, change the Save location to UDISK 2.0 (E:). (Your USB flash drive may have a different name and letter.)

- Click the Save as type box arrow and then click Single File Web Page.

- Click the Change Title button to display the Set Page Title dialog box.

- Type `Canaan Resume` in the Page title text box (Figure 3).

Figure 3

- Click the OK button in the Set Page Title dialog box.

- Click the Save button in the Save As dialog box to save the resume as a Web page and display it in the document window (Figure 4). (If Word displays a dialog box about compatibility with Web browsers, click the Continue button in the dialog box.)

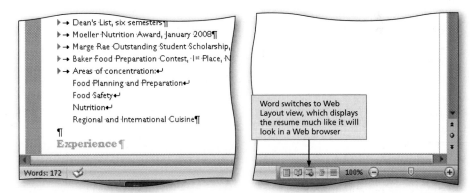

Figure 4

Other Ways

1. Press F12

Saving to a Web Server

If you have access to and can save files to a Web server, then you can save the Web page directly to the Web server by clicking the appropriate network location in the File list in the Save As dialog box. If you have access to a Web server that allows you to save to an FTP site, then you can save to the FTP site by selecting the site below FTP locations in the File list in the Save As dialog box. To learn more about saving Web pages to a Web server or FTP site using Microsoft Office programs, refer to Appendix D.

Formatting a Web Page

In this feature, the e-mail address on the Canaan Resume Web page is formatted as a hyperlink. Also, the background color of the Web page is blue. The following sections modify the Web page to include these enhancements.

To Format Text as a Hyperlink

The e-mail address in the resume Web page should be formatted as a hyperlink. When a Web page visitor clicks the hyperlink-formatted e-mail address, his or her e-mail program starts automatically and displays an e-mail window with the e-mail address already filled in (shown in Figure 1b on page WD 217). The following steps format the e-mail address as a hyperlink.

- Select the e-mail address (lhc@world.net, in this case).

- Display the Insert tab.

- Click the Insert Hyperlink button on the Insert tab to display the Insert Hyperlink dialog box (Figure 5).

- Click E-mail Address in the Link to bar so that the dialog box displays e-mail address settings instead of Web page settings.

- In the 'Text to display' text box, if necessary, type lhc@world.net, which specifies the text that shows on the screen for the hyperlink.

- Click the E-mail address text box and then type lhc@world.net to specify the e-mail address that the Web browser uses when a user clicks the hyperlink.

- Click the ScreenTip button to display the Set Hyperlink ScreenTip dialog box.

- In the text box, type Send e-mail message to Lana Halima Canaan, which is the text that will be displayed when a user points to the hyperlink (Figure 6).

Figure 5

Figure 6

- Click the OK button in each dialog box to format the e-mail address as a hyperlink (Figure 7).

Q&A

How do I know if the hyperlink works?

In Word, you can test the hyperlink by holding down the CTRL key while clicking the hyperlink. In this case, CTRL+clicking the e-mail address should open an e-mail window. If you need to make a change to the hyperlink, right-click it and then click Edit Hyperlink on the shortcut menu.

Figure 7

Other Ways
1. Right-click selected text, click Hyperlink on shortcut menu   2. Select text, press CTRL+K

To Add a Background Color

The next step is to add background color to the Web page so that it looks more eye-catching. Select a color that best represents your personality. This Web page uses a light shade of blue. The following steps add a background color.

- Display the Page Layout tab.

- Click the Page Color button on the Page Layout tab to display the Page Color gallery.

- Point to the sixth color in the second row (Ice Blue, Accent 2, Lighter 80%) to display a live preview of the background color (Figure 8).

🔍 **Experiment**

- Point to various colors in the Page Color gallery and watch the background color change in the document window.

❷

- Click the sixth color in the second row to change the background color to a light shade of blue.

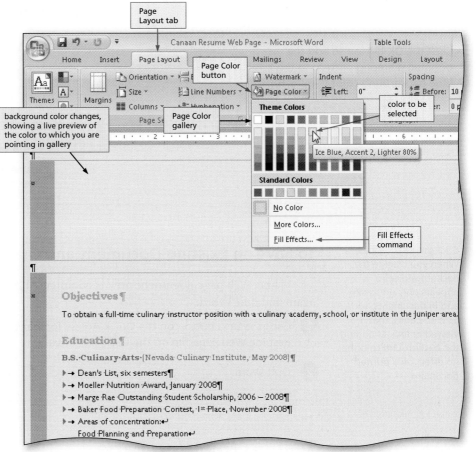

Figure 8

To Add a Pattern Fill Effect to a Background

When you changed the background color in the previous steps, Word placed a solid background color on the screen. For this resume Web page, the solid background color is a little too intense. To soften the background color, you can add patterns to it. The following steps add a pattern to the blue background.

- Click the Page Color button on the Page Layout tab (shown in Figure 8 on the previous page) to display the Page Color gallery again.

- Click Fill Effects in the Page Color gallery (shown in Figure 8) to display the Fill Effects dialog box.

- Click the Pattern tab to display the Pattern sheet in the dialog box.

- Click the Outlined diamond pattern (rightmost pattern in the fifth row) to select it (Figure 9).

Figure 9

- Click the OK button to add the outlined diamond pattern to the blue background color (Figure 10).

Figure 10

Background Colors
When you change the background color, it appears only on-screen and in documents, such as Web pages, that are viewed online. Changing the background color has no effect on a printed document.

To Save an Existing Document and Quit Word

The Web page document now is complete. The following steps save the document again and quit Word.

1 Click the Save button on the Quick Access Toolbar to overwrite the previous Canaan Resume Web Page file on the USB flash drive.

2 Quit Word.

Testing the Web Page

After creating and saving a Web page, you will want to test it in at least one browser to be sure it looks and works the way you intended.

To Test the Web Page in a Web Browser

The following steps use Windows Explorer to display the resume Web page in the Internet Explorer Web browser.

 1

- Click the Start button on the Windows Vista taskbar to display the Start menu.

- Click Computer on the Start menu to display the Computer window.

- If necessary, maximize the Computer window (Figure 11).

Figure 11

 2

- Double-click the USB flash drive icon in the Computer window to display the contents of the USB flash drive (Figure 12).

3

- Double-click the file name, Canaan Resume Web Page, to start the Internet Explorer Web browser and display the file in the browser window (shown in Figure 1a on page WD 217).

- With the Web page document displaying in the Web browser, click the e-mail address link to ensure it displays the e-mail window, as shown in Figure 1b on page WD 217.

Figure 12

 4

- Close all open windows.

BTW

Quick Reference
For a table that lists how to complete the tasks covered in this book using the mouse, Ribbon, shortcut menu, and keyboard, see the Quick Reference Summary at the back of this book, or visit the Word 2007 Quick Reference Web page (scsite.com/wd2007/qr).

Feature Summary

In this feature, you have learned how to save a Word document as a Web page, insert a hyperlink, add background color, and view a Web page. The items listed below include all the new Word skills you have learned in this feature.

1. Save a Word Document as a Web Page (WD 218)
2. Format Text as a Hyperlink (WD 220)
3. Add a Background Color (WD 221)
4. Add a Pattern Fill Effect to a Background (WD 222)
5. Test the Web Page in a Web Browser (WD 223)

If you have a SAM user profile, you may have access to hands-on instruction, practice, and assessment. Log in to your SAM account (http://sam2007.course.com) to launch any assigned training activities or exams that relate to the skills covered in this feature.

In the Lab

Design and/or create a document using the guidelines, concepts, and skills presented in this chapter. Labs are listed in order of increasing difficulty.

Lab 1: Saving a Word Document as a Web Page and in Other Formats

Problem: You created the research paper shown in Figure 2-83 on pages WD 138 and WD 139 in Chapter 2. You decide to save this research paper in a variety of formats. For each of the saved documents, be sure to change the document properties, as specified by your instructor.

Instructions:

1. Open the Lab 2-1 Computer Forensics Paper shown in Figure 2-83. (If you did not create the research paper, see your instructor for a copy.)

2. Save the research paper as a single file Web page using the file name, Lab WF-1 Computer Forensics Paper Web Page A. Print the Web page.

3. Use Internet Explorer to view the Web page.

4. If you have access to a Web server or ftp site, save the Web page to the server or site (see Appendix D for instructions).

5. Using Windows Explorer, look at the contents of the USB flash drive containing the Web page. Write down the names of the files related to Lab 2-1. Open the original Lab 2-1 Computer Forensics Paper. Save it as a Web page (not as a Single File Web Page) using the file name, Lab WF-1 Computer Forensics Paper Web Page B. That is, change the file type in the Save as type box to Web Page. Again, look at the contents of the USB flash drive using Windows Explorer. Write down any additional file names. How many more files and folders are created by the Web Page format?

6. Open the original Lab 2-1 Computer Forensics Paper. Save it as plain text using the file name, Lab WF-1 Computer Forensics Paper Plain Text. That is, change the file type in the Save as type box to Plain Text. Click the OK button if Word displays a File Conversion dialog box. Open the plain text file. *Hint:* In the Open dialog box, click the Files of type box arrow and then click All Files. Write down the difference between the plain text file and the original file.

In the Lab

Lab 2: Creating a Web Page with a Hyperlink

Problem: You created the resume shown in Figure 3-90 on page WD 211 in Chapter 3. You decide to save it as a Web page with the e-mail address as a hyperlink.

Instructions:

1. Open the Lab 3-2 Marsh Resume shown in Figure 3-90. (If you did not create the resume, see your instructor for a copy.)

2. Save the resume as a single file Web page using the file name, Lab WF-2 Marsh Resume Web Page. Change the page title to Constance Marsh. Convert the e-mail address to a hyperlink. Apply the Orange, Accent 1, Lighter 80% background color to the document. Apply the Divot pattern fill effect to the background color. Change the document properties, as specified by your instructor. Save the resume Web page again. View the Web page in Internet Explorer. Test the e-mail address hyperlink. Print the Web page.

3. If you have access to a Web server or ftp site, save the Web page to the server or site (see Appendix D).

Appendix A
Project Planning Guidelines

Using Project Planning Guidelines

The process of communicating specific information to others is a learned, rational skill. Computers and software, especially Microsoft Office 2007, can help you develop ideas and present detailed information to a particular audience.

Using Microsoft Office 2007, you can create projects such as Word documents, Excel spreadsheets, Access databases, and PowerPoint presentations. Computer hardware and productivity software such as Microsoft Office 2007 minimizes much of the laborious work of drafting and revising projects. Some communicators handwrite ideas in notebooks, others compose directly on the computer, and others have developed unique strategies that work for their own particular thinking and writing styles.

No matter what method you use to plan a project, follow specific guidelines to arrive at a final product that presents information correctly and effectively (Figure A–1). Use some aspects of these guidelines every time you undertake a project, and others as needed in specific instances. For example, in determining content for a project, you may decide that a bar chart communicates trends more effectively than a paragraph of text. If so, you would create this graphical element and insert it in an Excel spreadsheet, a Word document, or a PowerPoint slide.

Determine the Project's Purpose

Begin by clearly defining why you are undertaking this assignment. For example, you may want to track monetary donations collected for your club's fundraising drive. Alternatively, you may be urging students to vote for a particular candidate in the next election. Once you clearly understand the purpose of your task, begin to draft ideas of how best to communicate this information.

Analyze Your Audience

Learn about the people who will read, analyze, or view your work. Where are they employed? What are their educational backgrounds? What are their expectations? What questions do they have?

> **PROJECT PLANNING GUIDELINES**
>
> **1. DETERMINE THE PROJECT'S PURPOSE**
> *Why are you undertaking the project?*
>
> **2. ANALYZE YOUR AUDIENCE**
> *Who are the people who will use your work?*
>
> **3. GATHER POSSIBLE CONTENT**
> *What information exists, and in what forms?*
>
> **4. DETERMINE WHAT CONTENT TO PRESENT TO YOUR AUDIENCE**
> *What information will best communicate the project's purpose to your audience?*

Figure A–1

Design experts suggest drawing a mental picture of these people or finding photographs of people who fit this profile so that you can develop a project with the audience in mind.

By knowing your audience members, you can tailor a project to meet their interests and needs. You will not present them with information they already possess, and you will not omit the information they need to know.

Example: Your assignment is to raise the profile of your college's nursing program in the community. How much do they know about your college and the nursing curriculum? What are the admission requirements? How many of the applicants admitted complete the program? What percent pass the state Boards?

Gather Possible Content

Rarely are you in a position to develop all the material for a project. Typically, you would begin by gathering existing information that may reside in spreadsheets or data-bases. Web sites, pamphlets, magazine and newspaper articles, and books could provide insights of how others have approached your topic. Personal interviews often provide perspectives not available by any other means. Consider video and audio clips as potential sources for material that might complement or support the factual data you uncover.

Determine What Content to Present to Your Audience

Experienced designers recommend writing three or four major ideas you want an audience member to remember after reading or viewing your project. It also is helpful to envision your project's endpoint, the key fact you wish to emphasize. All project elements should lead to this ending point.

As you make content decisions, you also need to think about other factors. Presentation of the project content is an important consideration. For example, will your brochure be printed on thick, colored paper or transparencies? Will your PowerPoint presentation be viewed in a classroom with excellent lighting and a bright projector, or will it be viewed on a notebook computer monitor? Determine relevant time factors, such as the length of time to develop the project, how long readers will spend reviewing your project, or the amount of time allocated for your speaking engagement. Your project will need to accommodate all of these constraints.

Decide whether a graph, photograph, or artistic element can express or emphasize a particular concept. The right hemisphere of the brain processes images by attaching an emotion to them, so audience members are more apt to recall these graphics long term rather than just reading text.

As you select content, be mindful of the order in which you plan to present information. Readers and audience members generally remember the first and last pieces of information they see and hear, so you should put the most important information at the top or bottom of the page.

Summary

When creating a project, it is beneficial to follow some basic guidelines from the outset. By taking some time at the beginning of the process to determine the project's purpose, analyze the audience, gather possible content, and determine what content to present to the audience, you can produce a project that is informative, relevant, and effective.

Appendix B

Introduction to Microsoft Office 2007

What Is Microsoft Office 2007?

Microsoft Office 2007 is a collection of the more popular Microsoft application software. It is available in Basic, Home and Student, Standard, Small Business, Professional, Ultimate, Professional Plus, and Enterprise editions. Each edition consists of a group of programs, collectively called a suite. Table B–1 lists the suites and their components. **Microsoft Office Professional Edition 2007** includes these six programs: Microsoft Office Word 2007, Microsoft Office Excel 2007, Microsoft Office Access 2007, Microsoft Office PowerPoint 2007, Microsoft Office Publisher 2007, and Microsoft Office Outlook 2007. The programs in the Office suite allow you to work efficiently, communicate effectively, and improve the appearance of the projects you create.

Table B–1

	Microsoft Office Basic 2007	Microsoft Office Home & Student 2007	Microsoft Office Standard 2007	Microsoft Office Small Business 2007	Microsoft Office Professional 2007	Microsoft Office Ultimate 2007	Microsoft Office Professional Plus 2007	Microsoft Office Enterprise 2007
Microsoft Office Word 2007	✓	✓	✓	✓	✓	✓	✓	✓
Microsoft Office Excel 2007	✓	✓	✓	✓	✓	✓	✓	✓
Microsoft Office Access 2007					✓	✓	✓	✓
Microsoft Office PowerPoint 2007		✓	✓	✓	✓	✓	✓	✓
Microsoft Office Publisher 2007				✓	✓	✓	✓	✓
Microsoft Office Outlook 2007	✓		✓				✓	✓
Microsoft Office OneNote 2007		✓				✓		
Microsoft Office Outlook 2007 with Business Contact Manager				✓	✓	✓		
Microsoft Office InfoPath 2007						✓	✓	✓
Integrated Enterprise Content Management						✓	✓	✓
Electronic Forms						✓	✓	✓
Advanced Information Rights Management and Policy Capabilities						✓	✓	✓
Microsoft Office Communicator 2007							✓	✓
Microsoft Office Groove 2007						✓		✓

Microsoft has bundled additional programs in some versions of Office 2007, in addition to the main group of Office programs. Table B–1 on the previous page lists the components of the various Office suites.

In addition to the Office 2007 programs noted previously, Office 2007 suites can contain other programs. Microsoft Office OneNote 2007 is a digital notebook program that allows you to gather and share various types of media, such as text, graphics, video, audio, and digital handwriting. Microsoft Office InfoPath 2007 is a program that allows you to create and use electronic forms to gather information. Microsoft Office Groove 2007 provides collaborative workspaces in real time. Additional services that are oriented toward the enterprise solution also are available.

Office 2007 and the Internet, World Wide Web, and Intranets

Office 2007 allows you to take advantage of the Internet, the World Wide Web, and intranets. The Microsoft Windows operating system includes a **browser**, which is a program that allows you to locate and view a Web page. The Windows browser is called Internet Explorer.

One method of viewing a Web page is to use the browser to enter the Web address for the Web page. Another method of viewing a Web page is clicking a hyperlink. A **hyperlink** is colored or underlined text or a graphic that, when clicked, connects to another Web page. Hyperlinks placed in Office 2007 documents allow for direct access to a Web site of interest.

An **intranet** is a private network, such as a network used within a company or organization for internal communication. Like the Internet, hyperlinks are used within an intranet to access documents, pages, and other destinations on the intranet. Unlike the Internet, the materials on the network are available only for those who are part of the private network.

Online Collaboration Using Office

Organizations that, in the past, were able to make important information available only to a select few, now can make their information accessible to a wider range of individuals who use programs such as Office 2007 and Internet Explorer. Office 2007 allows colleagues to use the Internet or an intranet as a central location to view documents, manage files, and work together.

Each of the Office 2007 programs makes publishing documents on a Web server as simple as saving a file on a hard disk. Once placed on the Web server, users can view and edit the documents and conduct Web discussions and live online meetings.

Using Microsoft Office 2007

The various Microsoft Office 2007 programs each specialize in a particular task. This section describes the general functions of the more widely used Office 2007 programs, along with how they are used to access the Internet or an intranet.

Microsoft Office Word 2007

Microsoft Office Word 2007 is a full-featured word processing program that allows you to create many types of personal and business documents, including flyers, letters, resumes, business documents, and academic reports.

Word's AutoCorrect, spelling, and grammar features help you proofread documents for errors in spelling and grammar by identifying the errors and offering suggestions for corrections as you type. The live word count feature provides you with a constantly updating word count as you enter and edit text. To assist with creating specific documents, such as a business letter or resume, Word provides templates, which provide a formatted document before you type the text of the document. Quick Styles provide a live preview of styles from the Style gallery, allowing you to preview styles in the document before actually applying them.

Word automates many often-used tasks and provides you with powerful desktop publishing tools to use as you create professional looking brochures, advertisements, and newsletters. SmartArt allows you to insert interpretive graphics based on document content.

Word makes it easier for you to share documents for collaboration. The Send feature opens an e-mail window with the active document attached. The Compare Documents feature allows you easily to identify changes when comparing different document versions.

Word 2007 and the Internet   Word makes it possible to design and publish Web pages on the Internet or an intranet, insert a hyperlink to a Web page in a word processing document, as well as access and search the content of other Web pages.

Microsoft Office Excel 2007

Microsoft Office Excel 2007 is a spreadsheet program that allows you to organize data, complete calculations, graph data, develop professional looking reports, publish organized data to the Web, and access real-time data from Web sites.

In addition to its mathematical functionality, Excel 2007 provides tools for visually comparing data. For instance, when comparing a group of values in cells, you can set cell backgrounds with bars proportional to the value of the data in the cell. You can also set cell backgrounds with full-color backgrounds, or use a color scale to facilitate interpretation of data values.

Excel 2007 provides strong formatting support for tables with the new Style Preview gallery.

Excel 2007 and the Internet   Using Excel 2007, you can create hyperlinks within a worksheet to access other Office documents on the network or on the Internet. Worksheets saved as static, or unchanging Web pages can be viewed using a browser. The person viewing static Web pages cannot change them.

In addition, you can create and run queries that retrieve information from a Web page and insert the information directly into a worksheet.

Microsoft Office Access 2007

Microsoft Office Access 2007 is a comprehensive database management system (DBMS). A **database** is a collection of data organized in a manner that allows access, retrieval, and use of that data. Access 2007 allows you to create a database; add, change, and delete data in the database; sort data in the database; retrieve data from the database; and create forms and reports using the data in the database.

Access 2007 and the Internet   Access 2007 lets you generate reports, which are summaries that show only certain data from the database, based on user requirements.

Microsoft Office PowerPoint 2007

Microsoft Office PowerPoint 2007 is a complete presentation graphics program that allows you to produce professional looking presentations. With PowerPoint 2007, you can create informal presentations using overhead transparencies, electronic presentations using a projection device attached to a personal computer, formal presentations using 35mm slides or a CD, or you can run virtual presentations on the Internet.

PowerPoint 2007 and the Internet   PowerPoint 2007 allows you to publish presentations on the Internet or other networks.

Microsoft Office Publisher 2007

Microsoft Office Publisher 2007 is a desktop publishing program (DTP) that allows you to design and produce professional quality documents (newsletters, flyers, brochures, business cards, Web sites, and so on) that combine text, graphics, and photographs. Desktop publishing software provides a variety of tools, including design templates, graphic manipulation tools, color schemes or libraries, and various page wizards and templates. For large jobs, businesses use desktop publishing software to design publications that are **camera ready**, which means the files are suitable for production by outside commercial printers. Publisher 2007 also allows you to locate commercial printers, service bureaus, and copy shops willing to accept customer files created in Publisher.

Publisher 2007 allows you to design a unique image, or logo, using one of more than 45 master design sets. This, in turn, permits you to use the same design for all your printed documents (letters, business cards, brochures, and advertisements) and Web pages. Publisher includes 70 coordinated color schemes; 30 font schemes; more than 10,000 high-quality clip art images; 1,500 photographs; 1,000 Web-art graphics; 340 animated graphics; and hundreds of unique Design Gallery elements (quotations, sidebars, and so on). If you wish, you also can download additional images from the Microsoft Office Online Web page on the Microsoft Web site.

Publisher 2007 and the Internet   Publisher 2007 allows you easily to create a multipage Web site with custom color schemes, photographic images, animated images, and sounds.

Microsoft Office Outlook 2007

Microsoft Office Outlook 2007 is a powerful communications and scheduling program that helps you communicate with others, keep track of your contacts, and organize your schedule. Outlook 2007 allows you to view a To-Do bar containing tasks and appointments from your Outlook calendar. Outlook 2007 allows you to send and receive electronic mail (e-mail) and permits you to engage in real-time communication with family, friends, or coworkers using instant messaging. Outlook 2007 also provides you with the means to organize your contacts, and you can track e-mail messages, meetings, and notes with a particular contact. Outlook's Calendar, Contacts, Tasks, and Notes components aid in this organization. Contact information is available from the Outlook Calendar, Mail, Contacts, and Task components by accessing the Find a Contact feature. **Personal information management (PIM)** programs such as Outlook provide a way for individuals and workgroups to organize, find, view, and share information easily.

Microsoft Office 2007 Help

At any time while you are using one of the Office programs, you can interact with **Microsoft Office 2007 Help** for that program and display information about any topic associated with the program. Several categories of help are available. In all programs, you can access Help by pressing the F1 key on the keyboard. In Publisher 2007 and Outlook 2007, the Help window can be opened by clicking the Help menu and then selecting Microsoft Office Publisher or Outlook Help command, or by entering search text in the 'Type a question for help' text box in the upper-right corner of the program window. In the other Office programs, clicking the Microsoft Office Help button near the upper-right corner of the program window opens the program Help window.

The Help window in all programs provides several methods for accessing help about a particular topic, and has tools for navigating around Help. Appendix C contains detailed instructions for using Help.

Collaboration and SharePoint

While not part of the Microsoft Office 2007 suites, SharePoint is a Microsoft tool that allows Office 2007 users to share data using collaborative tools that are integrated into the main Office programs. SharePoint consists of Windows SharePoint Services, Office SharePoint Server 2007, and, optionally, Office SharePoint Designer 2007.

Windows SharePoint Services provides the platform for collaboration programs and services. Office SharePoint Server 2007 is built on top of Windows SharePoint Services. The result of these two products is the ability to create SharePoint sites. A SharePoint site is a Web site that provides users with a virtual place for collaborating and communicating with their colleagues while working together on projects, documents, ideas, and information. Each member of a group with access to the SharePoint site has the ability to contribute to the material stored there. The basic building blocks of SharePoint sites are lists and libraries. Lists contain collections of information, such as calendar items, discussion points, contacts, and links. Lists can be edited to add or delete information. Libraries are similar to lists, but include both files and information about files. Types of libraries include document, picture, and forms libraries.

The most basic type of SharePoint site is called a Workspace, which is used primarily for collaboration. Different types of Workspaces can be created using SharePoint to suit different needs. SharePoint provides templates, or outlines of these Workspaces, that can be filled in to create the Workspace. Each of the different types of Workspace templates contain a different collection of lists and libraries, reflecting the purpose of the Workspace. You can create a Document Workspace to facilitate collaboration on documents. A Document Workspace contains a document library for documents and supporting files, a Links list that allows you to maintain relevant resource links for the document, a Tasks list for listing and assigning To-Do items to team members, and other links as needed. Meeting Workspaces allow users to plan and organize a meeting, with components such as Attendees, Agenda, and a Document Library. Social Meeting Workspaces provide a place to plan social events, with lists and libraries such as Attendees, Directions, Image/Logo, Things To Bring, Discussions, and Picture Library. A Decision Meeting Workspace is a Meeting Workspace with a focus on review and decision-making, with lists and libraries such as Objectives, Attendees, Agenda, Document Library, Tasks, and Decisions.

Users also can create a SharePoint site called a WebParts page, which is built from modules called WebParts. WebParts are modular units of information that contain a title bar and content that reflects the type of WebPart. For instance, an image WebPart would contain a title bar and an image. WebParts allow you quickly to create and modify a SharePoint site, and allow for the creation of a unique site that can allow users to access and make changes to information stored on the site.

Large SharePoint sites that include multiple pages can be created using templates as well. Groups needing more refined and targeted sharing options than those available with SharePoint Server 2007 and Windows SharePoint Services can add SharePoint Designer 2007 to create a site that meets their specific needs.

Depending on which components have been selected for inclusion on the site, users can view a team calendar, view links, read announcements, and view and edit group documents and projects. SharePoint sites can be set up so that documents are checked in and out, much like a library, to prevent multiple users from making changes simultaneously. Once a SharePoint site is set up, Office programs are used to perform maintenance of the site. For example, changes in the team calendar are updated using Outlook 2007, and changes that users make in Outlook 2007 are reflected on the SharePoint site. Office 2007 programs include a Publish feature that allows users easily to save file updates to a SharePoint site. Team members can be notified about changes made to material on the site either by e-mail or by a news feed, meaning that users do not have to go to the site to check to see if anything has been updated since they last viewed or worked on it. The search feature in SharePoint allows users quickly to find information on a large site.

Appendix C
Microsoft Office Word 2007 Help

Using Microsoft Office Word Help

This appendix shows how to use Microsoft Office Word Help. At any time while you are using one of the Microsoft Office 2007 programs, you can use Office Help to display information about all topics associated with the program. This appendix uses Microsoft Office Word 2007 to illustrate the use of Office Help. Help in other Office 2007 programs responds in a similar fashion.

In Office 2007, Help is presented in a window that has Web browser-style navigation buttons. Each Office 2007 program has its own Help home page, which is the starting Help page that is displayed in the Help window. If your computer is connected to the Internet, the contents of the Help page reflect both the local help files installed on the computer and material from Microsoft's Web site. As shown in Figure C–1, two methods for accessing Word's Help are available:

1. Microsoft Office Word Help button near the upper-right corner of the Word window

2. Function key F1 on the keyboard

Figure C–1

To Open the Word Help Window

The following steps open the Word Help window and maximize the window.

● Start Microsoft Word, if necessary. Click the Microsoft Office Word Help button near the upper-right corner of the Word window to open the Word Help window (Figure C–2).

Figure C–2

● Click the Maximize button on the Help title bar to maximize the Help window (Figure C–3).

Figure C–3

The Word Help Window

The Word Help window provides several methods for accessing help about a particular topic, and also has tools for navigating around Help. Methods for accessing Help include searching the help content installed with Word, or searching the online Office content maintained by Microsoft.

Figure C–3 shows the main Word Help window. To navigate Help, the Word Help window includes search features that allow you to search on a word or phrase about which you want help; the Connection Status button, which allows you to control where Word Help searches for content; toolbar buttons; and links to major Help categories.

Search Features

You can perform Help searches on words or phrases to find information about any Word feature using the 'Type words to search for' text box and the Search button (Figure C–4a). Click the 'Type words to search for' text box and then click the Search button or press the ENTER key to initiate a search of Word Help.

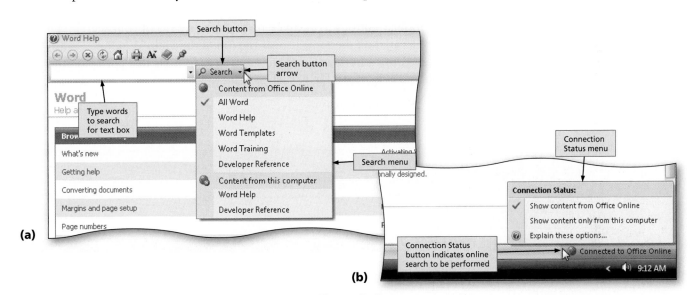

Figure C–4

Word Help offers the user the option of searching the online Help Web pages maintained by Microsoft or the offline Help files placed on your computer when you install Word. You can specify whether Word Help should search online or offline from two places: the Connection Status button on the status bar of the Word Help window, or the Search button arrow on the toolbar. The Connection Status button indicates whether Help currently is set up to work with online or offline information sources. Clicking the Connection Status button provides a menu with commands for selecting online or offline searches (Figure C–4b). The Connection Status menu allows the user to select whether Help searches will return content only from the computer (offline), or content from the computer and from Office Online (online).

Clicking the Search button arrow also provides a menu with commands for an online or offline search (Figure C–4a). These commands determine the source of information that Help searches for during the current Help session only. For example, assume that your preferred search is an offline search because you often do not have Internet access. You would set Connection Status to 'Show content only from this computer'. When you have Internet access, you can select an online search from the Search menu to search Office Online for information for your current search session only. Your search will use the Office Online resources until you quit Help. The next time you start Help, the Connection Status once again will be offline. In addition to setting the source of information that Help searches for during the current Help session, you can use the Search menu to further target the current search to one of four subcategories of online Help: Word Help, Word Templates, Word Training, and Developer Reference. The local search further can target one subcategory, Developer Reference.

In addition to searching for a word or string of text, you can use the links provided on the Browse Word Help area (Figure C–3 on page APP 10) to search for help on a topic. These links direct you to major help categories. From each major category, subcategories are available to further refine your search.

Finally, you can use the Table of Contents for Word Help to search for a topic the same way you would in a hard copy book. The Table of Contents is accessed via a toolbar button.

Toolbar Buttons

You can use toolbar buttons to navigate through the results of your search. The toolbar buttons are located on the toolbar near the top of the Help Window (Figure C–5). The toolbar buttons contain navigation buttons as well as buttons that perform other useful and common tasks in Word Help, such as printing.

Figure C–5

The Word Help navigation buttons are the Back, Forward, Stop, Refresh, and Home buttons. These five buttons behave like the navigation buttons in a Web browser window. You can use the Back button to go back one window, the Forward button to go forward one window, the Stop button to stop loading the current page, and the Home button to redisplay the Help home page in the Help window. Use the Refresh button to reload the information requested into the Help window from its original source. When getting Help information online, this button provides the most current information from the Microsoft Help Web site.

The buttons located to the right of the navigation buttons — Print, Change Font Size, Show Table of Contents, and Not on Top — provide you with access to useful and common commands. The Print button prints the contents of the open Help window. The Change Font Size button customizes the Help window by increasing or decreasing the size of its text. The Show Table of Contents button opens a pane on the left side of the Help window that shows the Table of Contents for Word Help. You can use the Table of Contents for Word Help to navigate through the contents of Word Help much as you would use the Table of Contents in a book to search for a topic. The Not On Top button is an example of a toggle button, which is a button that can be switched back and forth between two states. It determines how the Word Help window behaves relative to other windows. When clicked, the Not On Top button changes to Keep On Top. In this state, it does not allow other windows from Word or other programs to cover the Word Help window when those windows are the active windows. When in the Not On Top state, the button allows other windows to be opened or moved on top of the Word Help window.

You can customize the size and placement of the Help window. Resize the window using the Maximize and Restore buttons, or by dragging the window to a desired size. Relocate the Help window by dragging the title bar to a new location on the screen.

Searching Word Help

Once the Word Help window is open, several methods exist for navigating Word Help. You can search for help by using any of the three following methods from the Help window:

1. Enter search text in the 'Type words to search for' text box
2. Click the links in the Help window
3. Use the Table of Contents

To Obtain Help Using the Type Words to Search for Text Box

Assume for the following example that you want to know more about watermarks. The following steps use the 'Type words to search for' text box to obtain useful information about watermarks by entering the word, watermark, as search text. The steps also navigate in the Word Help window.

1

- Type watermark in the 'Type words to search for' text box at the top of the Word Help window.

- Click the Search button arrow to display the Search menu.

- If it is not selected already, click All Word on the Search menu to select the command. If All Word is already selected, click the Search button arrow again to close the Search menu.

Q&A Why select All Word on the Search menu?

Selecting All Word on the Search menu ensures that Word Help will search all possible sources for information on your search term. It will produce the most complete search results.

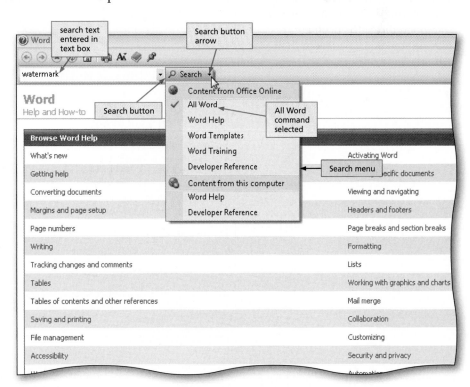

Figure C–6

2

- Click the Search button to display the search results (Figure C–7).

Q&A Why do my results differ?

If you do not have an Internet connection, your results will reflect only the content of the Help files on your computer. When searching for help online, results also can change as material is added, deleted, and updated on the online Help Web pages maintained by Microsoft.

Q&A Why were my search results not very helpful?

When initiating a search, keep in mind to check the spelling of the search text; and to keep your search very specific, with fewer than seven words, to return the most accurate results.

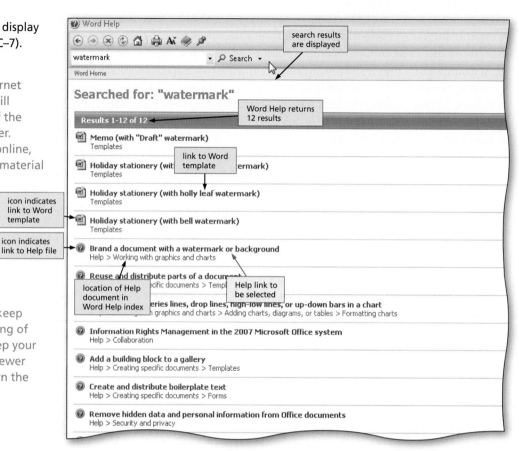

Figure C–7

3

- Click the 'Brand a document with a watermark or background' link to open the Help document associated with the link in the Help window (Figure C–8).

Figure C–8

4

- Click the Home button on the taskbar to clear the search results and redisplay the Word Help home page (Figure C–9).

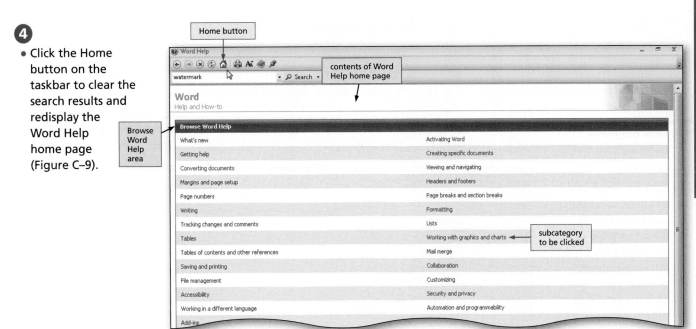

Figure C–9

To Obtain Help Using the Help Links

If your topic of interest is listed in the Browse Word Help area, you can click the link to begin browsing Word Help categories instead of entering search text. You browse Word Help just like you would browse a Web site. If you know in which category to find your Help information, you may wish to use these links. The following steps find the watermark Help information using the category links from the Word Help home page.

1

- Click the 'Working with graphics and charts' link to open the 'Working with graphics and charts' page.

- Click the 'Brand a document with a watermark or background' link to open the Help document associated with the link (Figure C–10).

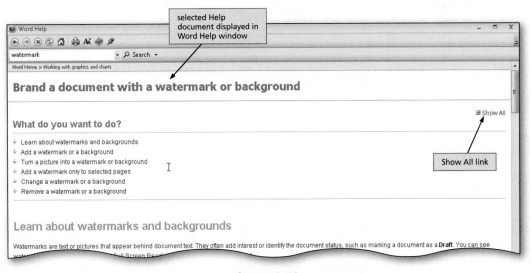

Figure C–10

Q&A

What does the Show All link do?

In many Help documents, additional information about terms and features is available by clicking a link in the document to display additional information in the Help document. Clicking the Show All link opens all the links in the Help document that expand to additional text.

To Obtain Help Using the Help Table of Contents

A third way to find Help in Word is through the Help Table of Contents. You can browse through the Table of Contents to display information about a particular topic or to familiarize yourself with Word. The following steps access the watermark Help information by browsing through the Table of Contents.

- Click the Home button on the toolbar.

- Click the Show Table of Contents button on the toolbar to open the Table of Contents pane on the left side of the Help window. If necessary, click the Maximize button on the Help title bar to maximize the window (Figure C–11).

Figure C–11

- Click the 'Working with graphics and charts' link in the Table of Contents pane to view a list of Help subtopics.

- Click the 'Brand a document with a watermark or background' link in the Table of Contents pane to view the selected Help document in the right pane (Figure C–12).

Q&A

How do I remove the Table of Contents pane when I am finished with it?

The Show Table of Contents button acts as a toggle switch. When the Table of Contents pane is visible, the button changes to Hide Table of Contents. Clicking it hides the Table of Contents pane and changes the button to Show Table of Contents.

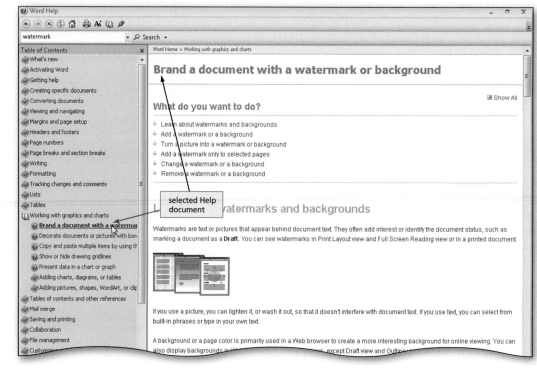

Figure C–12

Obtaining Help while Working in Word

Often you may need help while working on a document without already having the Help window open. For example, you may be unsure about how a particular command works, or you may be presented with a dialog box that you are not sure how to use. Rather than opening the Help window and initiating a search, Word Help provides you with the ability to search directly for help.

Figure C–13 shows one option for obtaining help while working in Word. If you want to learn more about a command, point to the command button and wait for the Enhanced ScreenTip to appear. If the Help icon appears in the Enhanced ScreenTip, press the F1 key while pointing to the command to open the Help window associated with that command.

Figure C–13

Figure C–14 shows a dialog box with a Get help button in it. Pressing the F1 key while the dialog box is displayed opens a Help window. The Help window contains help about that dialog box, if available. If no help file is available for that particular dialog box, then the main Help window opens.

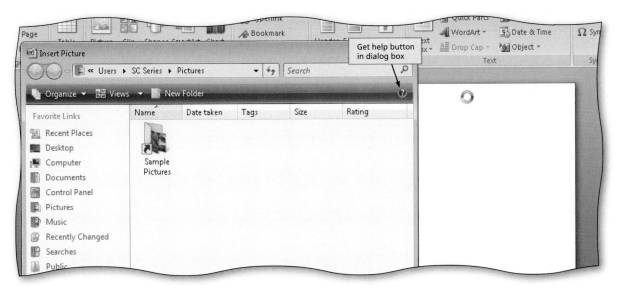

Figure C–14

Use Help

1 Obtaining Help Using Search Text

Instructions: Perform the following tasks using Word Help.

1. Use the 'Type words to search for' text box to obtain help about landscape printing. Use the Connection Status menu to search online help if you have an Internet connection.

2. Click Select page orientation in the list of links in the search results. Double-click the Microsoft Office Word Help window title bar to maximize it. Read and print the information. At the top of the printout, write down the number of links Word Help found.

3. Use the Search menu to search for help offline. Repeat the search from Step 1. At the top of the printout, write down the number of links that Word Help found searching offline. Submit the printouts as specified by your instructor.

4. Use the 'Type words to search for' text box to search for information online about adjusting line spacing. Click the 'Adjust the spacing between a list bullet or number and the text' link in the search results. If necessary, maximize the Microsoft Office 2007 Word Help window. Read and print the contents of the window. Close the Microsoft Office Word Help window. Submit the printouts as specified by your instructor.

5. For each of the following words and phrases, click one link in the search results, click the Show All link, and then print the page: page zoom; date; print preview; Ribbon; word count; and citation. Submit the printouts as specified by your instructor.

2 Expanding on Word Help Basics

Instructions: Use Word Help to better understand its features and answer the questions listed below. Answer the questions on your own paper, or submit the printed Help information as specified by your instructor.

1. Use Help to find out how to customize the Help window. Change the font size to the smallest option and then print the contents of the Microsoft Office Word Help window. Change the font size back to its original setting. Close the window.

2. Press the F1 key. Search for information about tables, restricting the search results to Word Templates. Print the first page of the Search results.

3. Search for information about tables, restricting the search results to Word Help files. Print the first page of the Search results.

4. Use Word Help to find out what happened to the Office Assistant, a feature in the previous version of Word. Print out the Help document that contains the answer.

Appendix D

Publishing Office 2007 Web Pages to a Web Server

With the Office 2007 programs, you use the Save As command on the Office Button menu to save a Web page to a Web server using one of two techniques: Web folders or File Transfer Protocol. A **Web folder** is an Office shortcut to a Web server. **File Transfer Protocol (FTP)** is an Internet standard that allows computers to exchange files with other computers on the Internet.

You should contact your network system administrator or technical support staff at your Internet access provider to determine if their Web server supports Web folders, FTP, or both, and to obtain necessary permissions to access the Web server. If you decide to publish Web pages using a Web folder, you must have the Office Server Extensions (OSE) installed on your computer.

Using Web Folders to Publish Office 2007 Web Pages

When publishing to a Web folder, someone first must create the Web folder before you can save to it. If you are granted permission to create a Web folder, you must obtain the Web address of the Web server, a user name, and possibly a password that allows you to access the Web server. You also must decide on a name for the Web folder. Table D–1 explains how to create a Web folder.

Office 2007 adds the name of the Web folder to the list of current Web folders. You can save to this folder, open files in the folder, rename the folder, or perform any operations you would to a folder on your hard disk. You can use your Office 2007 program or Windows Explorer to access this folder. Table D–2 explains how to save to a Web folder.

Table D–1 Creating a Web Folder

1. Click the Office Button and then click Save As or Open.

2. When the Save As dialog box (or Open dialog box) appears, click the Tools button arrow, and then click Map Network Drive... When the Map Network Drive dialog box is displayed, click the 'Connect to a Web site that you can use to store your documents and pictures' link.

3. When the Add Network Location Wizard dialog box is displayed, click the Next button. If necessary, click Choose a custom network location. Click the Next button. Click the View examples link, type the Internet or network address, and then click the Next button. Click 'Log on anonymously' to deselect the check box, type your user name in the User name text box, and then click the Next button. Enter the name you want to call this network place and then click the Next button. Click to deselect the 'Open this network location when I click Finish' check box, and then click the Finish button.

Table D–2 Saving to a Web Folder

1. Click the Office Button, click Save As.

2. When the Save As dialog box is displayed, type the Web page file name in the File name text box. Do not press the ENTER key.

3. Click the Save as type box arrow and then click Web Page to select the Web Page format.

4. Click Computer in the Navigation pane.

5. Double-click the Web folder name in the Network Location list.

6. If the Enter Network Password dialog box appears, type the user name and password in the respective text boxes and then click the OK button.

7. Click the Save button in the Save As dialog box.

Using FTP to Publish Office 2007 Web Pages

When publishing a Web page using FTP, you first must add the FTP location to your computer before you can save to it. An FTP location, also called an **FTP site**, is a collection of files that reside on an FTP server. In this case, the FTP server is the Web server.

To add an FTP location, you must obtain the name of the FTP site, which usually is the address (URL) of the FTP server, and a user name and a password that allows you to access the FTP server. You save and open the Web pages on the FTP server using the name of the FTP site. Table D–3 explains how to add an FTP site.

Office 2007 adds the name of the FTP site to the FTP locations list in the Save As and Open dialog boxes. You can open and save files using this list. Table D–4 explains how to save to an FTP location.

Table D–3 Adding an FTP Location
1. Click the Office Button and then click Save As or Open.
2. When the Save As dialog box (or Open dialog box) appears, click the Tools button arrow, and then click Map Network Drive... When the Map Network Drive dialog box is displayed, click the 'Connect to a Web site that you can use to store your documents and pictures' link.
3. When the Add Network Location Wizard dialog box appears, click the Next button. If necessary, click Choose a custom network location. Click the Next button. Click the View examples link, type the Internet or network address, and then click the Next button. If you have a user name for the site, click to deselect 'Log on anonymously' and type your user name in the User name text box, and then click Next. If the site allows anonymous logon, click Next. Type a name for the location, click Next, click to deselect the 'Open this network location when I click Finish' check box, and click Finish. Click the OK button.
4. Close the Save As or the Open dialog box.

Table D–4 Saving to an FTP Location
1. Click the Office Button and then click Save As.
2. When the Save As dialog box is displayed, type the Web page file name in the File name text box. Do not press the ENTER key.
3. Click the Save as type box arrow and then click Web Page to select the Web Page format.
4. Click Computer in the Navigation pane.
5. Double-click the name of the FTP site in the Network Location list.
6. When the FTP Log On dialog box appears, enter your user name and password and then click the OK button.
7. Click the Save button in the Save As dialog box.

Appendix E
Customizing Microsoft Office Word 2007

This appendix explains how to change the screen resolution in Windows Vista to the resolution used in this book. It also describes how to customize the Word window by changing the Ribbon, Quick Access Toolbar, and the color scheme.

Changing Screen Resolution

Screen resolution indicates the number of pixels (dots) that the computer uses to display the letters, numbers, graphics, and background you see on the screen. When you increase the screen resolution, Windows displays more information on the screen, but the information decreases in size. The reverse also is true: as you decrease the screen resolution, Windows displays less information on the screen, but the information increases in size.

The screen resolution usually is stated as the product of two numbers, such as 1024×768 (pronounced "ten twenty-four by seven sixty-eight"). A 1024×768 screen resolution results in a display of 1,024 distinct pixels on each of 768 lines, or about 786,432 pixels. The figures in this book were created using a screen resolution of 1024×768.

The screen resolutions most commonly used today are 800×600 and 1024×768, although some Office specialists set their computers at a much higher screen resolution, such as 2048×1536.

To Change the Screen Resolution

The following steps change the screen resolution from 1280×1024 to 1024×768. Your computer already may be set to 1024×768 or some other resolution.

1

- If necessary, minimize all programs so that the Windows Vista desktop appears.

- Right-click the Windows Vista desktop to display the Windows Vista desktop shortcut menu (Figure E–1).

Figure E–1

- Click Personalize on the shortcut menu to open the Personalization window.

- Click Display Settings in the Personalization window to display the Display Settings dialog box (Figure E–2).

Figure E–2

- Drag the slider in the Resolution area so that the screen resolution changes to 1024 × 768 (Figure E–3).

Figure E–3

4

- Click the OK button to change the screen resolution from 1280 × 1024 to 1024 × 768 (Figure E–4).

Figure E–4

5

- Click the Yes button in the Display Settings dialog box to accept the new screen resolution (Figure E–5).

Q&A

What if I do not want to change the screen resolution after seeing it applied after I click the OK button?

You either can click the No button in the inner Display Settings dialog box, or wait for the timer to run out, at which point Windows Vista will revert to the original screen resolution.

- Click the Close button to close the Personalization window.

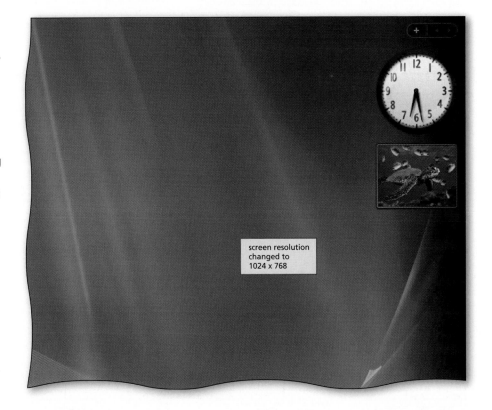

Figure E–5

Screen Resolution and the Appearance of the Ribbon in Word 2007

Changing the screen resolution affects how the Ribbon appears in Word 2007 programs. Figure E–6 shows the Word Ribbon at the screen resolutions of 800 × 600, 1024 × 768, and 1280 × 1024. All of the same commands are available regardless of screen resolution. Word, however, makes changes to the groups and the buttons within the groups to accommodate the various screen resolutions. The result is that certain commands may need to be accessed differently depending on the resolution chosen. A command that is visible on the Ribbon and available by clicking a button at one resolution may not be visible and may need to be accessed using its group button at a different resolution.

Figure E–6

Comparing the three Ribbons, notice changes in content and layout of the groups and galleries. In some cases, the content of a group is the same in each resolution, but the layout of the group differs. For example, the same buttons appear in the Font and Paragraph groups in the three resolutions, but the layouts differ. The buttons are displayed in three rows at the 800 × 600 resolution, and in two rows in the 1024 × 768 and 1280 × 1024 resolutions. In other cases, the content and layout are the same across the resolution, but the level of detail differs with the resolution. In the Clipboard group, when the resolution increases to 1280 × 1024, the names of all the buttons in the group appear in addition to the buttons themselves. At the lower resolution, only the buttons appear.

Changing resolutions also can result in fewer commands being visible in a group. Comparing the Editing groups, notice that the group at the 800 × 600 resolution consists of an Editing button, while at the higher resolutions, the group has three buttons visible. The commands that are available on the Ribbon at the higher resolutions must be accessed using the Editing button at the 800 × 600 resolution.

Changing resolutions results in different amounts of detail being available at one time in the galleries on the Ribbon. The Styles gallery in the three resolutions presented show different numbers of styles. At 800 × 600, you can scroll through the gallery three styles at a time, at 1024 × 768, you can scroll through the gallery four styles at a time, and at 1280 × 1024, you can scroll through the gallery six styles at a time.

Customizing the Word Window

When working in Word, you may want to make your working area as large as possible. One option is to minimize the Ribbon. You also can modify the characteristics of the Quick Access Toolbar, customizing the toolbar's commands and location to better suit your needs.

To Minimize the Ribbon in Word

The following steps minimize the Ribbon.

- Start Word.

- Maximize the Word window, if necessary.

- Click the Customize Quick Access Toolbar button on the Quick Access Toolbar to display the Customize Quick Access Toolbar menu (Figure E–7).

Figure E–7

- Click Minimize the Ribbon on the Quick Access Toolbar menu to reduce the Ribbon display to just the tabs (Figure E–8).

Figure E–8

Other Ways

1. Double-click the active Ribbon tab
2. Press CTRL+F1

Customizing and Resetting the Quick Access Toolbar

The Quick Access Toolbar, located to the right of the Microsoft Office Button by default, provides easy access to some of the more frequently used commands in Word (Figure E–7). By default, the Quick Access Toolbar contains buttons for the Save, Undo, and Redo commands. Customize the Quick Access Toolbar by changing its location in the window and by adding additional buttons to reflect which commands you would like to be able to access easily.

To Change the Location of the Quick Access Toolbar

The following steps move the Quick Access Toolbar to below the Ribbon.

- Double-click the Home tab to redisplay the Ribbon.

- Click the Customize Quick Access Toolbar button on the Quick Access Toolbar to display the Customize Quick Access Toolbar menu (Figure E–9).

Figure E–9

2

- Click Show Below the Ribbon on the Quick Access Toolbar menu to move the Quick Access Toolbar below the Ribbon (Figure E–10).

Figure E–10

To Add Commands to the Quick Access Toolbar Using the Customize Quick Access Toolbar Menu

Some of the more commonly added commands are available for selection from the Customize Quick Access Toolbar menu. The following steps add the Quick Print button to the Quick Access Toolbar.

1

- Click the Customize Quick Access Toolbar button to display the Customize Quick Access Toolbar menu (Figure E–11).

Figure E–11

- Click Quick Print on the Quick
  Access Toolbar menu to add the
  Quick Print button to the Quick
  Access Toolbar (Figure E–12).

Figure E–12

To Add Commands to the Quick Access Toolbar Using the Shortcut Menu

Commands also can be added to the Quick Access Toolbar from the Ribbon. Adding an existing Ribbon command that you use often to the Quick Access Toolbar makes the command immediately available, regardless of which tab is active.

- Click the Review tab on the
  Ribbon to make it the active tab.

- Right-click the Spelling &
  Grammar button on the Review
  tab to display a shortcut menu
  (Figure E–13).

Figure E–13

2

- Click Add to Quick Access Toolbar on the shortcut menu to add the Spelling & Grammar button to the Quick Access Toolbar (Figure E–14).

Figure E–14

To Add Commands to the Quick Access Toolbar Using Word Options

Some commands do not appear on the Ribbon. They can be added to the Quick Access Toolbar using the Word Options dialog box.

1

- Click the Office Button to display the Office Button menu (Figure E–15).

Figure E–15

- Click the Word Options button on the Office Button menu to display the Word Options dialog box (Figure E–16).

Figure E–16

- Click Customize in the left pane.

- Click the 'Choose commands from' box arrow to display the 'Choose commands from' list.

- Click Commands Not in the Ribbon in the 'Choose commands from' list.

- Scroll to display the Web Page Preview command.

- Click Web Page Preview to select it (Figure E–17).

Figure E–17

4

- Click the Add button to add the Web Page Preview button to the list of buttons on the Quick Access Toolbar (Figure E–18).

Figure E–18

5

- Click the OK button to add the Web Page Preview button to the Quick Access Toolbar (Figure E–19).

Figure E–19

Other Ways

1. Click Customize Quick Access Toolbar button, click More Commands, select commands to add, click Add button, click OK button

To Remove a Command from the Quick Access Toolbar

● Right-click the Web Page Preview
button on the Quick Access
Toolbar to display a shortcut menu
(Figure E–20).

Figure E–20

● Click Remove from Quick Access
Toolbar on the shortcut menu to
remove the button from the Quick
Access Toolbar (Figure E–21).

Figure E–21

Other Ways

1. Click Customize Quick
   Access Toolbar button,
   click More Commands, click
   the command you wish to
   remove in the Customize
   Quick Access Toolbar list,
   click Remove button, click
   OK button

2. If the command appears
   on the Customize Quick
   Access Toolbar menu, click
   the Customize Quick Access
   Toolbar button, click the
   command you wish to
   remove

To Reset the Quick Access Toolbar

1

- Click the Customize Quick Access Toolbar button on the Quick Access Toolbar.

- Click More Commands on the Quick Access Toolbar menu to display the Word Options Dialog box.

- Click the Show Quick Access Toolbar below the Ribbon check box to deselect it (Figure E–22).

Figure E–22

- Click the Reset button, click the Yes button in the dialog box that appears, and then click the OK button in the Word Options dialog box, to reset the Quick Access Toolbar to its original position to the right of the Office Button, with the original three buttons (Figure E–23).

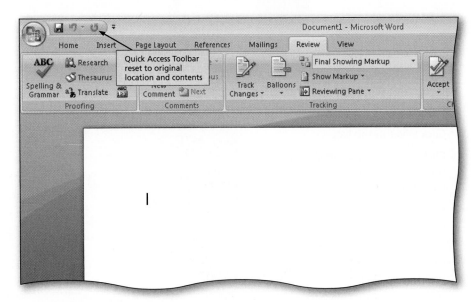

Figure E–23

Changing the Word Color Scheme

The Microsoft Word window can be customized by selecting a color scheme other than the default blue one. Three color schemes are available in Word.

To Change the Word Color Scheme

The following steps change the color scheme.

1

- Click the Office Button to display the Office Button menu.

- Click the Word Options button on the Office Button menu to display the Word Options dialog box.

- If necessary, click Popular in the left pane. Click the Color scheme box arrow to display a list of color schemes (Figure E–24).

Figure E–24

2

- Click Silver in the list.

- Click the OK button to change the color scheme to silver (Figure E–25).

 How do I switch back to the default color scheme?

Follow the steps for changing the Word color scheme, and select Blue from the list of color schemes.

Figure E–25

Appendix F
Steps for the Windows XP User

For the XP User of this Book

For most tasks, no differences exist between using Word under the Windows Vista operating system and using Word under the Windows XP operating system. With some tasks, however, you will see some differences, or need to complete the tasks using different steps. This appendix shows how to Start Word, Save a Document, Open a Document, Insert a Picture, and Insert Text from a File while using Microsoft Office under Windows XP.

To Start Word

The following steps, which assume Windows is running, start Word based on a typical installation. You may need to ask your instructor how to start Word for your computer.

1 Click the Start button on the Windows taskbar to display the Start menu.

• Point to All Programs on the Start menu to display the All Programs submenu.

• Point to Microsoft Office on the All Programs submenu to display the Microsoft Office submenu (Figure F–1).

Figure F–1

- Click Microsoft Office Word 2007 to start Word and display a new blank document in the Word window (Figure F–2).

- If the Word window is not maximized, click the Maximize button next to the Close button on its title bar to maximize the window.

- If the Print Layout button is not selected, click it so that your screen layout matches Figure F–2.

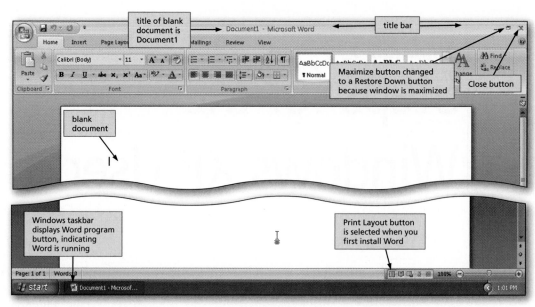

Figure F–2

Other Ways	
1. Double-click Word icon on desktop, if one is present	2. Click Microsoft Office Word 2007 on Start menu

To Save a Document

After editing, you should save the document. The following steps save a document on a USB flash drive using the file name, Horseback Riding Lessons Flyer.

- With a USB flash drive connected to one of the computer's USB ports, click the Save button on the Quick Access Toolbar to display the Save As dialog box (Figure F–3).

Q&A

Do I have to save to a USB flash drive?

No. You can save to any device or folder. A **folder** is a specific location on a storage medium. You can save to the default folder or a different folder. You also can create your own folders, which is explained later in this book.

Figure F–3

2

- Type the name of your file (Horseback Riding Lessons Flyer in this example) in the File name text box to change the file name. Do not press the ENTER key after typing the file name (Figure F–4).

Q&A What characters can I use in a file name?

A file name can have a maximum of 255 characters, including spaces. The only invalid characters are the backslash (\), slash (/), colon (:), asterisk (*), question mark (?), quotation mark ("), less than symbol (<), greater than symbol (>), and vertical bar (|).

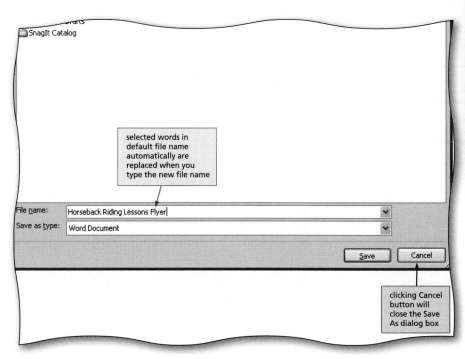

Figure F–4

3

- Click the Save in box arrow to display a list of available drives and folders (Figure F–5).

Q&A Why is my list of files, folders, and drives arranged and named differently from those shown in the figure?

Your computer's configuration determines how the list of files and folders is displayed and how drives are named. You can change the save location by clicking shortcuts on the **My Places bar**.

Q&A How do I save the file if I am not using a USB flash drive?

Use the same process, but be certain to select your device in the Save in list.

Figure F–5

4

- Click UDISK 2.0 (E:) in the Save in list to select the USB flash drive, Drive E in this case, as the new save location (Figure F–6).

- Click the Save button to save the document.

Q&A

What if my USB flash drive has a different name or letter?

It is very likely that your USB flash drive will have a different name and drive letter and be connected to a different port. Verify the device in your Save in list is correct.

Figure F–6

Other Ways

1. Click Office Button, click Save, type file name, select drive or folder, click Save button

2. Press CTRL+S or press SHIFT+F12, type file name, select drive or folder, click Save button

To Open a Document

The following steps open the Horseback Riding Lessons Flyer file from the USB flash drive.

1

- With your USB flash drive connected to one of the computer's USB ports, click the Office Button to display the Office Button menu.

- Click Open on the Office Button menu to display the Open dialog box.

- If necessary, click the Look in box arrow and then click UDISK 2.0 (E:) to select the USB flash drive, Drive E in this case, in the Look in list as the new open location.

- Click Horseback Riding Lessons Flyer to select the file name (Figure F–7).

- Click the Open button to open the document.

Q&A

How do I open the file if I am not using a USB flash drive?

Use the same process, but be certain to select your device in the Look in list.

Figure F–7

Other Ways

1. Click Office Button, double-click file name in Recent Documents list

2. Press CTRL+O, select file name, press ENTER

To Insert a Picture

The following steps insert a centered picture, which, in this example, is located on the same USB flash drive that contains the saved flyer.

1 Position the insertion point where you want the picture to be located. Click Insert on the Ribbon to display the Insert tab.

2 Click the Insert Picture from File button on the Insert tab to display the Insert Picture dialog box.

3 With your USB flash drive connected to one of the computer's USB ports, if necessary, click the Look in box arrow and then click UDISK 2.0 (E:) to select the USB flash drive, Drive E in this case, in the Look in list as the device that contains the picture. Select the file name of the picture file.

4 Click the Insert button in the dialog box to insert the picture at the location of the insertion point in the document.

To Insert Text from a File

The following steps insert text from a file located on the USB flash drive.

1 Click where you want to insert the text. Click Insert on the Ribbon to display the Insert tab.

2 Click the Object button arrow to display the Object menu. Click Text from File to display the Insert File dialog box.

3 With your USB flash drive connected to one of the computer's USB ports, if necessary, click the Look in box arrow and then click UDISK 2.0 (E:) to select the USB flash drive, Drive E in this case, in the Look in list as the device that contains the file. Select the file name of the file to be inserted.

4 Click the Insert button in the dialog box to insert the file at the location of the insertion point in the document.

Appendix G
Microsoft Business Certification Program

What Is the Microsoft Business Certification Program?

The Microsoft Business Certification Program enables candidates to show that they have something exceptional to offer – proved expertise in Microsoft Office 2007 programs. The two certification tracks allow candidates to choose how they want to exhibit their skills, either through validating skills within a specific Microsoft product or taking their knowledge to the next level and combining Microsoft programs to show that they can apply multiple skill sets to complete more complex office tasks. Recognized by businesses and schools around the world, more than 3 million certifications have been obtained in more than 100 different countries. The Microsoft Business Certification Program is the only Microsoft-approved certification program of its kind.

What Is the Microsoft Certified Application Specialist Certification?

The Microsoft Certified Application Specialist certification exams focus on validating specific skill sets within each of the Microsoft Office system programs. Candidates can choose which exam(s) they want to take according to which skills they want to validate. The available Application Specialist exams include:

- Using Microsoft® Windows Vista™
- Using Microsoft® Office Word 2007
- Using Microsoft® Office Excel® 2007
- Using Microsoft® Office PowerPoint® 2007
- Using Microsoft® Office Access 2007
- Using Microsoft® Office Outlook® 2007

> For more information and details on how Shelly Cashman Series textbooks map to Microsoft Certified Application Specialist certification, visit scsite.com/off2007/cert.

What Is the Microsoft Certified Application Professional Certification?

The Microsoft Certified Application Professional certification exams focus on a candidate's ability to use the 2007 Microsoft® Office system to accomplish industry-agnostic functions, for example Budget Analysis and Forecasting, or Content Management and Collaboration. The available Application Professional exams currently include:

- Organizational Support
- Creating and Managing Presentations
- Content Management and Collaboration
- Budget Analysis and Forecasting

Index

Quick Reference Summary

In the Microsoft Office Word 2007 program, you can accomplish a task in a number of ways. The following table provides a quick reference to each task presented in this textbook. The first column identifies the task. The second column indicates the page number on which the task is discussed in the book. The subsequent four columns list the different ways the task in column one can be carried out.

Table 1 Microsoft Office Word 2007 Quick Reference Summary

Task	Page Number	Mouse	Ribbon	Shortcut Menu	Keyboard Shortcut
1.5 Line Spacing	WD 86		Line spacing button on Home tab	Paragraph | Indents and Spacing tab	CTRL+5
AutoCorrect Entry, Create	WD 93	Office Button | Word Options button | Proofing | AutoCorrect Options button			
AutoCorrect Options Menu, Display	WD 92	Point to text automatically corrected, point to small blue box, click AutoCorrect Options button			
Background Color, Add	WD 221		Page Color button on Page Layout tab		
Bibliographical List, Create	WD 113		Bibliography button on References tab | Insert Bibliography		
Bibliographical List, Modify Source and Update List	WD 117		Manage Sources button on References tab | select source | Edit button		
Bibliography Style, Change	WD 95		Bibliography Style box arrow on References tab		
Bold	WD 34	Bold button on Mini toolbar	Bold button on Home tab	Font | Font tab | Bold in Font style list	CTRL+B
Border, Paragraph	WD 161		Page Borders on Page Layout tab | Borders tab		
Building Block, Create	WD 170		Quick Parts button on Insert tab | Save Selection to Quick Part Gallery		ALT+F3

Table 1 Microsoft Office Word 2007 Quick Reference Summary *(continued)*

Task	Page Number	Mouse	Ribbon	Shortcut Menu	Keyboard Shortcut
Building Block, Insert	WD 172		Quick Parts button on Insert tab | building block name		F3
Bullets, Apply	WD 32	Bullets button on Mini toolbar	Bullets button on Home tab	Bullets	ASTERISK KEY | SPACEBAR
Capital Letters	WD 86		Change Case button on Home tab | UPPERCASE	Font	CTRL+SHIFT+A
Case of Letters, Change	WD 86		Change Case button on Home tab	Font | Font tab	SHIFT+F3
Center	WD 26	Center button on Mini toolbar	Center button on Home tab	Paragraph | Indents and Spacing tab	CTRL+E
Citation Placeholder, Insert	WD 101		Insert Citation button on References tab | Add New Placeholder		
Citation, Insert and Create Source	WD 96		Insert Citation button on References tab | Add New Source		
Citation, Edit	WD 98	Click citation, Citation Options box arrow | Edit Citation			
Close Document	WD 60	Office Button | Close			
Count Words	WD 107	Word Count indicator on status bar	Word Count button on Review tab		CTRL+SHIFT+G
Color Text	WD 152	Font Color button arrow on Mini toolbar	Font Color button arrow on Home tab		
Content Control, Change Text	WD 187	Triple-click content control, change text			
Copy	WD 189		Clipboard Dialog Box Launcher on Home tab	Copy	CTRL+C
Cut	WD 121		Cut button on Home tab	Cut	CTRL+X
Date, Insert	WD 168		Insert Date and Time button on Insert tab		
Delete	WD 59				DELETE
Dictionary, Custom, View or Modify Entries	WD 127	Office Button | Word Options button | Proofing | Custom Dictionaries button			
Dictionary, Set Custom	WD 127	Office Button | Word Options button | Proofing | Custom Dictionaries button | select desired dictionary name | Change Default button			
Document Properties, Set or View	WD 51	Office Button | Prepare | Properties			
Documents, Switch Between	WD 189	Program button on Windows taskbar	Switch Windows button on View tab		ALT+TAB

Table 1 Microsoft Office Word 2007 Quick Reference Summary *(continued)*

Task	Page Number	Mouse	Ribbon	Shortcut Menu	Keyboard Shortcut
Double-Space Text	WD 87		Line spacing button on Home tab	Paragraph | Indents and Spacing	CTRL+2
Double-Underline	WD 35		Font Dialog Box Launcher on Home tab	Font | Font tab	CTRL+SHIFT+D
Envelope, Address and Print	WD 203		Envelopes button on Mailings tab | Envelopes tab | Print button		
File, Create from Existing File	WD 165	Office Button | New | New from existing			
Find Text	WD 124	Select Browse Object button on vertical scroll bar | Find icon	Find button on Home tab		CTRL+F
Find and Replace Text	WD 123	Select Browse Object button on vertical scroll bar | Find icon | Replace tab	Replace button on Home tab		CTRL+H
First-Line Indent Paragraphs	WD 88	Drag First Line Indent marker on ruler	Paragraph Dialog Box Launcher on Home tab | Indents and Spacing tab	Paragraph | Indents and Spacing tab	TAB
Font Size, Change	WD 28	Font Size box arrow on Mini toolbar	Font Size box arrow on Home tab	Font | Font tab	CTRL+SHIFT+P
Font Size, Decrease	WD 152	Shrink Font button on Mini toolbar	Shrink Font button on Home tab	Font | Font tab	CTRL+SHIFT+<
Font Size, Decrease 1 Point	WD 86			Font | Font tab	CTRL+ [
Font Size, Increase	WD 151	Grow Font button on Mini toolbar	Grow Font button on Home tab		CTRL+SHIFT+>
Font Size, Increase 1 Point	WD 86			Font | Font tab	CTRL+]
Font, Change	WD 29	Font box arrow on Mini toolbar	Font box arrow on Home tab	Font | Font tab	CTRL+SHIFT+F
Footnote Reference Mark, Insert	WD 100		Insert Footnote button on References tab		CTRL+ALT+F
Footnote, Delete	WD 106	Delete note reference mark in document window	Cut button Home tab		BACKSPACE | BACKSPACE
Footnote, Edit	WD 106	Double-click note reference mark in document window	Show Notes button on References tab		
Footnote, Move	WD 106	Drag note reference mark in document window	Cut button on Home tab | Paste button on Home tab		
Footnote Style, Modify	WD 102		Click footnote text | Styles Dialog Box Launcher | Manage Styles button | Modify button	Style | Footnote Text | Modify button	
Formatting Marks	WD 14		Show/Hide ¶ button on Home tab		CTRL+SHIFT+*

Table 1 Microsoft Office Word 2007 Quick Reference Summary (continued)

Task	Page Number	Mouse	Ribbon	Shortcut Menu	Keyboard Shortcut
Formatting, Clear	WD 162		Clear Formatting button on Home tab		CTRL+ SPACEBAR
Graphic, Insert	WD 153		Clip Art button on Insert tab		
Graphic, Recolor	WD 156		Recolor button on Format tab	Format Picture | Picture | Recolor button	
Graphic, Resize	WD 46	Drag sizing handle	Format tab in Picture Tools tab or Size Dialog Box Launcher on Format tab	Size | Size tab	
Graphic, Set Transparent Color	WD 157		Recolor button on Format tab | Set Transparent Color		
Hanging Indent, Create	WD 116	Drag Hanging Indent marker on ruler	Paragraph Dialog Box Launcher on Home tab | Indents and Spacing tab	Paragraph | Indents and Spacing tab	CTRL+T
Hanging Indent, Remove	WD 86		Paragraph Dialog Box Launcher on Home tab | Indents and Spacing tab	Paragraph | Indents and Spacing tab	CTRL+SHIFT+T
Header & Footer, Close	WD 83	Double-click dimmed document text	Close Header and Footer button on Design tab		
Header, Display	WD 80	Double-click dimmed header	Header button on Insert tab | Edit Header		
Help	WD 60		Office Word Help button		F1
Hyperlink, Format Text As	WD 220		Insert Hyperlink button on Insert tab	Hyperlink	CTRL+K
Hyperlink, Remove	WD 163		Hyperlink button on Insert tab | Remove Link button	Remove Hyperlink	
Indent Paragraph	WD 196	Drag Left Indent marker on ruler	Increase Indent button on Home tab	Paragraph | Indents and Spacing sheet	CTRL+M
Insertion Point, Move to Beginning of Document	WD 24	Scroll to top of document, click			CTRL+HOME
Insertion Point, Move to End of Document	WD 25	Scroll to bottom of document, click			CTRL+END
Italicize	WD 36	Italic button on Mini toolbar	Italic button on Home tab	Font | Font tab	CTRL+I
Justify Paragraph	WD 86		Justify button on Home tab	Paragraph | Indents and Spacing tab	CTRL+J
Left-Align	WD 86		Align Text Left button on Home tab	Paragraph | Indents and Spacing tab	CTRL+L
Line Break, Enter	WD 194				SHIFT+ENTER
Move Selected Text	WD 121	Drag and drop selected text	Cut button on Home tab | Paste button on Home tab	Cut | Paste	CTRL+X; CTRL+V